The Exploration of Outer Space with Cameras

A History of the NASA
Unmanned Spacecraft Missions

by
Michael M. Mirabito

McFarland 1983
Jefferson, North Carolina, and London

Photo credits. The 37 photographs appearing on 32 plates between pages 122 and 123 are from three sources:
NASA: plates 1 bottom, 2, 3, 7 bottom, 8, 10, 11 bottom, 14 top, 16, 17, 18, 19, 20, 23, 24 bottom, 26, 30
NASA/JPL: plates 1 top, 4 top, 6, 7 top, 9, 11 top, 12, 13, 14 bottom, 15, 27
National Space Science Data Center: plates 4, 5, 21, 22, 24 top, 25, 31, 32

The illustrations on pages 44, 45, 68 and 78 are all courtesy of NASA.

Library of Congress Cataloguing-in-Publication Data

Mirabito, Michael M., 1956–
  The exploration of outer space with cameras.

  Bibliography: p.
  Includes index.
  1. Outer space — Exploration — History — United States.
2. United States. National Aeronautics and Space
Administration — History. 3. Space probes. I. Title.
TL789.8.U5M57 1983   629.43'54'09   83-776

ISBN 0-89950-061-7

Manufactured in the United States of America

McFarland & Company, Inc., Publishers
  Box 611, Jefferson, North Carolina 28640

Dedicated to the memory of
Edward White, Virgil Grissom,
and Roger Chaffee of Apollo 1,
and to all of the past, present, and future
pioneers who have kept the dream alive.
And to Barbara,
who is part of this dream to me.

Acknowledgment

I wish to thank the following individuals for their assistance in the preparation of this manuscript: Dr. Denise Trauth and the staff members of NASA, JPL, the National Space Science Data Center, and the Government Document Division of Bowling Green State University. I am also grateful to Drs. Michael Carr, Eugene Shoemaker, Armand Delsemme, and Ben Ruben, and to Judy Phillips of Colorado Video, Inc., for their valuable time. Finally, I wish to acknowledge my family, friends, Ayn Miralano, and especially my wife and colleague Barbara, for her patience and assistance.

Table of Contents

Guide to the Plates
(following page 122)

1. Ranger Moon probe (top, spacecraft; bottom, camera)
2. Lunar Orbiter
3. Surveyor Moon probe
4. Surveyor photo of Moon
5. Lunar Orbiter 4 photo of Moon
6. Ranger 9 photo of Moon crater
7. Mariner 4 Moon probe (top, spacecraft; bottom, camera)
8. Earth-based photo of Moon
9. Mariner 4 photo of Moon
10. Mariner 9
11. Viking Orbiter Mars probe (top, spacecraft; bottom, cameras)
12. Viking Orbiter 1 photo of Mars
13. Viking Orbiter 1 photo of Mars
14. Viking Lander Mars probe (top, spacecraft; bottom, photo on Mars)
15. Viking Lander 1 photo of Mars
16. Viking Lander 1 photo of Mars
17. Mariner 9 photo of Phobos
18. Mariner 9 photo of Phobos
19. Earth-based photo of Mercury
20. Mariner 10 photos of Mercury
21. Mariner 10 photo of Mercury
22. Mariner 10 photo of Mercury
23. Mariner 10 Venus/Mercury probe
24. Top: Pioneer Venus photo of Venus; bottom: Pioneer Venus Orbiter
25. Pioneer 10 photo of Jupiter
26. Voyager 1 photos of Jupiter
27. Voyager 1 photo of Jupiter
28. Voyager 1 (top) and 2 (bottom photos of Jupiter
29. Voyager 2 photo of Jupiter's ring
30. Voyager 1 photo of Io
31. Voyager 2 photo of Saturn
32. Voyager 2 photo of Saturn's rings

CHAPTER 1

Introduction

On July 27, 1964, at 6:47 am, Ranger 7, America's first successful moon probe, was launched from Cape Canaveral. An important feature of the Ranger probe was a television subsystem designed to relay high resolution photographs of the moon back to earth. When the mission was over, 4,316 pictures had been transmitted, revealing details of the lunar surface far beyond the capabilities of any earth-bound instruments. The use of television cameras on outer space probes had made its first major contribution in the National Aeronautics and Space Administration's (NASA) exploration of the solar system.

The Ranger series was followed by probes that also used television and other visual imaging subsystems as integral components of their scientific packages to image the planetary bodies. The first Surveyor probe, for example, landed on the moon on June 2, 1966, with its camera, while a Lunar Orbiter spacecraft circled and photographed the moon with its film system. These two probes and the Rangers comprised a triad system to map and explore the moon with unmanned spacecraft.

In 1964, Mariner 4 was launched by NASA to explore the planet Mars. The mission's goals, in terms of its camera, was to initiate high resolution mapping of the planet to determine if any of the photographed regions contained life forms and to enable scientists to use the data as a base for more intensive studies of the planet. Mariner 4 was followed by Mariners 6 and 7 in 1969 and Mariner 9 in 1971. In 1976, two Viking craft landed on Mars and transmitted the first stereoscopic and color images from the surface of another planet. At the same time, two Viking Orbiter spacecraft orbited Mars and relayed the Viking Landers as well as their own photographs to earth. The planet Venus was also surveyed, at this time, by the Mariner 10 spacecraft. The probe also photographed Mercury during another phase of the mission.

In other missions, Pioneer Venus was inserted into an orbital position around the planet and transmitted photographs of Venus' dense cloud cover. Two other Pioneer spacecraft, Pioneers 10 and 11, penetrated the asteroid belt between Mars and Jupiter to investigate the planets of the outer solar system. The probes were followed a few years later by Voyagers 1 and 2. These spacecrafts' photographs revealed

1

details of Jupiter, Saturn, and their moons that had hitherto remained hidden from telescopic observations on earth. Proposed missions will possibly incorporate visual imaging subsystems to investigate other planetary bodies in the solar system, such as comets and asteroids.

This study, therefore, chronicles the use of television cameras and other visual imaging systems by NASA on unmanned outer space probes in the exploration of the solar system's planetary bodies. The missions and the spacecrafts' visual imaging devices are discussed as well as the systems' technological development and the criteria that influenced their designs. Furthermore, the image processing and enhancement techniques that converted the spacecrafts' transmissions into black and white and color photographs, the discoveries made through the use of these pictures, potential planetary missions, and the terrestial applications of the space program's technology are described.

CHAPTER 2

Flights Prior to Ranger 7

Ranger 7 was NASA's first spacecraft to image and transmit photographs of the moon to earth. The development of Ranger, however, was evolutionary in nature in that earlier inner and outer space probes contributed to its design and mission. Therefore, in order to place Ranger 7 and all subsequent outer space probes within the proper context of space exploration, a brief overview of spacecraft prior to Ranger 7's flight will be presented.

Inner/Outer Space

According to an early 1960's NASA report, there are essentially two types of space probes. The first are those satellites which orbit the earth or are placed in geostationary positions or slots.[1]* In an orbital mode, a satellite physically orbits and circles the earth at a rate determined by the satellite's velocity and altitude. In a geostationary mode, however, a satellite does not orbit the earth at a velocity that exceeds the earth's rotational period. Rather, because of its altitude of approximately 36,000 kilometers, the satellite's orbital velocity is identical to the earth's rotational motion around its axis. A satellite in a geostationary slot, therefore, remains stationary over a specific portion of the earth's surface.[2] Thus, a satellite positioned above the eastern portion of the United States, for example, will remain stationed above this sector of the country.

With only a few exceptions, satellites in either orbital or geostationary positions explore what is called inner space.[3] These probes, such as the Landsat remote sensing series or the Intelsat communication satellites, remotely "sense" the earth for its natural resources or provide international communication links.[4] Consequently, these spacecraft are employed to examine or to provide services for countries on the earth itself.

The second category of NASA probes are those which explore the interplanetary medium, which is the region of space between the

*See Chapter Notes, beginning on page 133.

planetary bodies, or those that flyby, orbit, or land on a planetary body.[5] It is this latter class of spacecraft or those that explore outer space, such as the Ranger 7 moon and the Mariner 4 Mars probes, that this book investigates.

Pre-Imaging Era of Space Exploration

Inner and outer spacecraft had been launched for nearly a decade before Ranger 7 completed its mission. A majority of these flights, however, were concerned with inner space activities. Explorer 1, for example, was launched in 1958 and through the data generated from its scientific package, the Van Allen Belt, which is the radiation zone that envelops the earth, was discovered.[6] Additional probes were launched to further investigate this natural phenomena. Another probe or satellite, Telstar 2, achieved orbit in 1962 to create the first international television link between the United States and Europe.[7] Other inner space probes, such as the Echo series, provided additional communication conduits and investigated the earth during this era,[8]

The use of space probes by NASA in the exploration of outer space at this time included the Pioneer series, the first of which was launched by the Advanced Research Projects Agency in 1958.[9] The Jet Propulsion Laboratory's version of this probe originally called for the use of a photographic subsystem to image and transmit a photograph of the moon to earth during the probe's lunar encounter.[10] The subsystem was deleted, however, before the first spacecraft was launched. Thus, like the first inner space satellites, the Pioneers did not employ television cameras or any other type of visual imaging device.

Television on Space Probes

In 1960, however, a Tiros weather satellite became NASA's first spacecraft to successfully operate in space with a television subsystem. This satellite was similar to its predecessors, such as Explorer 1, in that the objective of its subsystem was the exploration of inner, not outer, space. The Tiros' cameras photographed meteorological phenomena such as the earth's cloud formations and transmitted data about them to receiving stations.[11]

Even though Tiros was an inner space probe, it played a role in the development of imaging subsystems used on outer space probes, for the design of its television cameras influenced the Ranger spacecraft which followed it several years later. An example of this was the use of a slow scan vidicon tube as the imaging sensor for the Ranger and several subsequent outer space probe series after its initial use on a Tiros satellite.[12] In addition, the format of the photographic data generated from the Tiros was likewise adopted by NASA for its outer space probes. Unlike conventional television equipment used on earth, a Tiros did not produce pictures with motion, like a television show or a movie. Rather, an individual photograph was produced. The camera subsystem incorporated a shutter assembly whereby a single exposure was made every several seconds.[13] This photographic information was then converted into electronic signals and transmitted to earth where it was eventually reconstructed to produce separate photographs as though they were prints from a still film camera.[14] The Tiros satellite, therefore, was not capable of producing moving pictures. This was due, in part, to the operational parameters and design of the slow scan vidicon, which was itself a reflection of a spacecraft's limited power supply.[15]

This process of producing individual images was also employed on the Ranger and other outer space missions, since, like the Tiros satellite, these probes were subject to electrical power constraints. Hence, there was a transfer or evolution of technology from the Tiros, or an inner space probe, to those spacecraft used in the exploration of outer space.

Rangers 1 Through 6

When NASA drafted the final plans for the Ranger spacecraft in the early 1960's, it chose to incorporate a television camera subsystem on the probe to photograph the lunar surface.[16] A controversy arose within the scientific community, however, as to the value of these photographs in lieu of other types of data.[17] Some scientists suggested that the Rangers' television cameras be eliminated in favor of a different set of instruments, including a seismometer that was to have been placed on the moon via a Ranger.[18] This issue became even more volatile when the first five Ranger moon probes did not complete their missions and Ranger 6's television subsystem failed to operate.[19]

Yet, even with the failure of Ranger 6's television cameras, a similar subsystem with modifications was used on the next mission. The Ranger television imaging team insisted that the cameras could potentially reveal important geological features of the moon and that imaging was as important a tool in space exploration as any other scientific activity or instrument.[20]

Design Criteria

The television subsystem, therefore, was retained on Ranger 7, and its design was influenced by a general set of criteria which similarly affected all future spacecraft and their visual imaging subsystems. The probes had to survive a sterilization procedure, the launch phase of the mission with its accompanying vibrations and G-forces, and the environment of space itself. When the Mariner 4 mission was planned, for example, components of its television subsystem, including the tape for the magnetic tape recorder, were sterilized. The tape, therefore, had to physically function after this process without any deterioration of its recording ability.[21] In fact, it was heat sterilization, in part, which caused the first Rangers to fail. The high temperatures damaged some of the spacecrafts' parts, which contributed to their unsuccessful flights.[22]

Hence, this sterilization procedure was conducted with all outer space probes which were designed to land on or impact upon, or which might accidentally crash onto, the surface of another planetary body during a mission. The sterilization was employed to destroy any earth organisms on the probe which might have survived the flight through space.[23] If a spacecraft such as a Viking Lander which soft-landed on Mars was not free of these organisms, the area surrounding the probe might become contaminated. This would have biased or negated the results of the Lander's experiments designed to detect native Martian life forms.[24] In a larger sense, sterilization ensured that not only a small region but the whole planetary body itself did not become infested. Consequently, the safeguards to prevent the contamination of other worlds by earth life-forms influenced the design of a spacecraft's electro-optical subsystem since it had to survive this sterilization process.

The stress of the launch and the environment of space, namely, its temperature variance and vacuum, also affected an imaging subsystem's design. This included the selection of a vidicon tube as the imaging sensor for a probe's television cameras. The slow scan vidicon was chosen not only for its ability to operate under restricted transmission and power constraints, but also for its ruggedness. Furthermore, the tube was physically small and lightweight. This fulfilled other criteria, including the payload capacity of the launch vehicle and the size limitation imposed on a probe and its television subsystem.[25] The operation of this sensor will be described in the next chapter.

Another criterion which influenced the development of an imaging subsystem was the mission objectives for a spacecraft's camera and its optical system or lens. Different optical designs exhibited a variety of characteristics and responses. Consequently, based upon the objectives for the imaging system established by the Imaging Science Team, the engineers designed an appropriate optical system or modified an existing lens for the camera.[26] Several factors, however, limited this operation. These included the weight allowance imposed upon the lens and the technical feasibility of producing an optical design which satisfied all of the Imaging Team's requirements.

Conclusion

The technological evolution of inner and outer space probes prior to and including Rangers 1 through 6 eventually led to the success of Ranger 7's mission. Furthermore, the imaging subsystem carried by this spacecraft and all of the space probes described in the next four chapters were influenced by a number of general criteria. In addition to the factors listed, there were also specific influences which dictated the design of a particular spacecraft's electro-optical subsystem, including the initial selection of its imaging sensor. Therefore, when these subsystems are described, the specific elements which affected their designs must be outlined. These may include the in-flight operational characteristics of a spacecraft series, the transmission power and capacity of a probe, and the sensitivity of the receiving antennas on earth.

Finally, the design characteristics and operation of the imaging subsystems carried by the moon probes, which were the Ranger, Surveyor, and Lunar Orbiter series, will be described in Chapter 3. It was due, in part, to the success of the Ranger 7 mission and the photographs it relayed to earth that visual imaging devices were employed on the later moon series. Consequently, the Ranger spacecraft and its television subsystem will initially be discussed in Chapter 3.

CHAPTER 3

Moon Probes

Ranger Series

Introduction

After the failure of Ranger 6, changes were implemented on Ranger 7's television subsystem. These modifications proved successful, for Ranger 7 became NASA's first outer space probe to photograph and transmit images of the lunar surface. The spacecraft's imaging subsystem consisted of six television cameras subdivided into two operational groups designated as F and P.[1] These cameras were activated and initiated the transmission of their photographic data in the form of electronic signals when the probe began its final approach toward the moon prior to its impact. The signals were received on earth and were subsequently recorded on both magnetic tape and by a kinescope recorder on film. When the mission was completed, the magnetic tape and film were computer and chemically processed respectively to produce the final hard copy black and white photographic prints of the moon.[2]

Design Criteria

The design of the television subsystem was influenced by criteria other than the photographic requirements of the mission. The first of these was the payload capacity of the Atlas D/Agena rocket which was the probe's launch vehicle. The rocket's maximum payload allowance was 800 pounds, and it was determined that the television subsystem could not exceed approximately 380 of these pounds. The balance of the weight consisted of Ranger 7's body, structural components, and the probe's other subsystems and scientific instruments.[3]

Another constraint was the limited generating capacity of the probe's electrical subsystem. As with the television cameras and ancillary components, the electrical assembly was restricted in size and weight. Two external solar panels and a series of internal batteries generated the spacecraft's electrical power. The wattage, however, was not sufficient to operate a conventional transmission system. This necessitated the use of slow scan vidicons as the cameras imaging sensors. The data output from this type of vidicon was compatible with the probe's low transmission rate which was itself a reflection of the limited electrical power.[4]

Slow Scan Vidicon

The term slow scan vidicon referred to the light sensitive vidicon image sensors employed on the Ranger's television subsystem. In its operation, a lens from one of Ranger 7's cameras focused the region of the moon it was imaging onto the vidicon's light sensitive screen or photoconductor. The photoconductor itself was composed of thousands of light sensitive dots called picture elements. When the light from the image came into contact with the individual picture elements, they became electrically charged in proportion to the brightness of the imaged region.[5] An electron gun then discharged a beam of electrons at the charged elements in a scanning motion. The electrons neutralized the picture elements' charge and generated a current proportionate in strength to the electrical charge of each picture element.[6] This current, known as the video signal, was then processed and relayed by the spacecraft's transmission subsystem. When it was finally recorded on earth, the signals' strength varied in accordance with the charge of the elements and thus the brightness of the lunar terrain the camera had originally imaged.[7] The signal, therefore, was the electronic equivalent of the specific region of the moon the camera had just imaged.

As was previously stated, the use of the slow scan vidicon was a reflection of the probe's limited power supply. Its video signal or output was modulated prior to its transmission. It was then relayed over a narrow bandwidth channel which functioned as a carrier vehicle for the video output. This bandwidth was narrow when compared with the wide bandwidths employed with conventional communication devices on earth. Such a full bandwidth, however, would have required a power supply and transmission system which exceeded the capacity of the Ranger's subsystems.[8] Consequently, because of the slow scan vidicon's ability to generate its data at a rate accommodated by this narrow bandwidth and the transmission parameters, its was adopted by NASA for its outer space missions.

The narrow bandwidth, in turn, required a greater period of time to transmit a scanned image than a comparable system which employed a full bandwidth. The vidicon's photoconductor, therefore, stored the image until the scanning process was completed.[9] Depending upon the camera which was activated, one scanning period lasted up to 2.5 seconds for one picture in contrast with 1/30th of a second for one scan for conventional television systems used on earth.[10]

The operation and characteristics of the slow scan vidicon was analogous to the following situation. There were two hourglasses filled with precisely the same quantity of sand. One hourglass, however, had a larger aperture than the other. The sand in this hourglass, therefore, flowed more rapidly than the hourglass with the smaller hole. Hence, when both vessels were inverted, the hourglass with the larger aperture was emptied before the other.

The amount of sand and the size of the apertures were analogous to the physical quantity of data and the size of the bandwidths respectively. The transmission system with the wide bandwidth, therefore, relayed the identical quantity of data in a shorter period of time than the system with a narrow bandwidth. Thus both systems relayed equal amounts of data, yet the narrow bandwidth, analogous to the hourglass with the constricted opening, required a greater period of time to transmit its information.

Finally, the rate in which the sand fell through the large and small openings were similarly analogous to the 1/30th and 2.5 second scanning rates. The former scanning time produced video data at a much faster rate and volume than the latter. Due to the wider bandwidth, however, this quantity of data was capable of being transmitted in a shorter period of time just as the greater volume of sand was able to flow through the larger opening in a comparable amount of time. The 2.5 second scan period produced its video data at a much slower rate. Nevertheless, it matched the capacity of the transmission system and was relayed over the narrow bandwidth during this longer scanning period just as the reduced volume of sand fell through the narrow opening in a comparable amount of time. In summation, the slow scan vidicon produced its data at a sufficiently slow rate that they could be transmitted over the narrow bandwidth.

A final facet of the slow scan system was a shutter mechanism which prevented image blurring from the spacecraft's motion and provided a correct exposure time for the photographs.[11] The shutter was activated which permitted the camera lens to focus the light from the scene it was imaging onto the photoconductor. This image was then frozen on the photoconductor while the scanning process occurred. Since the image was stationary, it prevented any picture blurring due to the Ranger's forward velocity.[12]

Finally, once the scanning was completed and the video signal was generated, the image was erased from the photoconductor, the camera shutter was again activated, and a new image was focused on the vidicon. This cycle repeated itself until Ranger crashed onto the lunar surface during the mission's final phase.[13]

Full and Partial Scan Cameras

The television cameras which employed the slow scan vidicons were two F cameras, which operated in a full-scan mode, and four P, or partial scan, cameras. A full scan camera's photoconductor was 0.44 x 0.44 inches in size, in contrast with 0.11 x 0.11 inches for the partial scan system.[14] Implicit in this size difference was the physical area of the moon each camera photographed. From the same altitude, an F camera imaged a region 16 times greater in size than a P camera. The F camera also produced photographs with a higher resolution and definition. Consequently, smaller lunar surface features were depicted and identified from these photographs in contrast with those from a P camera.[15]

The two camera types also operated as two separate chains, namely, the F and P chains. Each chain had its own power supply, control circuit, and supporting electronic components.[16] The television subsystem, therefore, was designed as two independent systems. If one chain failed to function, photographs could still be produced and transmitted from the other one. This replication of the camera electronics was a design consideration and served as a back-up system or redundancy factor for the Ranger spacecraft.[17]

The individual cameras in each chain also functioned in conjunction with the other cameras in its own chain. In the P group, for example, the four cameras were not activated simultaneously. Rather, the cameras operated in sequence.[18] This was due, in part, to the nature of the slow scan vidicon. After each exposure and scanning period, a residual or ghost image remained on the photoconductor. Since it would have taken too long for the image to disappear naturally, a series of lamps flooded the photoconductor with light after each exposure. This erased the image and the photoconductor in preparation for the next exposure.[19]

The camera sequencing was conducted in the following manner. Camera P1 initially imaged the lunar surface. After the photoconductor was scanned and the video signal was produced, the erase lamps were activated. When the camera was in the process of being scanned and erased, P2 initiated its imaging cycle. When this camera's photoconductor was scanned and erased, P3 imaged the moon. This process was repeated until it was time for P1 to be activated again. At this point, the residual image was erased, the lamps were shut off, and the photoconductor was primed for the next photograph.[20] This cycle, therefore, provided sufficient buffer time for a camera to complete its scanning and erasing phases.

With this system, the P chain transmitted four pictures every 0.8 seconds. This represented an advantage over the F chain, which required 2.5 seconds for each photograph. The F chain, however, produced images that covered a greater surface area of the moon and had a higher resolution.[21] The camera subsystem, therefore, generated both a large volume of photographs via the P chain and highly resolved wide angle views of the moon with the F chain.

Finally, the video data for each photograph were transmitted directly to earth following the scanning of the photoconductor. This was called a real-time transmission in that the data were relayed as they were produced. This was in contrast with other space probes, which recorded their video data on magnetic tape prior to transmission.[22]

Camera Optics

The lenses mounted on the cameras determined the field of view, or the physical area of the lunar surface a camera could photograph at one time, as well as the size of the camera's photoconductor. A 25mm F/0.95 wide angle and a 76mm F/2.0 telephoto lens were fitted to the F cameras, while two wide angle and two telephotos were mounted on the P cameras.[23] The F chain's 25 and 76mm lenses provided respective fields of view of 25 and 8.4 degrees whereas the P cameras with their smaller photoconductors yielded 2.1° and 6.3° fields of view with their 25 and 76mm lenses respectively.

As the Ranger approached the moon, its photographs covered an 118 by 118 mile section of the lunar surface with a resolution of several hundred meters. Surface features which were at least several hundred meters in size, therefore, were resolved in the photographs. As the probe plummetted toward the moon prior to its impact, the area the cameras imaged decreased in size as the resolution increased.[24]

Central Computer and Sequencer

The CCS was the Ranger's central control system which issued commands to the spacecraft and the television subsystem at appropriate times during the mission. The television subsystem, for example, was not fully operational at the time of the launch and its flight toward the moon to conserve the internal batteries' power.[25] Approximately 20 minutes before lunar impact, however, the television subsystem was activated in one of three ways. In the first mode, a real-time command from the earth turned the system on. If the probe did not respond to the command, the CCS activated the system after a predetermined number of hours had elapsed.[26] If these procedures failed, a third and final back-up device was employed. When the Ranger spacecraft separated from the Agena rocket, an internal clock aboard the probe was activated.[27] At approximately 67 hours and 45 minutes into the flight, the computed time for the spacecraft's trajectory prior to its impact, the clock automatically switched the F chain on. Thus, even if the two primary systems failed, the full scan cameras would have produced and transmitted their photographs.[28]

Deep Space Network

Once the television subsystem was powered on and had initiated the relay of its photographs, they were received on earth by one of the Deep Space Network's antennas. The Deep Space Network was an organ of NASA responsible for the two-way communication between the earth and an unmanned spacecraft travelling 16,000 kilometers or more beyond the earth. This included the Ranger and all subsequent probes described in this book.[29] Furthermore, the two-way communication process was the relay of commands to a spacecraft and the return transmissions from the probe, including the photographic data.

The Network's antennas were parabolic receiving dishes outwardly resembling conventional satellite dishes employed by television stations on earth to receive transmissions from earth satellites. The Deep Space Network's antennas, however, were much larger, more sensitive, and also transmitted signals. The antenna which received the Ranger's signals had a diameter of 85 feet, or 25.9 meters. It was also steered so it could be properly positioned to maintain the two-way communication link with the probe.[30] A series of these antennas were located around the world so NASA could constantly monitor the probe. When the earth's rotation carried one antenna beyond its telecommunication link, another antenna transmitted and received the signals.

Conclusion

The Ranger's television subsystem was a technical and practical success, as the cameras operated according to their design specifications. Its full and partial scan cameras, slow scan vidicons, and optical systems, enabled NASA to procure its first high resolution photographs of the moon with one of its spacecraft.

The Ranger 7 probe also demonstrated the viability of its design configuration. It was a three axis stabilized spacecraft in that a series of electro-optical sensors and jets maintained the position of the Ranger's solar cells toward the sun to ensure the production of electricity from this system. The three axis stabilization design also made the Ranger a steady platform for its cameras. Furthermore, the probe's transmitting antenna remained positioned toward the earth while it relayed its photographic data during its descent toward the lunar surface.[31] The operation of this type of spacecraft will be described in detail in Chapter 4.

Ranger 7 was followed by Rangers 8 and 9 on February 16 and March 21, 1965, respectively.[32] The television subsystems carried by these craft were essentially identical to Ranger 7's system. It was with the Surveyor series which soft-landed on the moon, however, that a new television subsystem was introduced on an unmanned lunar probe.

Surveyor Series

Introduction

Approximately a year after Ranger 9 completed its mission, Surveyor 1 soft-landed on the moon. It was one of five probes in this series and represented NASA's first attempt to land a spacecraft on a planetary body other than the earth.[33] In addition, each Surveyor carried one television camera in contrast with a Ranger's six camera system. By the time the last Surveyor transmitted its final photograph in 1968, all five probes had relayed a total of 87,674 images of the moon to earth.[34]

Design Criteria

The Surveyor probe's television subsystem was designed with a constraint similar to its predecessor. The slow scan vidicon was adopted as the camera's imaging sensor, in part because of its reduced data rate. As previously described, the vidicon's extended scanning period and consequently the output of its video signal permitted its data to be transmitted on a compressed bandwidth.[35]

In summation, the rate of data from the vidicon was reduced to meet a constraint imposed by a Surveyor's power and transmission subsystems. Its photographic data, like that of the Rangers, were also directly transmitted to earth in real time without first being stored on a magnetic tape recorder.[36]

The harsh lunar environment also played a role in the design of the television subsystem. The vidicons chosen for the missions had to operate during the lunar day when temperatures rose to approximately 250°F, survive the − 250° lunar nights in a standby mode for the equivalent of 14 earth days, and then begin functioning during the next lunar day.[37] A series of tests, therefore, were conducted on earth which subjected the vidicons to lunar conditions. It was believed, for example, that the extreme cold would cause the seal on a vidicon to break, which would create a leak in the tube and impair its photographic properties. Another fear was that the cold would cause the photoconductor material to peel away from the vidicon's faceplate.[38] This too would have disabled the camera.

It was discovered, however, that if a tube initially survived its exposure to the cold temperatures during the test, it would continue to operate during subsequent cold periods. Thus, before a vidicon was employed on a spacecraft, it had to survive the cold exposure test. As an additional safeguard, flights after Surveyor 1 employed a heater system to keep the photoconductor warm to prevent its physical deterioration.[39]

A similar series of tests were also conducted which subjected the vidicons to high temperatures to simulate the lunar day. The concern of mission personnel for the possible effects of heat damage eventually led to the design and use of a passive radiator system to dissipate heat accumulated in the camera subsystem.[40]

The ability of the television subsystem to survive the physical stress of the launch and the effects of the lunar landing were the final primary design criteria for the subsystem. When a Surveyor landed on the moon, for example, its landing velocity was approximately 3.4 feet per second.[41] Even though the spacecraft's aluminum landing pads that crushed on contact with the lunar surface and a series of shock absorbers incorporated in the landing gear were designed to absorb the physical impact of a landing, nevertheless, the television subsystem had to be rugged enough to survive the vibrations and jarring not dampened by these two systems.[42]

Camera Design

Each Surveyor spacecraft, with only one exception, carried a single television camera with a 11mm square photoconductor as part of its scientific package. Since the probe operated on the moon for an extended period of time, one camera was capable of completing all of the mission's photographic requirements.[43] Only Surveyor 1 carried an additional camera. It was designed to photograph the lunar surface during the probe's descent. The camera was not used during the mission, however, and was replaced with other scientific instruments on subsequent missions.[44]

A Surveyor's television camera was housed in a mast-like appendage mounted on the probe at a 16° angle. The mast, approximately 65 inches tall, increased the overall height of the subsystem and permitted the camera to survey the surrounding terrain and the spacecraft's other scientific devices.[45] The top of the mast was fitted with a mirror which rotated 360° in azimuth and + 50° in an upward and − 60° in a downward motion relative to the normal plane of the camera.[46]

The camera's lens was located beneath the mirror and relayed the scene the mirror was imaging to the vidicon near the bottom of the mast.[47] Thus, the lens and vidicon remained in stationary positions while the mirror moved up and down in elevation or in a 360° circular motion. As the mirror pointed at a specific region of the surrounding landing site, for example, the light from this area was reflected to the lens below and finally to the vidicon's photoconductor. Finally, this whole system was inclined on a 16° angle or tilt relative to the probe's vertical axis.[48] This configuration and the mirror permitted the camera to image regions above and below the horizon, the surrounding terrain, and other areas of the probe itself.[49]

The camera was also capable of producing both 200 and 600 line frames or photographs.[50] A 600 line frame, for example, meant that there were 600 scan lines in that particular photograph. The number of lines per frame, in turn, determined the resolution or sharpness of the image. Consequently, as the number of lines increased, the resolution of the image improved.[51]

The quality of the pictures produced by the Surveyor's 600 line mode was slightly greater than the pictures aired on a conventional television set in the United States. Depending upon the television system a country adopted, the number of scan lines varied. The United States standard, for example, was 525 lines per frame.[52] A Surveyor's 600 and 200 line images, therefore, were technically superior and inferior respectively to the images produced by the American television system.

The Surveyor's 200 line frames were transmitted by an omnidirectional antenna immediately following the spacecraft's lunar landing. Each photograph required 61.8 seconds for its scanning cycle in contrast with 3.6 seconds for the 600 line images. These time periods included the erasure of the photoconductor in preparation for the next exposure.[53]

Furthermore, the 600 line frame was the camera's normal operational mode and this photograph was transmitted when the Surveyor's powerful planar array antenna was properly positioned toward the earth. Because of its greater number of scan lines, a 600 line image necessitated the use of a wider transmission bandwidth than a 200 line picture and was accommodated only by the planar array antenna.[54] Hence, in order for the higher resolution 600 line frames to be transmitted, the planar array had to be operational. If this antenna malfunctioned, all of the transmissions were made on the omnidirectional antenna in 200 line frames. This mode, therefore, also served as an auxiliary transmission system for the spacecraft.[55]

In addition, the television subsystem incorporated a shutter to expose each photograph. The nominal shutter speed was 150 milliseconds, and a camera was also capable of making time exposures in the subsystem's integration mode. During this operation, the shutter remained open for extended periods of time, up to approximately 30 minutes, to enable the light energy from faint images to be accumulated and recorded by the vidicon.[56]

The camera was also equipped with polarizing and color filters arrayed on a moveable filter wheel. Commands issued from earth activated the wheel and placed a specific filter in the lens' optical path when a photograph was taken.[57]

Color pictures of the lunar surface were produced and transmitted through the use of these filters. The identical region of the lunar surface was photographed three times through different filters. The first exposure was made through the red filter. The wheel was rotated and a picture was then taken through a blue filter, which was followed by another rotation of the wheel and an exposure through a green filter.[58] The colors of these filters represented the three primary colors which, when mixed, created a color image.[59] The sequence of these three black and white photographs, therefore, was received on earth and reconstructed to create the final composite photograph which depicted the true color of the lunar surface.[60]

Camera Optics

The television subsystem's lens which created these black and white and color images was a 25 to 100mm variable focal length lens with an aperature range of F/4 to F/22. It resolved objects as small as one millimeter in size at four meters and had a focusing capability of 1.23 meters to infinity.[61] The lens was housed in the probe's mast and was positioned between the mirror and the vidicon tube.

Even though the lens was variable focal length in design, its full zoom ratio was not employed during the mission. Rather, the lens operated at the two extreme ends of its range, or the 25 and 100mm settings, which yielded respective field of views of 25.3° and 6.4°.[62] Consequently, both wide- and narrow-angle views of the surrounding terrain in addition to closeup photographs through the 100mm setting were accommodated by this optical system.

The lens' iris or aperture setting was adjusted by a servomechanism or by commands from earth. In the automatic mode, a photocell similar to that employed on conventional cameras measured the intensity of light reflected from the scene the camera was imaging. Once the light level was determined, the iris was automatically adjusted to provide a correct exposure.[63] In the manual mode, a command was transmitted to the spacecraft to change the aperture to one of six F/stops. This permitted the mission personnel to manipulate the F/stop to complete any desired photographic task.[64]

Camera Control Operation

The manual control of the aperture and all of the spacecraft's operations were conducted by a series of command signals transmitted from the earth to the Surveyor. This was a reflection of a design criterion for the probe. The harshness of the lunar environment, the payload weight restriction, the duration of the mission, and a philosophy to minimize the complexity of the Surveyor's subsystems dictated the use of commands from earth in lieu of onboard computers to control the craft.[65] This reliance upon earth commands was illustrated during the Surveyor 7 mission. The probe received over 150,000 orders in contrast with only 11 commands issued for a Ranger probe which used an onboard control system.[66] It must be noted, however, that the Ranger mission was a less sophisticated operation.

The Surveyor's television subsystem was capable of receiving, decoding, and implementing 25 commands. These included signals to turn the camera on and off, to rotate the filter wheel, to change focus, and to open or close the iris.[67] Some command sequences were also prerecorded on tape. When they were played back, a series of commands were sequentially issued to the Surveyor to complete a specific photographic survey. An example of this was a series of five tapes with 200 commands each to produce a 100-picture 360° panoramic survey of the landing site. Thus, the tapes provided the Surveyor's operators with a preprogrammed system to initiate complex camera movements.[68]

Furthermore, to ensure the camera completed its assigned commands, potentiometers were connected with the mirror and filter motors to monitor their movements. If a command was issued to the camera to change the mirror's position, for example, the potentiometer registered this change and this information was relayed to earth.[69]

In summation, the Surveyor's camera control system functioned as a closed loop. Commands were relayed from the earth and were received by the spacecraft. These orders were then decoded and implemented by the Surveyor, at which point the potentiometers registered the movement of the camera's components and transmitted this information to earth. In addition to this data, other camera functions and conditions, such as the temperature of the vidicon's faceplate or the focal length of the lens for a specific photograph were also monitored and relayed to earth in a digital form.[70]

Finally, the video information was transmitted prior to the digitized signals. Thus, each photograph was mated with the digital information which identified the F/stop, for example, at which a specific photograph was taken. The video data or the transmitted photographs were permanently recorded on magnetic tape and 70mm film. These were processed to eventually produce the hard copy prints.[71] The video data were also monitored by a real-time television system which displayed the images as they were received. Polaroid and "paper camera" devices also produced instant hard copy prints of these images if it was so desired.[72]

Conclusion

The design of the Surveyors' television subsystem employed for all five spacecraft was only slightly modified in the two years the probes explored the lunar surface. Consequently, the only major alteration was the deletion of the second camera which was mounted on Surveyor 1 to image the probe's descent.[73] Other minor changes included the placement of additional mirrors on a Surveyor's frame to permit the camera to image the instruments mounted on its bottom, an alteration of the camera's filters, and the elevation limit of the mirror was increased.[74]

When Surveyor 7, the last in the series, completed its transmission at 00:24 Universal Time on February 21, 1968,[75] it signalled the end of the second stage of NASA's triad system of unmanned lunar exploration. The final phase was the imaging of the moon by the Lunar Orbiter series. Their photographs yielded high resolution views of the moon and were used to complement the Surveyors' images.

Lunar Orbiter Series

Introduction

The Lunar Orbiter series of spacecraft consisted of five probes which orbited the moon and photographed its surface much like a satellite would have orbited and photographed the earth.[76] The visual imaging subsystem of the spacecraft was a hybrid design unlike its predecessors. The Ranger and Surveyor probes' imaging sensors were slow scan vidicons while the Lunar Orbiters employed a film and photomultiplier readout system.[77]

Design Criteria

That the film/photomultiplier subsystem was adopted instead of a slow scan vidicon was due, in part, to the mission goal of obtaining high resolution photographs of the lunar surface in preparation for the Apollo manned landings.[78] Even though the vidicons were capable of resolving features to a high degree, nevertheless, the photographic requirement of producing high resolution pictures of selected lunar sites and slightly lower resolution pictures of the moon's remaining surface areas was deemed to be best fulfilled by the use of both high contrast and fine grain film.[79]

Since film was selected as the imaging and recording medium, a method had to be devised to return the data to earth. One option was to have a spacecraft take the photographs and return to earth with the exposed film. This system, however, was expensive to design and implement.[80] A second and less costly method was therefore selected whereby the film was developed on the probe and its data was transmitted while the spacecraft remained in lunar orbit.[81]

After this decision was made, it was necessary to shield the film/readout system from the environmental conditions of space. Hence, the project engineers designed a pressurized metal shell to encase and protect the photographic system.[82]

Two clear windows were built into the shell as shooting ports for the cameras.[83] Laboratory tests revealed, however, that when a thermal door protecting the windows was opened prior to the shooting sequence, the cameras' lenses experienced a temperature loss which impaired their performance. This problem was eventually alleviated by the placement of a heater system between the window and the lenses' front elements.[84] This helped stabilize the temperature in the system.

A final design criterion was the configuration and inflight operation of the Lunar Orbiter itself. Since the probe's primary goal was to transmit high resolution photographs of the moon, it was necessary that the visual imaging was conducted from a stable platform.[85] Thus, a three axis stabilization control similar to the one employed on the Mariner probes and which was originally pioneered by the Rangers was incorporated on the Lunar Orbiter. This ensured its stability as a camera platform for the duration of its mission.

The Lunar Orbiter also used a Canopus star sensor which "locked onto" or maneuvered the spacecraft to keep the star within the field of view of this electro-optical sensor. Like the Ranger spacecraft, this maintained the position of the solar panels toward the sun and the antenna toward the earth for the transmission of its data.[86] The operation of three axis stabilized spacecraft will be described in depth in Chapter 4, on the Mariner Spacecraft Series.

Camera Design

A Lunar Orbiter's visual imaging system consisted of a 610mm or 24-inch and a 80mm or 3-inch lens, a Bimat film processor, a scan tube, and a video amplifier.[87] In addition, a velocity-to-height ratio sensor measured the probe's speed and altitude, which varied during its orbital rotations. This sensor, in turn, activated an image motion compensation mechanism which prevented image smearing due to the probe's low altitude and forward motion.[88]

In its operational mode, the camera subsystem was capable of taking 20 photographs per orbital pass over the target area. Each camera exposed one-half of the 70mm film. Thus, there were two pictures on every frame, namely, one from the 610mm and one from the 80mm lens.[89]

When each orbital pass was completed, the exposed film was stored on a film looper. The film was developed by the Bimat processor at a rate of 2.4 inches a minute, while it was exposed, at times, at a rate of 7 inches a second. The Bimat processor, therefore, could not develop the film as rapidly as the pictures were taken.[90] Because of this discrepancy, the film looper served as a buffer which stored pictures until they could be processed.

After the film was exposed and stored on the looper, it subsequently passed through the Bimat unit.[91] In a conventional photographic system, an exposed negative was immersed in a tank containing a liquid developing solution.[92] With the Bimat system the exposed film was physically laminated and sandwiched against another piece of film that was saturated with a developing agent.[93] This process initiated and completed the developing cycle without using the containers of liquids which rendered a conventional processing system impractical for operations in outer space. Another advantage of this system was that it was capable of surviving the physical force of the launch and the flight through space which might have damaged a processing unit normally employed on earth.[94]

When the developing cycle was completed, the two pieces of film were separated. The film with the negatives was then dried and stored on a readout looper. Just as the film looper was a buffer between the shooting and processing stages, so too was the readout looper a buffer between the developed film and the readout process.[95]

One component of the readout system was a scan tube. This device produced a high intensity light which was focused upon and scanned across the developed film by a lens. As the lens scanned or moved across the film, therefore, it caused the light to move in this same motion. The length of each scan was 2.54 millimeters, or 0.1 inches. The scanning was initiated at the top of the film and continued in a downward motion until the bottom end of the film was reached. This completed the first scan. The film was then mechanically advanced 2.54 millimeters, and the scanning commenced in the opposite or upward direction.[97] When the top of the film was reached, the film was again advanced another 2.54 millimeters or one framelet.[98] Consequently, the lens moved vertically up and down the film until one negative which represented one photograph was fully scanned. It required 40 minutes to scan and transmit a single picture.[99]

As the scanning took place, the light from the tube passed through and was modulated by the density of the film. Furthermore, as the film's density varied, so too did the light's modulation.[100] The light then passed through a condenser lens and was diffused onto a photomultiplier. This sensor created an electrical output in proportion to the strength of the modulated light.[101]

The photomultiplier's output was subsequently channeled to a video amplifier which augmented and converted this signal to one compatible with the Lunar Orbiter's transmission system. The amplifier also mixed a sync signal with the reconverted data which provided calibration information when the photographs were reconstructed on earth.[102]

In order for the pictures to be relayed, the Lunar Orbiter had to be in view of the sun for its solar cells to generate the electricity for its transmission system. The spacecraft had to be simultaneously in view of the earth for the Deep Space Network to receive its signals.[103] When the probe was thus positioned, a command was issued from earth which activated the readout system and began the 40 minute transmission for each photograph.[104] The signals were then processed in the Lunar Orbiter's Ground Reconstruction Electronics (GRE) which was a component of the Ground Reconstruction System (GRS).[105]

The photographic data was initially channeled into the GRE and was converted to a line display on a cathode-ray tube. The line display was then photographed with a 35mm motion picture camera by means of a kinescope display system. The 35mm film was then processed and evaluated. If there were any technical defects due to the processing, they were detected and corrected at this time.[106]

The Lunar Orbiter had originally scanned the film in framelets and the pictures were received in this form. Once the individual framelets were received on earth, however, they were enlarged 7.2 times their original size prior to their recording on the 35mm film.[107] When the processing and evaluation stages were completed, therefore, the film with the framelets entered a Reassembly Printer. This device rejoined all of the framelets which composed one photograph and produced a 9.5 inch negative from which the final black and white prints were made.[108]

To sum up, the Lunar Orbiter's photographic subsystem operated in the following manner. Two camera lenses imaged the lunar surface and recorded the pictures on film. The film was processed on the probe, scanned by light which was modulated by the film's density, and was then diffused onto a photomultiplier. The photomultiplier generated a signal which was proportinate to the modulated light, channeled the output to a video amplifier whereby the photographic data were relayed to earth. The data were then processed and the enlarged framelets were assembled into negatives, each of which was composed of 14 framelets.[109] These final negatives were then used to produce the final hard copy prints of the Lunar Orbiter's photographic data.

Camera Optics

The optical systems were 610mm and 80mm lenses which photographed respective 16.6 by 4.15 and 37.4 by 31.6 kilometer sections of the moon.[110] Depending upon the orbital altitude, the high resolution 610mm telephoto resolved surface features as small as one meter, while the moderate 80mm wide angle lens' maximum resolution was approximately eight meters.

The lenses also produced two separate pictures on each frame of the Lunar Orbiter's 70mm film. The regions of the moon photographed by the high resolution lens were similarly photographed in the moderate resolution wide angle photograph. The telephoto lens, therefore, provided a detailed and highly resolved view of portions of the lunar surface covered in the wide angle survey and were nested within the wide angle's images.[111]

The photographs were taken individually or in clusters of 4, 8, or 16 frames per orbital pass. The multiple frame sequences provided continuous coverage of the lunar surface along the probe's flight path.[112] They also produced an overlap between successive frames of up to 86% depending upon the frame rate. The overlap not only ensured the specific target area was visually imaged, but it also provided stereoscopic views of these surface regions.[113]

The final optical component of the subsystem was the sensor for the image motion compensation mechanism which prevented image smearing from the probe's motion. Its operation was integrated with the 610mm lens in that it used a portion of the lens for its field of view of the moon.[114] The sensor surveyed the lunar surface ahead of and before the cameras were activated. Based upon this view, it measured the probe's height and velocity. This information was used by the Lunar Orbiter to manipulate a drive mechanism which controlled the platens or bases the cameras were mounted on.[115] The platens were then moved in such a manner as to compensate for the forward motion of the spacecraft.

Conclusion

The Lunar Orbiter's unique photographic subsystem's design yielded high and moderate resolution photographs of the entire visible surface area of the moon, which was the side that always faced the earth, in addition to regions of its far side. The film supply for a probe was also designed to produce 194 frames per mission, yet, during an actual flight, this system generated over 210 photographs.[116]

The use of film as the recording medium in contrast with the real-time transmissions of the Ranger and Surveyor series and magnetic tape recorders on other missions was due to film's high resolution and information storage capabilities. Moreover, the Lunar Orbiter produced photographs with 8,360 lines per frame in contrast with only 700 lines per frame for one of the Mars probes which employed a vidicon subsystem.[117] This line per frame figure for the Lunar Orbiters translated into highly resolved images, and because of the high resolution, more photographic information was incorporated in each frame.[118] The probes were also capable of preserving the high information content during the readout and eventual transmission of the data.

This system was never used again, however in any of NASA's outer space probes. Yet, if the resolution and information content of this imaging subsystem were superior to those of a television assembly, the question arose as to why the Lunar Orbiter's design was not incorporated into other missions. After investigating the available sources, this researcher believes there are several possible explanations.

One reason was the nature of the Lunar Orbiter's mission. Its visual imaging subsystem was designed to photograph wide areas of the lunar surface and specific sites, in part, for the future Apollo landings.[119] The requirements for a manned landing were more stringent than the general mapping of a planet's surface features, since NASA required the high resolution photographs to determine if specific sites could safely accommodate the Lunar Landing Module.[120] The missions to the other planets such as Mercury, however, were preliminary reconnaissance flights to map major geological features. Thus, the detailed observations of the Lunar Orbiter were not a primary mission goal.[121]

Another possible explanation relates to the limitations imposed by the use of a film subsystem. The complete Lunar Orbiter unit had to be protected in the pressurized metal shell.[122] Some missions, such as Voyagers 1 and 2, required several years of interplanetary flight before they encountered their objectives.[123] The shell, therefore, had to provide this protective environment for an extended period of time. If it was breached during the flight, the film and chemicals might have been damaged by the extreme physical conditions of space in a way similar to that in which film and chemicals are affected by conditions on earth.[124]

The possibility of environmental damage was potentially great even if the shell was not damaged during a flight. The Lunar Orbiter's film was lightly shielded to protect it from the radiation of the earth's Van Allen Belt.[125] During the Pioneer and Voyager flights to Jupiter and Saturn, however, the spacecraft encountered radiation levels powerful enough to damage several of a probe's instruments.[126] and would potentially have damaged any film carried aboard the craft. A heavier radiation shield would have been needed, therefore, if a Lunar Orbiter type probe attempted to visually image these outer planets. Yet, the additional weight for this shielding might have exceeded a launch vehicle's payload capacity,[127] thus preventing its use.

A film subsystem also produced a limited number of photographs. The Lunar Orbiter was capable of generating approximately 210 pictures in one mission.[128] In contrast with this, Mariner 10's television subsystem produced approximately 3,000 photographs of the planet Mercury. The spacecraft stored images on its tape system in addition to operating in a real-time mode like the Ranger and Surveyor probes. The ability of the tape recorder to record and subsequently transmit photographs more than once in addition to the almost unlimited capacity of the real-time transmissions far outstripped the Lunar Orbiter's film system in the number of photographs produced per mission.[129] If the film supply was enlarged to yield more photographs, it would have necessitated a redesign of the subsystem to accommodate this additional footage. This, in turn, would have added weight to the probe and might have exceeded the launch vehicle's payload capacity.

Two final possible reasons for the use of television subsystems in lieu of film were economic and technological in nature. On Mariner 4, NASA employed a slow scan vidicon television camera. This probe was its first Mars explorer. Subsequent spacecraft evolved from Mariner 4 in that instead of designing a new probe for each mission, Mariner 4's basic configuration and scientific instruments were retained. In a later flight, for example, Mariner 9's television subsystem was similar to that of Mariners 6 and 7. Since only limited funds were available for the missions, preexisting hardware and tested designs were employed on the Mariner 9 probe.[130] Thus, an economic factor influenced the design of outer space probes, and in part, contributed to the continued use of television subsystems.

A technological criterion was the computer image processing and enhancement of photographic information from television subsystems that became more sophisticated with each successive flight.[131] The computer manipulation of the data enabled scientists to produce detailed photographs of the planetary bodies in a number of formats. (This will be elaborated upon in subsequent chapters.) Hence, even though film was still a superior recording medium in terms of its information content and resolution abilities, nevertheless the images from television sub-systems were capable of yielding important information through the use of computers.

In conclusion, the Lunar Orbiter's visual imaging subsystem was specifically designed to meet its mission objectives. Even though its sub-system produced high resolution and detailed images, its limited film capacity and other criteria apparently precluded its use on other missions.

The Lunar Orbiter series was also the last of the unmanned space-craft to explore the moon with visual imaging devices. The next major phase of the exploration of the planetary bodies with electro-optical subsystems described in this study was the exploration of the planet Mars. The first mission was initiated in 1964 with the Mariner 4 space-craft. This probe mounted a solitary television camera to image the planet's surface during the spacecraft's encounter. It was also the first of eight probes to visually explore the planet.

CHAPTER 4

Mariner Spacecraft Series

Introduction

While the Lunar Orbiters were photographing the moon, a Mariner outer space probe, Mariner 4, had already initiated the visual imaging of Mars by this spacecraft series.[1] The probe's immediate predecessor was slated for this first mission, but like the first Rangers, it failed. During Mariner 3's launch, the protective shroud or shield that housed and protected the spacecraft did not eject. Thus, the probe was entombed within the shroud and never fully deployed.[2] Three weeks after the aborted flight, the reason for the malfunction was discovered, and a new shroud was designed. It was installed on another rocket and on November 28, 1964, Mariner 4 was successfully launched toward Mars.[3] The probe was followed by Mariner 6 and 7 in 1969, Mariner 9 in 1972, and finally by the Viking Orbiters, which were the last orbiting spacecraft to investigate the planet. Even though the Vikings and the Voyager probes which will be discussed in Chapter 6 were not designated as Mariners, nevertheless, they belonged to the same class of spacecraft.[4]

General Design Criteria

A design criterion that influenced the Mariner series was the probes' mission objectives. In contrast with the Surveyors, which soft-landed on the moon, for example, a Mariner imaged a planetary body during its flyby or orbits around the celestial body. The spacecraft, therefore, was designed to provide a steady platform for the photographic reconnaissance and the other experiments conducted during the mission. It was a three axis stabilized probe much like a Lunar Orbiter whereby nitrogen jets located on the spacecraft's body enabled it to roll, yaw, and pitch or to move in three different directions during the flight.[5] These maneuvers were employed to align a Mariner and its transmitting antenna toward the earth for the relay of its data and toward the planetary body for the deployment of its experiments. With the exception of the Voyagers, the three axis stabilization system also ensured that a probe's solar panels remained directed at the sun to generate the spacecraft's electricity.[6]

Through the use of the jets, therefore, a Mariner maintained its proper orientation in space. The jets, in turn, were controlled by commands from earth or a series of sensors, including a sun and Canopus star sensor which were also employed on the Ranger and Lunar Orbiter series respectively. The sensors were electro-optical devices which detected these bright celestial objects. If the spacecraft deviated from its predetermined position in space or what was called its attitude, the sun and Canopus drifted out of the sensors' field of view. This triggered a series of events in which the nitrogen jets were eventually activated to maneuver the spacecraft to acquire its celestial references and thus regain its proper attitude.[7]

Once the probe was properly oriented, it remained "locked" in this position during its encounter with the planetary body pending subsequent commands from earth or an onboard computer. Consequently, the probe was stabilized during its rendezvous, which ensured the maximum return from its television cameras since the craft was not subject to any extreme movements other than its forward velocity as it passed over a planet.

Image smearing which would have been created by erratic motions was essentially eliminated. Furthermore, even the effect of the spacecraft's forward motion was minimized by the use of a fast shutter speed. A Mariner, therefore, was a stable visual imaging platform, which was a prerequisite for the production of highly resolved and technically acceptable photographs from a television subsystem. This was in contrast with other outer space probe series, such as the Pioneers, that employed a different type of electro-optical subsystem to deal with the spacecraft's rolling motion as it visually imaged a planet.[9] The probe and its imaging photopolarimeter will be discussed in Chapter 5.

Before this general description of the inflight characteristics of the Mariner series can be completed, two additional points must be noted. The first was that a Mariner's design was not based solely upon the requirements of its television camera subsystem. Rather, a combination of other criteria such as the other scientific instruments, economics, and a Mariner's payload capacity and flexibility contributed to its configuration.[10] In this book, which is concerned with visual electro-optical subsystems, however, the only criteria elaborated upon in the general description of the Mariners are those that influenced the design and operation of a Mariner's television subsystem. Secondly, the Mariner 10 spacecraft that explored Venus and Mercury chronologically followed the Mariner 9 Mars' probe. Nevertheless, to preserve the unity of this chapter and the development and progression of electro-optical subsystems on probes which explored the planet Mars, Mariner 10 will be described after the Viking missions. These spacecraft were the last probes to visually image Mars.

Mariner 4

Introduction

Mariner 4 was NASA's first spacecraft to successfully photograph Mars. Eight months after it was launched, Mariner approached the planet from a distance of 16,900 kilometers and initiated its photographic survey of the planet's surface. A total of 22 pictures were transmitted to earth.[11] Once these images were processed, they revealed geological details of the Martian surface not visible from earth. In this respect, the mission was analogous to that of Ranger 7's when this spacecraft transmitted pictures depicting lunar features for the first time.

Design Criteria

The Mariner 4 space probe carried one television camera with a slow scan vidicon as its imaging sensor. The subsystem's design was influenced by criteria similar to those of the moon probes, such as the camera's ability to operate in the extreme temperature range of outer space, which varied throughout Mariner 4's mission between $+5°$ to $-12°C$.[12] The television subsystem was also influenced by one specific criterion that did not affect the lunar probes. This was the 120 million mile distance across which Mariner 4 had to transmit its photographs, in contrast with only 239,000 miles for the lunar missions.[13]

This distance necessitated the use of a magnetic tape recorder on Mariner 4 to record and store the spacecraft's photographs for transmission at a later time. Like the Orbiter probes, the Mariner's transmission system was not capable of relaying its photographs in real time or as rapidly as they were exposed. Thus, the photographs were recorded on magnetic tape.[14] This served as a buffer, much like the film on the Lunar Orbiters: since the pictures could not be transmitted in real time, they were stored and relayed at a slower rate that was compatible with Mariner 4's transmission subsystem.[15]

The television subsystem's second design criterion was Mariner 4's camera, the first digital television camera used on an outer space probe. The camera originally generated its picture information in analog form. The analog data were then channelled through an analog-to-digital converter aboard the probe, digitized, and transmitted to earth in a binary code.[16] Once the data were received and recorded on magnetic tape, computers manipulated the digital information during processing to enhance the photographs and correct their technical errors to better reveal Mars' surface features.[17]

Mariner 4's digital format for its photographic data was different from the one employed by the lunar probes. These spacecraft transmitted their pictures in their original analog form. Nevertheless, since the data were recorded on both magnetic tape and on film, the tape was capable of being digitized. This system permitted the lunar probes' photographs to similarly undergo computer processing.[18]

The primary reason why Mariner 4 and all subsequent spacecraft described in this study employed digital subsystems was the distance the photographs and other data had to be transmitted.[19] It was discovered that when signals were transmitted over long distances, pulse code modulation, which was a digital relay method like Mariner 4's, was superior to the analog mode. Because of the distance the signal had to travel from Mars, there was the possibility that there would be a data loss. By using pulse code modulation, however, the picture information was coded into binary digits.[20] Thus, if portions of the photographic data were lost during transmission, the coding enabled operators on earth to complete the pictures through the reconstruction of lost data by the interpolation of the photographic data that were received.[21] A digital system, therefore, was more secure than analog systems in data transmissions over long distances.

Digital transmissions also helped maintain the high signal-to-noise ratio of the slow scan vidicon's output, the electronic signals that constituted its photographs.[22] Both conventional television equipment used on earth and a spacecraft's subsystem were subject to electronic interference or noise. This noise was an electronic byproduct of the television system and always accompanied and interfered with the video signal. A digital subsystem, however, preserved a high or strong video signal relative to a weak or low level of interference. This produced technically superior signals and ultimately better images.[23] The digital transmission was also capable of being sampled in that only selective picture elements (bits) that composed a photograph were transmitted. The sampling, therefore, was a form of data compression.

Camera Design

The television subsystem that produced this high signal-to-noise ratio initiated its photographic sequence by focusing onto the slow scan vidicon's photoconductor the light reflected from the region of Mars the camera was imaging. The shutter was then activated to produce a single exposure.[24] A shutter speed of 200 milliseconds was employed both to reduce image blurring due to the spacecraft's forward motion and to provide the correct exposure level for the pictures based upon the general illumination level of the Martian surface. The camera was also equipped with an automatic exposure control system capable of changing the shutter speed to 80 milliseconds.[25] This faster speed was a supplementary mode that was to be used if the light level of the planet was greater than expected and necessitated the use of a faster speed to produce a properly exposed photograph.[26]

Once the exposure was made, the scanning process began whereby the video signal was produced much in the same manner as the Ranger and Surveyor subsystems. It required 24 seconds to scan one frame or photograph with Mariner 4's camera.[27] After the video signal was generated, the photoconductor was erased in preparation for the next exposure. Unlike the lunar spacecraft that used lamps to flood the photoconductor, Mariner 4 erased its camera with an electronic beam. The beam charged the photoconductor so it returned to a physical state known as the cathode potential.[28] This meant that the previous electronic charge or image stored on the photoconductor was neutralized or erased and the camera was primed to receive the next exposure. The erasing and priming procedures required 24 seconds in addition to the camera's 24 second scan rate. Hence, 48 seconds elapsed between pictures.[29]

When the scanning was completed, the video signal was amplified and channelled through the analog-to-digital converter where the photographic data were digitized.[30] Like the Ranger and Surveyor television subsystems, Mariner 4's slow scan vidicon's photoconductor was composed of thousands of picture elements. During the digital transformation, each one of the Mariner's 40,000 picture elements was translated into a single six digit binary code or "word." A six digit word, in turn, represented the black through white brightness level of the individual picture elements on a 0 to 63 scale. A series of six zeroes, for example, was equivalent to white while six ones represented black. This system accommodated a color range of black through white with intermediate levels of gray in a graduated series of 64 steps.[31]

In summation, as the picture elements became electrically charged in proportion to the brightness and shade levels of a scene the camera was imaging, the binary words represented in a digital format the brightness and shade for every picture element that constituted this scene. Every photograph the spacecraft transmitted was in the form of a binary code whereby zeroes and ones were the digital counterparts of the picture elements and thus of the black through white representation of the specific area of Mars the camera had photographed.[32] The final black and white hard copy prints of the planet, therefore, were originally transmitted and composed of binary words.

With this digital format, it required approximately 240,000 bits to create one of Mariner 4's pictures. This figure was computed on the basis of the following formula: 40,000 picture elements for the vidicon's photoconductor was multiplied by the six bits per element. This was equal to 240,000 bits per picture. In turn, each one of Mariner 4's photographs was also composed of 200 scan lines, each line being the equivalent of 200 picture elements.[33] The resolution of the photographs, therefore, was lower than the pictures produced in the United States by 525 line commercial television systems.[34]

When the Mariner's television subsystem originally digitized its photographic data, the 240,000-bit photographs were recorded at only 10,700 bits per second by the onboard magnetic tape recorder. This slow acquisition rate was one of the reasons the probe used a slow scan vidicon. The sensor was capable of generating its video data at a reduced rate so it could match the tape recording. The Ranger and Surveyor series relayed their photographs in real time and their vidicons produced data at a rate compatible with their transmission systems. In a similar manner, since Mariner 4 and all subsequent Mariner spacecraft stored their data, in part, on tape recorders, their vidicons generated and channelled the photographic data into the recorders at a rate compatible with these devices.[35] Mariner 4's recorder, for example, accepted 10,700 bits per second. Therefore, its vidicon generated the same number of bits per second. This rate also accounted for the camera's 24 second scanning time per frame.

The recording capacity of Mariner 4's system was 5.24×10^6 bits of data or a minimum of 20 photographs on the 100 meters of tape.[36] Due to payload restrictions, the recorder was limited to this storage capacity, as additional tape would have required a larger and heavier subsystem. When the mission was completed, the television subsystem actually recorded 21 complete photographs and a portion of another picture.[37]

After these photographs were recorded, the magnetic tape was replayed and the images were relayed by the spacecraft's transmission subsystem. Because of power limitations, only 8⅓ bits per second were transmitted. Consequently, one photograph was relayed in approximately eight hours, while the complete photographic sequence was transmitted over a period of eight to ten days. Furthermore, the data were replayed once both to ensure its reception on earth and to compare the two transmissions to detect and correct any discrepancies between both sets of information.[38]

The photographic data were relayed over the probe's high gain antenna on an S-band communication channel. This was the first time an S-band channel was used by an outer space probe, and its use was due, in part, to the distance the signals had to travel between Mars and the earth.[39] It functioned as an accurate and reliable communications conduit between Mariner 4 and the Deep Space Network's receiving stations. The data were subsequently recorded on magnetic tape for later computer processing and enhancing.[40]

After the photographic data were computer manipulated, the

images were still technically inferior to those produced by the lunar spacecraft. This was partially due to the limiting factor of Mariner 4's 200 lines per frame. It appeared however, that there were several reasons why the Mariner's television subsystem was not designed to produce more highly resolved photographs. First, the storage capacity of the tape recorder was limited. If a picture was composed of more than 200 scan lines, the number of picture elements and bits would have proportionately increased. Hence, with its tape storage capacity, the spacecraft would have produced only a few high resolution photographs of Mars instead of the 22 images it did produce since the photographic information in several high resolution images was equivalent to a larger number of low resolution pictures. This would have defeated one of the mission objectives, which was to provide a preliminary reconnaissance of Mars. The few high resolution pictures would have exhausted the tape supply without generating enough images to constitute a preliminary survey of the planet.[41] A solution to this dilemma was to increase the tape's length. Yet, since the probe had a weight limit, this option was not available.

Another limiting factor was Mariner 4's tape recorder. Its acquisition rate was so slow that if higher resolution photographs were produced, only a few pictures would have been recorded by the time the probe completed its flyby. One of the mission's goals, however, was to produce a swath of photographs across the planet.[42] The 200 line frames with their lower volume of photographic information and bits were capable of being recorded at a rapid enough pace to produce this swath even with the recorder's low acquisition rate.

Camera Optics

The lens which produced these photographs was an F/8 12-inch Cassegrain telephoto. A Cassegrain lens is a telescopic device incorporating a primary mirror at the rear of the lens assembly. Light reflected from Mars entered the lens and was reflected off of the primary mirror. It was then directed to a smaller secondary mirror located at the center and in front of the lens tube. The secondary mirror, in turn, reflected the light back through a hole in the primary mirror at the rear of the lens. The light passed through the hole and was focused onto the vidicon's photoconductor.[43] The mirrors produced a folded optical path which made the Cassegrain a more compact lens than a conventional telephoto of the same magnification power. That a Cassegrain, therefore, was chosen for the Mariner 4 mission was due to its light weight and compact design in addition to its large aperture of F/8 for a telephoto.[44]

The lens had a field of view of 1.05° × 1.05°. From an altitude of approximately 11,000 kilometers which was Mariner 4's closest approach to the planet's surface during its flyby, each photograph covered a 202 by 202 kilometer square of Mars. The Cassegrain's maximum resolution was approximately three kilometers, meaning that geological formations or other surface markings smaller than three kilometers would not have been resolved, or clearly defined, in the photographs.[45]

The optical subsystem also incorporated a series of colored filters on a moveable wheel that was placed in the lens' optical path immediately before the shutter mechanism. There were four filters on the wheel that alternated between green and red. Since the Mariner television subsystem was designed to return photographs providing geological as well as color information about Mars' surface, all of the photographs were imaged through the filters. The first picture was taken through a red filter, the filter wheel was rotated, and the second image that was recorded was taken through a green filter.[46] The pictures were also taken in pairs since 15% of the surface area of two successive photographs, one through a red and one through a green filter, overlapped.

The color filters did not permit the television subsystem to produce color photographs of Mars. Rather, the red and green filters made color features of the Martian surface more visible since they enhanced the geological formations in the Mariner's transmitted black and white photographs.[47] The red filter, for example, darkened any green regions of the Martian landscape while it simultaneously lightened any red surface areas or features. The green filter produced the opposite effect. Red areas became more pronounced and green regions appeared lighter. The 15% overlap region which was photographed through a red and a green filter in their respective photographs, permitted scientists to determine the general coloration of Mars' surface features.[48]

Central Computer and Sequencer

The operation of Mariner 4's television subsystem was controlled either by an onboard computer system or by commands from earth. The central computer and sequencer (CCS) performed tasks on Mariner 4 similar to its counterpart on a Ranger spacecraft. The Mariner's CCS automatically initiated specific operations, such as the playback of the recorded pictures at a predetermined time during the flight.[49] Mariner 4 also received direct command signals from ground stations on earth to complete assigned programs. These orders were received by the probe and channelled to the command subsystem and thus to the appropriate subsystem to complete the task.[50]

During the flight, the spacecraft received a command to activate the science subsystem when it approached Mars. The scan platform was also powered on at this time. This platform was designed to aim the television cameras at Mars during the flyby. Unlike a Ranger's cameras, which remained stationary, Mariner 4's solitary camera was mounted on the mobile scan platform.[51] It was designed to rotate in an 180° arc so the camera could be positioned properly in relation to Mars' surface.

In addition to the television camera, the platform mounted a wide angle sensor. This device was designed to initially locate Mars within its field of view as the platform moved through its search pattern. When the planet was detected, a signal was generated which aimed the platform, and thus the camera, toward the specific area of Mars that was to be photographed during the flight.[52]

A narrow angle Mars "gate" instrument was similarly located on the platform. This electro-optical device had a narrow field of view and did not sense the light reflected from Mars at the same time as the aforementioned wide angle sensor. It was only when Mariner 4 was 43.5 minutes from its closest approach to the planet, which was the optimum visual imaging distance for the spacecraft's camera, that the narrow angle Mars gate device detected the planet. At this time, another signal was generated and the photographic survey began.[53] After the pictures were recorded, they were not transmitted immediately since the probe's trajectory led to Mariner's occultation by Mars.[54] It was only eight hours after Mariner 4 passed out of the occultation region that the CCS activated the tape recorder and began relaying the photographs.[55]

To sum up, Mariner 4's operation was controlled both by earth and preprogrammed commands stored in the CCS. When the spacecraft neared its encounter with Mars, the scan platform received a command to begin its search pattern to locate the planet. The wide angle sensor detected the planet and moved the platform to aim the television camera at Mars. After this, the narrow angle Mars gate sensed the planet and initiated the picture taking phase of the mission.

When Mariner 4 completed its mission, there were no other spacecraft launched to investigate Mars until the late 1960's. This next series of flights was designated the Mariner–Mars 1969 mission. Twin Mariner spacecraft were launched within four weeks of each other and their television subsystems were designed to return a quantity of photographic data significantly in excess of Mariner 4's single camera system.[56]

Mariners 6 and 7

Introduction

Mariners 6 and 7 were launched after three years of preparation. The basic configuration of the spacecraft was similar to Mariner 4.

The octagonal shape of the main structure which housed the electronic subsystems, the use of solar panels to produce electricity, and the use of gas jets to make the probes three axis stabilized craft were retained from their predecessor.[57] These twin probes, however, mounted two television cameras each in contrast with Mariner 4's solitary instrument. This dual system permitted a probe to produce both wide angle and telephoto images of Mars.[58] Mariners 6 and 7 also carried both digital and analog tape recorders and were capable of relaying photographs in real time, much like the Ranger and Surveyor probes.[59]

Design Criteria

The two primary design criteria for Mariners 6 and 7 that influenced the television subsystems' design were the photographic results of the Mariner 4 flight and economic considerations. Based upon Mariner 4's photographs, for example, it was discovered that Mars' surface, in terms of its photographic qualities, was low in contrast. It was determined that the placement of minus blue filters on Mariners 6 and 7's telephoto lenses would increase the contrast of their photographs. Consequently, the minus blue filters enhanced the photographs by making surface features more distinguishable.[60]

The economic criterion was the limited funds that were available for the mission. Instead of designing and constructing a new television subsystem, existing hardware was used on the probes. To increase the photographic storage capacity, for example, two tape recorders based on Mariner 4's design were modified and carried aboard each spacecraft. This system eliminated the necessity of designing a new recorder with a large enough capacity to store the data.[61] Thus, an economic criterion influenced the technological design and operation of the television subsystems.

Mariners 6 and 7 also mounted two cameras whereas Mariner 4 was limited by its launch vehicle, an Atlas D–Agena B rocket, and could only carry one television camera.[62] Mariners 6 and 7, however, were each launched on an Atlas–Centaur rocket which had a larger payload capacity. This enabled project designers to add the second television camera on the spacecraft.[63]

Camera Design

In addition to permitting two cameras to be mounted on each spacecraft, the more powerful launch vehicles also made it possible to use a hybrid tape recorder system consisting of two magnetic tape recorders. A digital recorder stored the precision photographic data in a digital format while an analog recorder stored a larger volume of data in its original analog form. This recorder type was used instead of another digital device because it could store a greater number of photographs in analog form than a digital recorder could store in a digital format on equal lengths of tape.[64] Hence, the mission requirement for precise digital data and a large photographic capacity was satisfied by the digital and analog system.[65]

The photographic acquisition and recording sequences consisted of the following steps. A camera's shutter was activated and depending upon the intensity, or brightness of the light reflected from Mars' surface, a shutter speed of 90 or 180 milliseconds for the wide angle camera and 6 or 12 milliseconds for the telephoto camera was selected. An automatic aperture control, which was an electronic sensor, measured the light's intensity and chose the appropriate shutter speed.[66]

After the shutter was triggered, the light that entered through a camera's lens was focused onto the slow scan vidicon's photoconductor. The photoconductor was then scanned at a rate of 42.2 seconds for one frame for both the wide angle and telephoto cameras. Each frame consisted of 704 scan lines.[67] This represented a 504 line increase over Mariner 4's photographs and consequently, a greater amount of detail was visible in Mariners 6 and 7's pictures.

Both cameras also operated sequentially, much like the cameras on the Ranger spacecraft. When one camera was being scanned, the other was in the process of being erased in preparation for the next exposure. An electron beam erased a photoconductor in 31.68 seconds.[69]

After the photoconductor was scanned, the video signal was amplified and split into digital and analog streams which led to digital and analog recorders respectively.[70] The digital stream was "sampled," that is, only every seventh picture element was selected and each sampled element was digitized into an eight bit "word." The sampling for these and the other outer space probes was a data compression technique. Since the data were sampled, as on Mariner 4, not all of the pictorial information was processed, transmitted, or stored. Thus, because of the lower quantity of data that had to be transmitted, for example, the information was accommodated by the spacecraft's transmission subsystem.

The digital data were then further processed in several additional steps until they were either stored on the tape recorder for transmission at a later time or a segment of a complete photograph was transmitted in real time. In the real-time operation, the photographic data were relayed to earth as soon as they were processed.[71] Because of power limitations and the spacecrafts' transmission subsystems, however, only these partial photographs were capable of transmission in this mode.

The realtime transmission was also made possible through the use of the Deep Space Network's powerful 210 foot (64 meter) receiving antenna at Goldstone, California, which had not existed during the Mariner 4 mission. Furthermore, Mariners 6 and 7 were equipped with larger antennas and more powerful transmitters. The spacecraft, therefore, were able to relay more data and stronger signals.[72] In addition, when Goldstone was in position to receive Mariners 6 and 7's photographic data, a transmission rate of up to 16,200 bits per second for recorded data was possible in contrast with Mariner 4's 8⅓ bits per second rate. At other times, the smaller 25.9 meter antennas were employed and received the data at a lower rate.

In the analog stream, the data were channelled through an automatic gain control which maintained the signal at a constant and steady level. The signal was then fed through a cubing circuit which enhanced the signal. After undergoing an additional process, the signal was stored on the analog tape recorder.[73] Unlike the digital data, however, the analog information was not relayed in real time.

When the analog data were ready for transmission, they first passed through an analog-to-digital converter. In this way each picture element was transformed into a six bit word. The data were then at times temporarily stored on the digital tape recorder and later transmitted. Because of the higher volume of pictures the analog recorder stored in contrast with its digital counterpart, it required several recordings on the part of the digital recorder to accommodate the analog's photographic data.[74]

In terms of its storage capacity, Mariners 6 and 7's digital/analog system stored 1.8×10^8 bits of information in contrast to Mariner 4's 5×10^6 bits. Furthermore, each one of Mariners 6 and 7's photographs were composed of 665,280 picture elements in contrast with Mariner 4's 40,000 elements.[75] The latter spacecraft's pictures were also represented by only 64 levels or steps of gray, ranging from black through white with a six bits word per picture element. Mariner 6 and 7's digital data were encoded into 256 levels with an eight bit word per element and 254 intermediate levels of gray in the transmitted photographs.[76]

After the photographic data were relayed in real time or transmitted in the digital mode, e.g., at a rate up to 16,200 bits per second,[77] they were recorded on magnetic tape on earth and computer processed. It was during this image processing and enhancing stage that the flexibility of the analog/digital recording system was fully revealed. The original analog data in which all of the picture elements were digitized for transmission were used to produce maximum definition photographs. These pictures revealed detailed surface features of Mars, such as craters and other geological formations. The analog and digital data for the same photograph were also recombined: the analog and digital streams were merged to produce a photometric version of the data[78] — one in which the video information was quantitative as to the brightness level of the data measured.[79] The photometric pictures, therefore, depicted the brightness or the light and dark variations of the Martian surface in lieu of specific geological details.[80]

Camera Optics

The camera lenses which produced these photographs were a 508mm F/2.4 Schmidt Cassegrain telephoto and a 52mm F/5.5 wide angle lens, with respective field of views of 1.1° × 1.4° and 11° × 14°.[81] The telephoto's field of view was equal to a 100 × 100 kilometer area of Mars and the lens resolved surface features as small as 300 meters. The wide angle's nominal coverage was a 1000 × 1000 mile region with a maximum resolution of 3 kilometers.[82]

The television subsystem also produced nested photographs similar to those generated by the Lunar Orbiter probes. With this process, the regions photographed by the high resolution telephoto were also imaged by the wide angle lens. Thus, the high resolution pictures revealed small surface features within a wide angle view of these specific areas on Mars.[83] Successive wide angle images also overlapped each other much like the picture pairs produced by Mariner 4. It was within this overlapped region that the high resolution images were nested.[84]

The wide angle lens on each spacecraft was also fitted with red, green, and blue filters on a moveable wheel. After an exposure was made through one of the filters, the wheel was rotated and a different filter was placed within a lens' optical path. These filters served the same function as they did on the Mariner 4 flight in that they enhanced color, surface, and in this instance, atmospheric features of Mars.[85] They were also used to create color composites of the planet in a procedure pioneered by the Surveyor spacecraft. Three photographs of the same region were taken in succession through the red, blue, and green filters. The three images were recombined on earth to produce the final color print.[86]

Far and Near Encounters

The television cameras themselves were mounted on a scan platform that was similar in operation to that of Mariner 4's. There was a difference, however, in that Mariner 4's platform remained stationary during the probe's flyby, while Mariners 6 and 7's system was capable of moving 70° in an up and down motion and in a 215° arc. This movement was controlled by an onboard computer with programmed instructions which was also capable of implementing new commands transmitted from earth.[87] Consequently, mission operators were able to point the television cameras toward specific regions of Mars during the spacecrafts' flybys.

The photographic survey conducted by each Mariner was divided into a near and far encounter phase. The far encounter commenced when a spacecraft was still several days from its closest approach to Mars. At this time, the high resolution telephoto was activated and photographed full disc views of Mars as it rotated on successive days. Consequently, the whole planet's surface was visually imaged during the far encounter due to Mars' rotational movement.[88]

In the near encounter phase, the telephoto and wide angle cameras photographed the planet in both real time and recorded modes. The photographs relayed by Mariner 6 which preceded Mariner 7 also revealed an atmospheric anomaly in the region of the southern polar cap. The mission operators, therefore, programmed Mariner 7's scan platform to aim its cameras at this region during the flyby and its near encounter phase with the planet.[89]

When both missions were completed, Mariner 6 had transmitted 50 far encounter, 26 near encounter, and 428 real-time images. Mariner 7 relayed 93 far encounter, 33 near encounter, and 749 real-time photographs.[90] This constituted the most extensive survey of Mars by visual imaging subsystems up until that time, for not only were full disc images relayed, but the large number of both high and low resolution photographs that were taken during the near encounters mapped wide sections of the planet's surface.

Conclusion

The success of the Mariners 6 and 7 mission was due, in part, to the Mariner 4 flight. This spacecraft demonstrated that digital television equipment could function on outer space probes and that the digital transmission of photographic data was a viable means of communication.

Mariners 6 and 7 evolved from Mariner 4, using two television cameras instead of one. The single digital tape recorder was also replaced by a hybrid analoy/digital system in which the advantages of both types of recorders were realized. The spacecrafts' television subsystems also produced images with 704 scan lines per frame, 665,280 picture elements, and a 256-step, black through white color range—in contrast with Mariner 4's 200 scan lines, 40,000 picture elements, and 64-step photographs.[91]

This technological evolution and development of the Mariner series, however, did not stop with Mariners 6 and 7. The next step was achieved during Mariner 9's extended mission when the spacecraft orbited Mars and imaged the planet while its surface features went through the different Martian seasons.

Mariner 9

Introduction

When the mission objectives for Mariner 9 were originally drafted, NASA planned to use two spacecraft in the same manner as the Mariners 6 and 7 flights. A problem developed, however, during Mariner 8's launch. Before the Atlas/Centaur rocket could boost the spacecraft into its trajectory toward Mars, the rocket malfunctioned and plunged into the ocean, thus destroying the Mariner probe.[92] The mission of completing the photographic reconnaissance of Mars that was designed for two spacecraft was subsequently modified to be completed by only Mariner 9.

On May 30, 1971, 21 days after Mariner 8 was destroyed, NASA launched Mariner 9. After a six month flight, the probe was inserted into an orbital slot around Mars and became the first unmanned spacecraft to orbit another planet. When the mission was completed on October 27, 1972, Mariner 9 had visually imaged the complete surface area of Mars and transmitted 7,329 photographs to earth.[93]

Camera Design

Many of the television subsystem's components which produced these pictures were similar in design and operation to those used on the Mariner 6 and 7 probes. In order to avoid redundancy, therefore, only the distinguishing characteristics of Mariner 9's assembly will be described in depth.

Mariner 9 mounted two television cameras with slow scan vidicon tubes as the imaging sensors on a scan platform. When an exposure was made, the shutter speed was selected according to the brightness of the surface area that the probe was imaging. This operation was automatically controlled by the spacecraft or from a command relayed by the mission controllers. In its nominal operational mode, when a series of photographs was about to be taken, the shutter was first activated without actually producing a photograph. This initial exposure, however, permitted the spacecraft's sensor to measure the light level of the region of Mars the cameras were going to image. Based upon this information, the preselected shutter speed was increased or decreased one increment in speed, or it remained the same when the actual imaging sequence began.[94]

The cameras' shutter range was increased for this flight, anticipating Mariner 9's extended surveillance of Mars as it orbited the planet. The mission objective to map 70% of the Martian landscape over different seasons meant that the cameras would encounter a wide range of lighting conditions.[95] This variance in surface brightness and the information generated from the earlier missions dictated that a wide shutter speed range should be adopted, to produce accurate exposures of Mars in most situations.

After the shutter speed was selected and an actual exposure was made, a camera's photoconductor was scanned in 42 seconds and produced the video signal. The two cameras also operated sequentially. When one camera was making an exposure, the other was erasing its image. The elapsed time for a complete scan and erase cycle was 84 seconds per camera.[96] When the scanning was completed, the analog video signal passed through a an analog-to-digital converter and the picture elements were encoded into nine-bit words. The data was then stored on Mariner 9's single digital magnetic tape recorder.[97]

The use of a single digital recorder in place of Mariner 6 and 7's analog/digital system was one of the major design modifications of the Mariner 9 probe. This device, however, was capable of storing the same amount of bits as Mariner 6 and 7's two instruments.[98] For the Mariner 9 probe, which recorded its data only in digital form, this was equal to approximately 31 pictures in one recorder load. In an average day, the spacecraft was capable of recording and transmitting up to two tape recorder loads for a total of 62 pictures.[99] Each one of these photographs was composed of 700 scan lines per frame with 832 picture elements on a line. Thus, a picture consisted of 582,400 picture elements.[100]

After the recorder had stored one load of photographs, the data were transmitted to earth at a maximum speed of 16,200 bits per second on an S band communication channel pioneered by Mariner 4. In order for this high speed transmission to occur, Mariner 9's and Goldstone's antennas had to be properly aligned. Accordingly, a timetable was devised for the mission when it would be possible to achieve the high speed linkup between the spacecraft and the earth.[101] At other times, the photographic information was transmitted at a lower rate to one of the Deep Space Network's smaller receiving antennas.

Unlike Mariners 6 and 7, Mariner 9 did not relay its photographs in real time. In contrast to a flyby mission where the visual imaging sequence might have lasted only several days as a probe approached, encountered, and departed from a planetary body, Mariner 9 was in a long term orbit around Mars. Its active photographic survey period was measured in months. There was sufficient time, therefore, for the spacecraft to transmit its photographs in other than real time; that is, first recording the pictures then playing them back and relaying them to earth. As it was demonstrated during the Mariner 10 mission, which will be discussed in the final section of this chapter, real-time transmissions were valuable under certain circumstances.[102] In terms of a photograph's technical quality, however, other than real-time images, such as those produced by Mariner 9's television subsystem, were generally superior to the real-time pictures. Thus, the non-real-time mode was employed on Mariner 9 to yield the maximum data from its photographs.

Once the data were received on earth, they were recorded on magnetic tape for computer processing. The photographs were then manipulated like those from the earlier missions to produce both photometric and detailed images of Mars. The photometric images highlighted Mars' light and dark surface variations while the detailed pictures revealed the planet's geological features.[103]

Camera Optics

The lenses mounted on Mariner 9's two cameras were almost identical in design to those employed on the Mariner 6 and 7 spacecraft. The 50mm F/4.0 wide angle lens yielded a 11° × 14° field of view and the telephoto, which was a modified Cassegrain telescope, had a 1.1° × 1.4° field of view. The only alterations from the earlier mission were minor in nature. The wide angle's aperture was changed from F/5.5 to F4.0 and one of the telephoto's mirror mounts was modified.[104]

Furthermore, the minus blue filter originally fitted onto Mariner 6 and 7's telephoto lenses was likewise retained. The number of filters for the wide angle lens, however, was increased to eight. They were mounted on a moveable filter wheel which advanced one or two filters after every exposure. An override command also existed which hindered the wheel's movement. Consequently, the same filter remained in the lens' optical path for two or more consecutive exposures.[105]

Since Mariner 9 photographed Mars as it orbited around the planet, the surface area each lens imaged was determined by the orbital altitude. From a height of 2,000 kilometers, for example, the wide angle's 11° × 14° field of view photographed a 380 × 500 kilometer section of Mars. As the orbit increased in height, so too did the photographed region. Thus, from a 6,000 kilometer orbit, the lens covered an 1150 × 1500 kilometer section of the planet.[106.]

The wide angle lens resolved surface features between one and three

MARINER NARROW ANGLE TV CAMERA

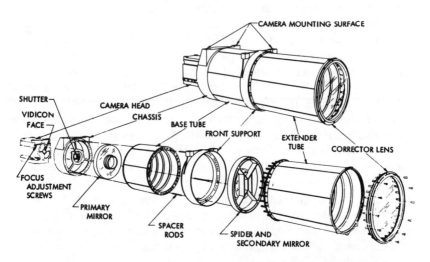

This camera has a modified Cassegrain telescope lens design (courtesy NASA).

kilometers while the telephoto had a resolution of 100 to 300 meters. During the spacecraft's photographic survey, 100% of its surface area was visually imaged by the low resolution wide angle lens. Approximately 1 to 2% of this area was photographed by the telephoto.[107] The low resolution images, therefore, produced a general survey of Mars while the high resolution frames depicted specific geological features and surface markings within the context of the wide angle frames.

The photographs from both lenses were also used to construct maps of Mars and control networks of the planet.[108] (A control network is a map with identifiable geological formations and the coordinates of these landmarks.)

The final technical component of Mariner 9's optics that merits discussion was the thermal protection afforded the lenses. Like all spacecraft, Mariner 9's optical components were constructed of materials relatively insensitive to temperature variations. This was especially vital for a telephoto lens which employed a Cassegrain design, due to its mirror system. A temperature shift could cause a mirror or its mount to expand or contract. This, in turn, could alter the preset focus of the lens and degrade the image quality of the transmitted photographs.[109]

On an extended mission such as Mariner 9's when the spacecraft was exposed to a number of temperature gradations during its orbit around Mars, an attempt was made to maintain the telephoto lens' temperature at a constant level. This would prevent the optical elements from expanding and contracting and would help to eliminate defocused images. One method of preserving the optimum environment was the placement of an

MARINER WIDE ANGLE TV CAMERA

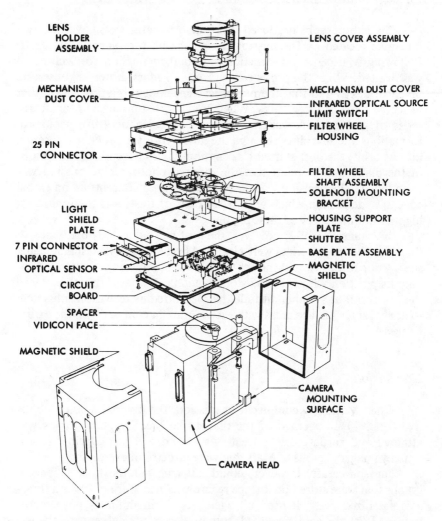

LENS HOLDER ASSEMBLY

LENS COVER ASSEMBLY

MECHANISM DUST COVER

MECHANISM DUST COVER

INFRARED OPTICAL SOURCE

LIMIT SWITCH

FILTER WHEEL HOUSING

25 PIN CONNECTOR

FILTER WHEEL SHAFT ASSEMBLY

SOLENOID MOUNTING BRACKET

LIGHT SHIELD PLATE

HOUSING SUPPORT PLATE

SHUTTER

7 PIN CONNECTOR

BASE PLATE ASSEMBLY

INFRARED OPTICAL SENSOR

MAGNETIC SHIELD

CIRCUIT BOARD

SPACER

VIDICON FACE

MAGNETIC SHIELD

CAMERA MOUNTING SURFACE

CAMERA HEAD

Almost identical to cameras on Mariners 6 and 7, but with an aperture of F/4.0 instead of F/5.5 (courtesy NASA).

electric heater system on the telephoto tube.[110] The heater helped maintain a constant temperature along the tube's length. This system was similarly employed during the Mariners 6 and 7 mission. Another solution was the use of thermal materials or insulation blankets constructed from aluminum mylar which were wrapped around the camera system. The blanket provided an insulation layer against the environment of outer space and helped stabilize the temperature of the cameras and their lenses.[111]

Photographic Sequence

The photographs produced from these cameras were governed by a timetable created by the mission designers and the planet Mars itself. Following Mariner 8's destruction, a modified mission for Mariner 9 was drafted. While the probe was en route to Mars, however, observers on earth discovered that the planet was enveloped in a dust storm that obscured most of its features. When Mariner 9 approached Mars, three series of photographs were taken which revealed only five geological formations and markings through the dust. After the probe was inserted into its orbit, the dust started clearing, but it still obscured observations of the planet to the point that the original photographic mission was abandoned. The decision was made, therefore, to concentrate on global coverage, determine which areas were clear of dust, and then initiate a high resolution survey of these regions.[112]

By January of 1972, however, the dust had sufficiently dissipated so that wide sections of Mars were clear and became suitable visual imaging sites. Prior to this time, Mariner 9's orbit was adjusted to better coordinate its position with the Goldstone antenna. Its new orbit also placed the spacecraft at a higher altitude that permitted its television subsystem to image larger surface areas with each picture in contrast with the earlier images.[113]

Conclusion

When Mariner 9 completed its mission, the original mission objective for a 70% coverage of the planet's surface by photographs was attained and surpassed.[114] Due to its extended flight, Mariner 9 also visually imaged regions of Mars that were hitherto unexplored.

The spacecraft, however, could not transmit the final 15 photographs that were stored on its tape recorder. Since Mariner 9 was a three-axis stabilized craft, it used nitrogen jets to maintain its proper attitude.[115] With the data generated from its electro-optical sensors, the jets maneuvered Mariner 9 durings its orbits to maintain its sun lock. Hence, the solar panels remained pointed toward the sun in order for the power subsystem to generate the probe's electrical energy. Before the 15 photographs could be transmitted, Mariner 9's nitrogen gas supply was depleted. Consequently, the sun lock was lost. This led to a series of steps whereby the solar panels and the transmitting antenna deviated from their positions, electricity was no longer generated, and the probe's recording and transmission subsystems' power supply was eliminated. This prevented the relay of Mariner 9's final photographs.[116]

Several years after the conclusion of this mission, NASA launched four more spacecraft for its final—up to the time this book was written—investigation of Mars. These probes were the two Viking Orbiters and Viking Landers. Their combined photographic output produced high resolution images of the planet from both its surface and orbital positions.

Viking Orbiter

Introduction

The Viking Mars mission encompassed four spacecraft. These were the two Viking Landers that soft-landed on the planet and the two Viking Orbiters that orbited around Mars. Viking Orbiters 1 and 2 are the concern of this section.

The two Viking Orbiters were twin spacecraft designed to transport the Viking Landers to Mars. They also initiated a photographic reconnaissance of the planet to locate suitable landing sites for the Landers, provided photographic data in support of the Landers' missions, and produced high resolution photographs of Mars' surface.[117] The Orbiters' missions were also divided into primary and extended phases. During the primary mission, a spacecraft remained in the proximity of its Lander to provide technical support. This included relaying a Lander's data at a high rate to earth. When the primary mission was completed and most of the Lander's mission objectives were satisfied, the extended mission began. During this phase, an Orbiter was no longer locked in a support position for a Lander and was able to shift its orbit to investigate other regions of Mars.[118]

An Orbiter's design was based upon the Mariner series. It was a three-axis stabilized spacecraft with a configuration similar to the earlier Mariner probes. The mission requirements of housing and transporting the Landers to Mars, however, necessitated a number of design modifications that made an Orbiter larger and heavier than the previous Mariners. Consequently, when Viking 1 and Viking 2 were launched on August 20 and September 9, 1975, respectively, a new launch vehicle, a Titan III/Centaur, was employed to boost each spacecraft toward its Martian rendezvous.[119]

The operational status of the twin Orbiters ended at different times during their missions. Orbiter 2's subsystems were powered down on July 25, 1978, while Orbiter 1 continued functioning through and beyond 1979.[120] Both spacecraft survived beyond their nominal life expectancies, which had been established as one year.

Design Criteria

The primary design criterion for an Orbiter's television subsystem was the mission objective of producing photographic data in support of the Viking Landers. Accordingly, an Orbiter had to photograph a contiguous 100 kilometer region of Mars that encircled each Lander.[121] The television subsystems on the earlier Mariner probes were not capable of fulfilling this criterion. Thus, even though the wide angle camera of Mariner 9's subsystem would have been able to photograph this area, because of its wide field of view, the lens' low resolution would not have satisfied the mission requirements. The telephoto camera, on the other hand, produced photographs with an acceptable resolution value, yet its field of view was so limited that by the time the camera completed its 84 second scan cycle the target would have already passed out of the lens' field of view because of the spacecraft's forward motion.[122] Even if the wide angle and the telephoto cameras were sequentially activated in order to reduce the time of the imaging cycle, the combination of the mismatched fields of view in addition to the low resolution of the wide angle camera would have negated the use of this particular television system.

An additional design criterion was the necessity that an Orbiter's television subsystem produce high resolution photographs depicting small geological features. This was accomplished, in part, because of an Orbiter's ability to visually image Mars from a low altitude.[123] The earlier Lunar Orbiters were also capable of generating highly resolved photographs of the moon through the use of film as its imaging sensor and the image motion compensation device. In a flyby or orbital mission, if a spacecraft approached too close to the surface of a planetary body as it began its picture taking sequence, a combination of the low altitude and the probe's motion over the terrain smeared the pictures. A Lunar Orbiter's compensation system helped eliminate image smear. The spacecraft, therefore, was technically able to photograph the moon from a low altitude and produce images which resolved small lunar features.[124]

A Viking Orbiter with its television subsystem was also able to provide its own form of image motion compensation. When the spacecraft imaged Mars from a low altitude, such as 300 and 800 kilometers, the cameras' scan platform moved in a predetermined direction throughout this sequence. These maneuvers served the same purpose as the Lunar Orbiter's motion compensation device. The slewing, or motion, of the scan platform compensated for a Viking Orbiter's motion and helped reduce image smearing.[125] A Viking Orbiter's television subsystem, therefore, was designed to provide contiguous high resolution photographs of Mars taken at low altitudes.

Camera Design

A Viking Orbiter's television subsystem consisted of two identical television cameras with slow scan vidicons as the imaging sensors. The cameras operated sequentially like those on earlier flights in that when one camera was being scanned, the other vidicon was being erased. It required 8.96 seconds for an Orbiter to image Mars, scan and erase its photoconductor, and read or feed the video data to a digital tape recorder.[126]

In summation, while one camera's photoconductor was erased, the other camera was in the process of activating its shutter and imaging Mars. After an Orbiter's camera had completed its 8.96 second cycle, therefore, the other camera had already imaged the planet. This meant that the Orbiter's television subsystem was capable of producing one photograph every 4.48 seconds.[127]

This high rate of picture acquisition permitted an Orbiter to produce contiguous picture sequences. The television subsystem was also modified to produce technically superior photographs. During the erase cycle, the photoconductor was not flooded with an electron beam as it was on Mariners 4, 6, 7, and 9. Rather, a system of flood lamps, much like those used on the lunar probes, erased the Orbiter's photoconductors. An inflight calibration of the system revealed that only 0.5% of the residual image's modulation, or its imprint on the photoconductor, remained after the erasing cycle was completed.[128] The electron beam procedure was abandoned because it never completely erased the residual image which technically impaired the next image imprinted on the photoconductor. The flood lamps, which were also used for the Mariner 10 mission, eliminated this source of technical interference.[129]

After a camera was scanned, its analog video signal was digitized. Each picture element was translated into a seven-bit word. There were also 1056 scan lines per frame and 1,182 picture elements per line. This was equal to 1,248,192 elements in every photograph. The brightness of each picture element ranged from 0 to 127, or black to white with graduated levels of gray.[130] Finally, the resolution of an Orbiter's television subsystem surpassed those on the earlier Mariner spacecraft. This was a reflection of both the development of the technology for camera assemblies and of the mission objectives for the Orbiter. The production of high resolution photographs was a necessity since mission personnel used the pictures to locate suitable landing sites for the Viking Landers.[131]

After the analog signal was digitized, it passed through a flight data subsystem which divided the signals into seven separate data streams. Each stream was then channelled to one of seven tracks on a magnetic tape recorder. In addition, because of the rapid camera sequencing and production of photographic data, the flight data system also functioned as a buffer between the acquisition of the video data at 2.112 million bits per second and its subsequent storage on one of the digital recorder's seven tracks at a rate of 314,000 bits per second. The video signal, therefore, was generated by the cameras at a rate surpassing the recording ability of a recorder. Consequently, the flight data system functioned to reduce the rate to a level that a recorder was capable of accommodating.[132] The storage capacity for one recorder was approximately 60 photographs.

The stored data on all seven tracks were then transmitted to earth one track at a time. This information was then recorded on magnetic tape upon its reception. It was subsequently processed in order to merge the tracks and reproduce the original picture.[133] In addition, the data were computer processed to create topographic relief maps, color composites, and other visual displays of Mars. The Orbiter transmitted its data at a maximum rate of 16,200 bits per second in conjunction with the Deep Space Network's 64 meter antenna. At this speed, it required ten minutes to relay one picture and this time period increased if a lower transmission rate was employed with one of the smaller receiving antennas.[134]

In summation, the Viking Orbiter television subsystem acquired data at a rate hitherto possible only with a film system such as the one employed on a Lunar Orbiter spacecraft. This probe stored its data at a rapid pace for, unlike a television subsystem, once a frame of film was exposed, it was not necessary to scan a photoconductor and then read the data into a recorder or channel them to a transmission system for a realtime relay. Rather, the Lunar Orbiter exposed a frame of film and it was immediatly advanced to position the next frame of unexposed film into the film gate.[135] This eliminated the steps of scanning a photoconductor, feeding the signal to a recorder or transmission system, and erasing the residual image, which were necessary operations with a television subsystem.

A Viking Orbiter's 8.96 second scan and erase cycle, however, helped alleviate the time delay factor inherent in television subsystems. Even though its imaging cycle was slower than that of a Lunar Orbiter, nevertheless, the television cameras were capable of operating sequentially at a rate rapid enough to satisfy the mission requirement of providing the contiguous coverage of Mars' terrain.[136]

The final component of the camera subsystem was its thermal protection. In addition to the usual thermal insulation materials, the top section of the cameras were fitted with moveable louvers. The louvers resembled and operated much like venetian blinds on windows. If the heat within the camera became too great because of environmental conditions and camera electronics, the louvers automatically opened to dissipate the heat and cool the equipment.[137]

Camera Optics

The lenses for the cameras were identical in focal length and design. When the optical system was initially drafted, the lenses were mated with image intensifiers. These components would have increased the sensitivity of the television cameras in terms of their ability to image Mars. The intensifiers were abandoned, however, when they failed to meet design specifications.[138]

The subsystem's final design, therefore, consisted of twin 475mm F/3.5 telephotos which were based upon a modified Cassegrain configuration. The cameras were mounted on a scan platform and were canted on a 1.38° angle from each other. A lens' field of view was 1.54° × 1.69° and represented a 40 × 44 kilometer region of Mars from an altitude of 1,500 kilometers. Since the cameras were canted, their combined field of view was 3.1° × 1.51° and produced a 80 kilometer wide swath of Mars.[139] Furthermore, the photographs that were produced by one camera overlapped each succeeding frame and yielded a continuous photographic strip of Mars' surface along the Orbiter's flight path and within the lens' field of view.[140]

Each camera was also fitted with a complement of six filters on a moveable filter wheel. They primarily served the same function as on the earlier probes and were also used to produce three-image color composites of Mars.[141]

Camera Command Subsystem

The television cameras were controlled by the Camera Command Subsystem (CCS), which was an advanced computer system. The CCS received and implemented commands from earth in addition to storing a series of commands to initiate and complete specific sequences. In terms of the television subsystem, the CCS controlled the recording and playback of the tape recorders, the movement of the scan platform, and the flight data subsystem (FDS). The FDS, in turn, functioned as a buffer for the tape recorders and activated the cameras' shutters and their erase cycles.[142] In its role as a buffer, the FDS received the photographic data as they were produced and then channelled them to a tape recorder at a rate compatible with this system. In summation, the CCS was the master control unit for an Orbiter while the FDS monitored and regulated the cameras' basic operations.

Camera Event Sequence

The deployment of the television subsystem during the actual mission was as follows. When Viking Orbiter 1 was within 120 hours of its insertion into a Mars orbit, it relayed its first far encounter photographs of the planet. This survey enabled scientists to determine the visual clarity of Mars' atmosphere in order to predict the visibility of its surface for the forthcoming pictures as the probe orbited the planet.[143] After seven days, the spacecraft achieved orbit and initiated its photographic reconnaissance in conjunction with earth based radar. Both the Orbiter's photographs and the information generated from the radar depicted the profile of Mars' surface at selected sites to locate a safe landing area for Viking Lander 1.[144] A northwest section of the Chryse region of Mars was then selected as the data from the pictures and radar revealed that this site appeared to be free of major geological obstructions that could have damaged the probe. The Viking Lander then separated from the Orbiter and soft-landed on Mars.

After the Lander was safely secured on the surface, the Orbiter was locked in a synchronous orbit about the Lander. In this mode, the spacecraft remained stationed over the general area of the Viking's landing site and functioned as a relay for the Lander's photographic data in addition to providing other mission support.[145] During the final stages of the primary mission and throughout the extended mission, the Orbiter was released from its synchronous orbit and visually imaged other regions of Mars. The same sequence of events was similarly followed by Viking Orbiter and Lander 2.

One of the Viking Orbiter's components that permitted the television subsystem to image these extensive areas of Mars and to produce the high resolution photographs throughout the primary and extended mission phases was the scan platform. This mechanism moved the cameras and the other instruments it mounted in two axes. The first movement was an arc between the angles of 80° and 310°. The second was an up and down or a cone motion whereby the platform moved between 90° and 175° in elevation. This freedom of movement permitted the platform, and thus the cameras, to image Mars in predetermined patterns in addition to reducing image smear at low altitudes.[146]

Conclusion

The success of the Viking Orbiters' scan platforms and their television subsystems enabled the spacecraft to transmit high resolution photographs of Mars and its moons, Phobos and Deimos, that surpassed those from any previous mission. Both spacecraft also survived their primary missions and commenced their extended operations. On July 25, 1978, however, Viking Orbiter 2 suffered a fate similar to that of Mariner 9. A leak and malfunction in the attitude jets' gas system depleted the spacecraft's gas supply and caused the probe to lose its sun lock. Shortly thereafter, it ceased all transmissions. Nevertheless, Viking 2 did relay 16,525 photographs to earth during its 700 orbits around Mars.[147]

Viking Orbiter 1 survived beyond its contemporary's operational period. In December of 1978, however, it photographic mission was curtailed to approximately four pictures a day. The Pioneer Venus and the Voyager probes were approaching Venus and Jupiter respectively. These missions were granted a priority status over the Viking mission since the Vikings had already completed their primary assignments. Therefore, mission personnel and the number of hours the Deep Space Network devoted to the Mars mission were reduced. Yet, even with the photographic transmission restriction, Orbiter 1 relayed over 24,000 photographs of Mars durings its lifetime.[148]

In conclusion, the Viking Orbiters constituted only half of the Viking mission. While these spacecraft surveyed the planet during their orbital rotations, the Viking Landers investigated Mars from its surface. A variety of instruments were carried by each Lander, including two cameras that were mounted on each probe.

Viking Lander

Introduction

The two Viking Landers, 1 and 2, were analogous to the Surveyor lunar probes in that they were NASA's first spacecraft to soft-land on another planet just as the Surveyors landed on the moon. A Viking also physically resembled a Surveyor in certain facets of its design, such as in the landing struts and pads. At the same time the Viking Lander represented a radical departure from the earlier spacecraft, especially in the design and operation of its visual imaging subsystem.

A Surveyor was also dependent upon commands from earth for the operation of its subsystems, and each probe functioned as an independent unit. The Viking Lander, on the other hand, incorporated a sophisticated onboard computer system and operated in conjunction with the Viking Orbiters. It was also capable of functioning independently of the Orbiters since the spacecraft could transmit its own data to earth or use an Orbiter as a communication relay between the earth and the Lander.[149]

A Lander's mission was divided into primary and extended mission phases just like an Orbiter's. Both Landers transmitted 1,076 photographs during the primary phase and a total of 3,388 photographs by July 31, 1979, which was the end of the extended mission.[150] Approximately four months before this time, the probes began operating in an automatic transmission mode as the constraints that reduced the personnel and the Deep Space Network's receiving hours for the Orbiters likewise affected the Viking Landers.[151] As of early 1983, Viking Lander 1 is still operational and periodically transmits meteorological data to earth upon command.

Design Criteria

The data a Lander transmitted during its primary and extended mission phases ranged from the results of biological experiments attempting to detect Martian lifeforms to photographs relayed by the spacecraft's cameras. As with the electro-optical subsystems used on earlier probes, the Viking's system was influenced by specific mission and technological criteria.

One such factor was the type of camera selected for the mission. Instead of designing an imaging system with a slow scan vidicon, the engineers and mission planners devised a facsimile scanning camera that employed 12 silicon photodiodes as the imaging sensors.[152] A photodiode was a sensor that measured the amount of light directed onto its surface. An electrical signal proportionate to the brightness of the light was then produced.

A facsimile camera was chosen primarily because of mechanical and electronic simplicity in comparison with a television camera and its slow scan vidicon. Hence, the facsimile camera was less prone to mechanical and electronic malfunctions.[153]

The camera also weighed less than a comparable television camera. This was an important feature for a Viking Lander since the craft was weight limited. The method in which the photographic data were transmitted by a facsimile system also permitted wide angle panoramic vistas of the Martian terrain to be produced as the data were received on earth.[154] In contrast with this, a television subsystem generated separate and individual photographs. If a panoramic image was therefore produced, a series of smaller photographs had to be combined to create the finished picture. This process was called mosaicking.[155]

As its name implies, mosaicking is a method of completing a picture of the lunar surface surrounding a Surveyor spacecraft, for example, or of a section of Mars that was visually imaged by an Orbiter and its television cameras. The photographs which constituted a panoramic picture or mosaic were not randomly exposed. In the case of a Surveyor, after one photograph was taken, the camera's mirror was slightly moved to photograph an adjacent area of the lunar surface. This sequence was then repeated in a programmed pattern until the preselected region was imaged. The photographs were combined on earth to create the finished mosaic which displayed the specific area of the moon in one continuous view.[156] This process was analogous to joining the individual pieces of a puzzle to complete a picture. In this instance, the puzzle pieces were the equivalent of the individual photographs while the completed puzzle was analogous to the panorama.

In addition to the task of joining the photographs, a spacecraft with a television subsystem, such as a Surveyor, had to be issued a complex series of commands to transmit the specific photographs required to produce the panorama. A Viking Lander, for example, created a 360° panorama with one photograph. The Surveyor, however, transmitted 130 individual wide angle or 1000 narrow angle pictures, in which the camera lens was set at the 25mm or 100mm settings respectively, to produce a similar view. This narrow angle survey also required a series of 5,000 commands to complete the picture sequence.[157] Thus, the work involved in generating wide angle views of Mars was simplified with the facsimile camera.

An additional advantage of this camera subsystem was the accuracy of its photogrammetric data. Photogrammetry was the process in which photographs were employed "to measure object sizes, distances, and altitudes."[158] This procedure was used to analyze photographs to reveal geological features, such as a field of rocks that surrounded a Viking Lander. The contours of the surface and the distance between objects was also measured. In essence, photogrammetry employed two-dimensional photographs to yield information in three dimensions.

The Viking Lander's camera also produced precise stereo views of Mars' surface. A photogrammetrist, a person who manipulates photogrammetric data, used the transmitted pictorial information from each of the probe's two cameras to create stereo images and topographic relief maps of the Viking's landing site.[159] Furthermore, in addition to the stereo information, which was itself a facet of photogrammetry, a facsimile camera produced accurate radiometric data. This was the measurement of the radiance of a scene a camera imaged.[160]

Besides the technological criteria that dictated the use of the facsimile camera, there was another criterion that influenced the Lander's imaging subsystem as a whole. This was the use of an auxiliary system permitting a probe to communicate directly with the earth. If the Viking Orbiters, which functioned as relay stations between the earth and a Lander, were unable to receive and transmit a Lander's photographic data, the Lander's own communication system relayed this information.[161]

A Lander also carried an onboard tape recorder to temporarily store its cameras' data. Prior to its launch, the spacecraft was subjected to a severe sterilization process in an attempt to destroy earth organisms it might harbor and thus to prevent the contamination of Mars. When the sterilization was initiated, the probe was already sealed in its bioshield, a shield or cocoon designed to maintain the sterile environment for the Lander and to prevent the Lander from becoming contaminated from the Viking Orbiter mother ship during the flight.[162]

There was therefore a possibility that the tape recorder system might have been damaged during the sterilization period. It was also impossible to test the system to determine its operational status since it was already sealed in the bioshield. Consequently, the Lander was also designed to transmit its photographs in real time to either an Orbiter or to the earth if the recorder malfunctioned.[163]

In summation, it appeared that the Lander's imaging subsystem was designed to fulfill two objectives. The first was the selection of a camera that was lightweight, reliable, and generated accurate radiometric and photographic data. The second objective was insuring that the output from the Lander's instruments reached earth. Thus, the spacecraft's telecommunication subsystem was designed to operate in three modes. The photographs were transmitted to the Viking Orbiter, they were relayed directly to earth, and if the recorder device failed, the Lander employed a real-time transmission procedure.

Camera Design

The two cameras each Lander carried were mounted on the spacecraft's frame in individual mastlike structures. The cameras were separated by .822 meters and the dual system was capable of photographing in stereo approximately one-half of the area in front of and to the rear of the cameras. Finally, a camera could also photograph regions from 40° above through 60° below the horizon and almost 360° in azimuth or in a circle on a horizontal plane.[164]

The top section of the camera's mast rotated in azimuth for the horizontal movement while a scanning mirror mounted at the mast's top generated the vertical motions. The scanning mirror also introduced light, from a scene the camera was imaging, into the mast and onto a photodiode.[165] The function of this mirror, however, was different from one used on a Surveyor spacecraft. A Surveyor's mirror reflected the light to a slow scan vidicon and initiated a series of steps whereby the video signal was generated. The mirror was then moved to another location and another photograph was produced.

The mirror on the Viking camera not only permitted the subsystem to image a scene, as was the case of the Surveyor, but was also an integral component of the imaging process itself. The mirror was constantly engaged in the vertical motion while the mast rotated in azimuth. Consequently, a photograph was gradually produced as the mirror and camera turret completed their movements[166] while a Surveyor's mirror was used to simply image different regions of the spacecraft's landing site or the sky.

Before a Viking Lander began its photographic survey, however, there were several decisions to be made, including the photograph's resolution, if it was going to be a color composite or a black and white picture, and the photograph's coverage or field of view of the landing site. The imaging sensors for a camera were the 12 photodiodes and depending upon the type of photograph selected, a specific diode or a combination of diodes were used to generate the picture.[167]

After the photographic format was determined, the imaging process was initiated. The scanning mirror moved upward in a vertical motion and the light from the scene was reflected through a lens in the mast onto the selected diode. The light was then transformed into an electrical signal. The signal varied in strength as the amount of light from the scene varied during one vertical scan. Each vertical scan, in turn, was divided into 512 separate steps. Once the vertical scan was completed and the data generated during the upward movement, the mirror moved down and the mast assembly was rotated one step in azimuth. The next vertical scan was then completed and the mast was again moved one step in azimuth. This process continued until the photograph was completed.[168] Each azimuth step was equivalent to one horizontal picture element and their number was determined by the width of the finished image. The 512 steps during the vertical scans similarly constituted the vertical picture elements.

The signal produced by the photodiode, with the exception of only one of the 12 sensors, was then amplified, sampled, and digitized into six-bit binary words. The digital encoding also provided for 64 levels of quantization, black to white with intermediate steps of gray, in the transmitted photographs.[169]

Before extensive photographic sequences were produced by the cameras, however, a preliminary survey of the landing site was conducted to measure the intensity of light of this region. Depending upon the measurement, a command was issued to a Lander to alter the gain or sensitivity control of a camera. The gain was the electronic equivalent of an aperture or F/stop on a conventional camera which permitted a greater or lesser quantity of light to fall on the imaging sensor. Since a Lander did not utilize a conventional lens with F/stops, the gain control was adjusted for the different light levels on Mars.[170]

Once the photographic data were generated, they were transmitted at primarily one of two rates. The 250 bits per second mode was employed when the spacecraft transmitted data directly to earth. The data were also relayed at 16,000 bits per second when a Viking Orbiter was

positioned in the vicinity of a Lander. The Lander transmitted its data
to the Orbiter at this high rate and this spacecraft stored the information
on a tape recorder. The Orbiter then relayed the data to earth during a
subsequent transmission.[171]

The transmission mode selected also determined the scanning rate of
the mirror and consequently the output of the photographic data. As the
scan rate increased, the data flow was proportionately upgraded. During
a 250 bits per second relay, therefore, the mirror scanned at a rate which
produced data at a level accommodated by the 250 bits per second transmission speed. As the transmission speed was increased, so did the
mirror's scanning motion and the data flow.[172] The scanning mirror,
therefore, was analogous to the scanning operation of a slow scan vidicon. The scan cycle was adjusted to match the transmission and recording subsystems' respective relay and acquisition rates the same way the
Lander's scanning mirror and transmission modes were coordinated.

Photodiodes

It was during the upward motion of the scanning mirror that the
data were produced and subsequently stored or transmitted in real time.
When the light entered the mast, it was directed at only one photodiode.
Since each of the 12 diodes exhibited different characteristics, a diode was
selected based upon the type of photograph to be created. Four of the
diodes, for example, produced high resolution black and white photographs. These four diodes, in turn, provided optimum focus points
for objects that were 1.9, 2.7, 4.5, and 13.3 meters respectively from the
camera. Thus, if a high resolution black and white photograph for a rock
field that stretched from 13.3 meters to infinity from a camera was desired, a command was issued to the Lander whereby the high resolution
diode for this specific focus range was selected and exclusively employed
throughout the scanning and the production of the picture.[173]

Six of the diodes were capable of yielding multispectral photographs, or those in color or the infrared region of light. In this instance,
if a color photograph was produced, a procedure was adopted analogous
to the creation of a color composite with a television subsystem. In a
similar process in which the identical region was imaged through three
successive filters, the Lander directed the light from the scene onto the
blue, green, and red filtered diodes in succession. Consequently, when a
vertical scan was completed for the blue filtered diode, the camera mast
did not move one step in azimuth. Rather, an identical vertical scan was
completed, but this time the light was directed onto the green filtered
photodiode. The process was then repeated for the red filtered sensor.[174]
The scene, therefore, was imaged through the three primary colors,

and when the data were transmitted to earth, they were processed to complete the final color composite.

An eleventh diode was employed to produce low resolution wide angle views of the Martian terrain. In this mode, the camera was able to produce a wide angle image in less time than one from the four high resolution diodes. The twelfth and final photodiode was designed to directly view the sun. It was fitted with a red filter and was used, in part, to help determine the Lander's position on Mars. The angle in which the sun was viewed at specific times helped to pinpoint the position in the same way a sextant was used to determine a ship's location on earth by the position of the sun in the sky.[175]

A final component of the photodiode assembly were pinholes placed over the diodes. The light first passed through a pinhole before it contacted a diode's surface. The pinholes served two purposes. In terms of the four high resolution diodes, for example, the distance each diode's pinhole was placed from the lens in the mast assembly determined the optimum focus point for a diode. The diameter of a pinhole also governed each diode's field of view. The wide angle, color, and spectral diodes were fitted with pinholes producing a 0.12° field of view. The high resolution diodes had pinholes that yielded a 0.04° field of view.[176]

The field of view also determined the degree in azimuth the camera mast rotated following a vertical scan. With the wide angle survey diode, for example, the mast moved 0.12° as this diode produced a 0.12° field of view per vertical scan. Accordingly, when the first vertical line was scanned, the mast was shifted 0.12° in azimuth and the next vertical scan was initiated.[177]

Finally, at a 16,000 bits per second transmission rate to a Viking Orbiter, the relay time for one picture depended upon the picture type and format. A 60° × 120° black and white panorama with the survey or wide angle photodiode, for instance, was transmitted in 3.68 minutes. A comparable photograph in color was relayed in 11.04 minutes. The number of bits in each photograph also varied with each picture type. Since a color photograph necessitated three vertical scans with three diodes, it required approximately 10.2 million bits to produce a 60° × 120° panorama, as opposed to 3.4 million bits for the black and white photograph.[178] Thus, the greater number of bits in the color composite necessitated the longer transmission time. Furthermore, the camera's maximum resolution was of objects two millimeters in size.

Conclusion

The photographs transmitted by the Viking Landers yielded geological information about Mars. The same visual imaging subsystem was also employed to monitor a spacecraft's other instruments and experiments. In one instance, photographs were relayed of the Lander's collector arm. This device dug trenches and carried samples of the Martian soil to the Lander's biological test package. The photographs were used to determine if the arm completed its assignment.[179]

The camera subsystem was also used to search the landing site for lifeforms in addition to producing color and stereo views of this region. The Lander's photographic data, when combined with that of the Orbiters, constituted the most extensive reconnaissance of a planet other than earth by electro-optical devices.

Prior to the launch of the Viking spacecraft, however, another Mariner mission had occurred. The Mariner 10 spacecraft rendezvoused with the planets Mercury and Venus during a multiple flyby mission. Nevertheless, in the present book the spacecraft and its television subsystem were not described in chronological order as it would have disrupted the sequence of the Mars' exploratory vehicles. Finally, even though the probe did photograph Venus and Mercury, it has been incorporated in this chapter since it was a member of the Mariner class of spacecraft.

Mariner 10

Introduction

Mariner 10 was NASA's first spacecraft to successfully photograph Venus and Mercury during a multiple flyby mission. The probe was launched on November 3, 1973, and after an encounter with Venus, was boosted by that planet's gravity toward its encounter with Mercury. Mariner 10's visual imaging subsystem consisted of two television cameras with slow scan vidicons as the imaging sensors. The probe transmitted thousands of photographs of the planets throughout its mission, and it relayed additional images of Mercury as it encountered the planet two more times in subsequent flybys.[180] Because the probe incorporated many of the features of the earlier Mariner spacecraft, only those facets of the television subsystem unique to Mariner 10 will be described.

Design Criteria

The primary design criterion for Mariner 10's television assembly were the mission's photographic objectives. During the Venus encounter, for example, the cameras were designed to image the planet in the ultraviolet region of light to better record Venus' cloud structures. The cameras were also designed to yield high resolution photographs of the cloud markings and also to Mercury's geological characteristics. These capabilities were in addition to their ability to generate photometric data and provide continuous coverate of sections of both planets.[181]

Mercury 10's television subsystem also incorporated a design modification employing erasure lamps that flooded the photoconductor after its scanning. The lamps erased the vidicons' residual images prior to the next exposure. Mariners 6, 7, and 9 employed a high current electron beam to erase and restore the photoconductor to a neutral state. The process did not completely erase the old image. Consequently, a lamp system was used on Mariner 10 and subsequent spacecraft.[182]

Another design criterion was the focal length of the cameras' lenses. In contrast to the earlier Mariner spacecraft that carried 500mm telephoto lenses, Mariner 10 mounted twin 1,500mm telephoto lenses of a Cassegrain configuration. Since the focal length was increased by a factor of three, these lenses were more powerful than their predecessors and were capable of resolving smaller physical features.[183]

Selected optical components of a lens were also treated with a special surface coating to increase the television subsystem's sensitivity to ultraviolet light, which had a shorter wavelength than visible light. Human vision and the conventional visual imaging systems could not perceive this shorter wavelength. The surface coatings on the optics thus allowed Mariner 10 to make exposures in the ultraviolet region.[184]

This coating was employed because photographs taken prior to the mission demonstrated that images taken through visible light revealed little of Venus' cloud formations and patterns. Imaging in the ultraviolet region, however, produced photographs with pronounced cloud features. Therefore, a lens' coating, in addition to an ultraviolet filter mounted in a lens' filter wheel, helped provide ultraviolet photographs during this mission.[185]

Camera Design

The operation of the television subsystem was similar to that for other dual camera configurations. The cameras imaged a planet sequentially, and when one camera's photoconductor was scanned, the other's was erased. Mariner 10 relayed these photographs in real time or stored the images on a tape recorder for retransmission at a later time. The scanning time for a camera was 42 seconds for one frame; therefore, both the real-time transmission and the recording rates matched this 42 second cycle.[186]

The cameras also were mounted on a moveable scan platform and the fastest shutter speed for the system was three milliseconds. The photographs themselves consisted of 832 scan lines per frame with 700 picture elements on a line. Thus, each fully transmitted photograph was composed of 582,400 picture elements. The picture elements, in turn, were encoded and digitized into eight-digit binary words with 256 quantization levels.[187]

After a camera initiated its imaging sequence and the photoconductor was scanned, the digitized photographic data were manipulated in one of several ways. The photographs were stored on Mariner 10's tape recorder, for example, during certain sequences. This device was capable of recording 36 pictures that were subsequently transmitted at a rate of 22,050 bits per second over a 2.24 hour period. This mode was one of the spacecraft's slower transmission rates. Nevertheless, the slow rate also produced photographs with low error rates and reduced signal-to-noise ratios.[188] These photographs were technically superior to those relayed at higher rates, such as the real-time transmissions.

In the real-time mode, the photographs were transmitted at a rate of 117,600 bits per second, permitting the probe to relay one photograph every 42 seconds. The 42 seconds matched the scanning and readout time for one of the cameras. Even though this mode increased the flexibility of the television subsystem in terms of its ability to generate a high volume of photographs, these images were inferior to those transmitted at the aforementioned 22,050 bits per second rate, or the second real-time mode option. This was called the edit mode whereby only a segment of a complete picture was transmitted at a real-time rate of 22,050 bits per second. The edit mode's transmissions produced technically superior photographs in contrast to the higher rate real-time relay. In this procedure, all the picture elements for an edit-mode photograph were encoded as six-bit words with a corresponding decrease in the gray levels.[189]

The real-time transmissions played an important role during the Mariner 10 mission even though their images were technically inferior to those which were initially recorded and subsequently transmitted. During the first Mercury rendezvous, for example, the close encounter with the planet lasted for approximately eight hours, or four hours of approach and four hours of departure from Mercury.[190] The tape recorder would have been capable of storing and transmitting approximately 128 photographs during this optimum visual imaging period. This was in contrast with the 592 real-time pictures that the spacecraft actually produced and which provided continuous coverage of the planet's surface.

The tape recorder, however, was used during different phases of the mission. In one instance, Mariner 10 passed behind Mercury during the close encounter and photographed its far side (that perpetually faced away from the earth). The planet blocked the spacecraft's transmissions from reaching the earth during this time, thus necessitating the use of the tape recorder.[191] The recorder system was also employed at other points in the mission to produce photographs relatively free of technical errors.

In summation, the television and transmission subsystems incorporated the best features of both real time and recorded relays. The real-time transmissions permitted Mariner 10 to image continuous swaths of the planets during an encounter lasting for only a short period of time. The tape recorder system, on the other hand, enabled the probe to store its photographs for retransmission when the real-time relays were impossible as was the case during the Mercury flyby. It also provided the most accurate method of transmitting the probe's photographs to earth.

When the pictorial information was received on earth, it was recorded on magnetic tape. The information was then processed by computers to enhance and correct any faults in the data, such as the loss of bits during the data's original transmission from Mariner 10.[192] Some of the spacecraft's photographs transmitted in real time were displayed on television monitors almost as rapidly as the data were received. In this procedure, the real-time data were initially stored on magnetic tape and immediately computer processed to yield the real-time displays.[193]

Camera Optics

The lenses which produced these photographs were identical 1,500mm telephotos. This lens system was unique in two ways. The first was in a telephoto's capability for ultraviolet imaging and the second was the method in which wide angle views were produced through an auxiliary lens system.

Each 1,500mm lens had a maximum aperture of F/8.5 and yielded a 0.36° × 0.48° field of view. The resolution of surface features changed as the distance in which the spacecraft imaged a planet changed. During one of the Mercury encounters, for example, the probe's close approach to the planet permitted the cameras to resolve features that ranged between 120 and 900 meters. As the distance between the probe and Mercury increased, however, the resolution decreased.[194] Furthermore, twin 1,500mm lenses were used primarily for the purpose of redundancy. If one camera malfunctioned or one lens was damaged during the flight, the other system was still capable of completing the mission's objectives.

Mariner 10 also carried 50mm F/4.0 wide angle lenses mounted on top of the telephotos' tube assemblies. They each produced an 11° × 14° field of view and were employed to create low resolution wide angle views of Venus and Mercury. To activate the wide angle system, a filter wheel located behind a telephoto's optics and mounting a mirror in one of the filter slots, was rotated. This positioned the mirror within the camera's optical path. Consequently, light from the scene the camera was imaging entered through the wide angle assembly. The light was then directed toward the mirror on the filter wheel, which reflected it, in turn, toward the vidicon. The image was then stored on the photoconductor prior to its scanning.[195] A wide angle lens, therefore, shared a camera assembly with a 1,500mm telephoto in that one telephoto and one wide angle lens both used the electronic components of a single camera.

One of the reasons this dual system was employed was the mission objective of obtaining high resolution images of Venus and Mercury. In order to yield these photographs, the Mariner television subsystem, which was typically composed of a wide angle and a telephoto lens, was abandoned in favor of two high resolution telephotos.[196] The wide angle lenses, therefore, were relegated to auxiliary roles and as such were used only occasionally.

A final component of the optical system was the filter wheel assembly fitted with eight filter slots. Upon the receipt of a command from the earth or Mariner 10's onboard computer, a specific filter or the mirror for the wide angle lens was dialed into place. The filters ranged from an ultraviolet to an orange filter and they were used for a variety of reasons.[197] The ultraviolet filter, for example, was employed when a planet was imaged in the ultraviolet region of light. In another instance, identical regions of Mercury were imaged through the ultraviolet and orange filters. Since their spectral characteristics were different, the photographs they produced highlighted color differences on the planet.[198] This process was analogous to the use of red and green filters during the Mariner 4 mission to identify the color variations of the Martian terrain.

Conclusion

Mariner 10 fulfilled the primary objectives devised for its television subsystem. The probe not only imaged Venus and Mercury as scheduled but because of a reserve supply of gas for its jets, was able to maintain its attitude and after a six month orbit around the sun, encountered and imaged Mercury for a second time. A third and final flyby occurred on March 16, 1975.[199]

These planetary encounters were subdivided into phases which can best be illustrated by Mariner 10's first Mercury encounter. The photographic sequencing was initiated when the space probe was six days away from its rendezvous. As Mariner 10 approached the planet, a series of photographs were taken through the filters at different exposure levels to calibrate the cameras for the next phase of the mission. This was the color mosaicking period when images through the ultraviolet and orange filters were taken to distinguish Mercury's surface coloration. Following this, the close encounter phase occurred, followed by another color mosaicking period and a final outgoing far encounter picture sequence.[200]

Five months after Mariner 10's mission was completed and the probe had expended its supply of attitude-correction gas, the first Viking spacecraft was launched. With the exception only of the Venus Pioneer spacecraft, the Viking mission signalled the end of the exploration of the inner solar system by unmanned spacecraft with visual imaging subsystems. The next two chapters of this book, therefore, are devoted to the technological development of the imaging subsystems used on the probes that explored the outer planets, namely, Pioneers 10 and 11 and Voyagers 1 and 2. Finally, even though the Pioneer Venus spacecraft photographed Venus, which was a member of the inner solar system, its imaging subsystem will be described in Chapter Five since its electro--optical device was similar to those employed on the Pioneer 10 and 11 spacecraft.

CHAPTER 5

Pioneer Series

Introduction

On March 2, 1972, when Mariner 10 was in the final stages of preparation for its launch, the first of the Pioneer probes designed for the study of the outer planets, Pioneer 10, was launched. It was followed a little over one year later by Pioneer 11, which was launched on April 5, 1973.[1] These probes were also designated as Pioneers F and G.

The first of the Pioneer series, however, were originally designed and launched in the 1950's to explore the moon. The culmination of the series were Pioneers 10, 11, and the Pioneer Venus spacecraft. Pioneer 10 investigated Jupiter while Pioneer 11 explored both this planet and Saturn. The Pioneer Venus spacecraft orbited, and in early 1983 still orbits, Venus. This probe has so far transmitted over 1,000 photographs of Venus' clouds in the ultraviolet region of light.[2]

All three probes were spin-stabilized craft, in contrast with the three-axis-stabilized Ranger, Lunar Orbiter, and Mariner class of spacecraft. This design feature, in turn, enabled the project engineers to incorporate spin scan imaging photopolarimeters instead of the conventional television subsystems which were normally employed on three-axis-stabilized spacecraft.[3] The use of this type of electro-optical device on the Pioneers was due, in part, to the spacecrafts' inflight characteristics and the design criteria that influenced the missions. Finally, even though all three spacecraft were similar in specific areas of their design and operation, nevertheless, due to their mission objectives and the planets they explored, Pioneers 10 and 11 were also different from Pioneer Venus in other respects. Hence, the first section of this chapter will describe the operation of Pioneers 10 and 11 and the traits similarly shared by Pioneer Venus, while the second part of the chapter is devoted to Pioneer Venus and its specific design characteristics.

Design Criteria

The primary design criterion of all three Pioneer spacecraft was that they be spin-stabilized. In contrast with a three-axis-stabilized probe, a spin-stabilized Pioneer rotated around a central or spin axis. Thus, this spinning motion stabilized the craft during its mission.[4]

Pioneers 10 and 11 were also fitted with a series of thrusters that permitted operators on earth to alter the probes' direction or the rate of their rotation from the normal 4.48 revolutions per minute. The spacecraft also employed a Canopus star and a sun sensor to maintain their attitude in relation to the earth in addition to a series of controls that kept the probes' high gain antennas pointing toward the earth for the transmission of their photographic data.[5]

Since a Pioneer type of spacecraft rotated during its flight, its motion provided the optimum environment for several scientific devices that measured, for example, the magnetic field in the interplanetary region of space. The rotation permitted a probe to rapidly scan different sections of the sky.[6]

This same movement that was beneficial for certain instruments was detrimental to certain types of electro-optical imaging devices since a spacecraft's motion did not create a stable photographic platform. Consequently, an electro-optical subsystem that was originally employed on spin stabilized earth satellites was adopted for the Pioneers. This was a spin scan photopolarimeter. This device was designed to visually scan and image a planet as the probe rotated around its spin axis during its flight.[7]

The Pioneers' motion, therefore, prevented a television subsystem from being used on Pioneers 10, 11, and Pioneer Venus, since these electro-optical devices produced their highest resolved images from a stabilized platform. The Pioneers, however, incorporated their spinning motion in the operation of their photopolarimeters and in the eventual production of their photographs.

The design philosophy of the photopolarimeters was also a reflection of the Pioneer spacecraft themselves. Unlike the Mariner probes, the Pioneers were simple in design and operation. Their spin stabilization method, for example, eliminated the three-axis-stabilization system. This, in turn, made the Pioneers a less complex and a lighter spacecraft series. Thus, they were also less expensive to build.[8] In essence, a Pioneer probe was analogous to a Ford Model T automobile. Like the Model T, which was less expensive and less sophisticated in contrast with other automobiles, the Pioneer did not carry the sophisticated electro-optical devices and powerful transmission subsystems as did more expensive and larger spacecraft.

Therefore, due to the general criteria to build a less complex probe, Pioneers 10 and 11, for example, did not incorporate multiple camera units or onboard tape recorders to store the photographic data once they were generated. Rather, the imaging information was produced by a single electro-optical device and was transmitted in what was essentially

PIONEER/JUPITER MAJOR SUBSYSTEMS

① RADIOISOTOPE THERMOELECTRIC GENERATORS (2)
② THRUSTERS
③ MEDIUM-GAIN ANTENNA
④ HIGH-GAIN ANTENNA
⑤ COMMAND DISTRIBUTION UNIT
⑥ STELLAR REFERENCE ASSEMBLY
⑦ LOW-GAIN ANTENNA
⑧ TRAVELING WAVE TUBES (2)
⑨ DIGITAL TELEMETRY UNIT

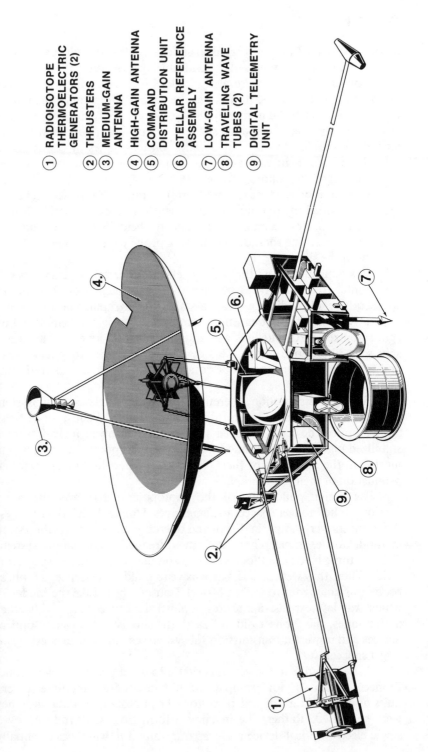

a real time mode.[9] Furthermore, the Pioneers' transmission subsystem was also less powerful and less sophisticated than those incorporated on a Mariner class spacecraft, such as the Voyagers. Hence, the Pioneers were capable of transmitting their data at only low bits-per-second rates. When this factor was combined with the absence of an onboard recorder and the limited amount of time the data were capable of being transmitted, only a portion or sample of the picture elements that constituted a fully scanned photograph were transmitted. Other spacecraft series' photographic data similarly underwent sampling, but not to the extent of the Pioneers.[10]

A final criterion was determined by the mission objectives. Pioneers 10 and 11 were the first spacecraft to approach and image Jupiter, and Pioneer 11 additionally rendezvoused with Saturn after the probe was boosted by Jupiter's gravity towards its Saturn encounter. The flight exposed the probes and their subsystems to what was believed to have been the high radiation levels surrounding Jupiter. Furthermore, the distance the probes had to travel and to transmit their data exceeded any previous mission.[11]

Thus the visual subsystems, in addition to Pioneers 10 and 11's other components, were specifically designed to survive and continue operating throughout the prolonged missions and to withstand the environment they would encounter. In light of this, the physical characteristics and possible effects of Jupiter on the spacecraft and their instruments for example, were determined. This information was then used to draft a set of design criteria for the probes.[12]

Imaging Operation

As previously described, the visual imaging device carried by the Pioneers was a photopolarimeter. Since the Pioneer Venus unit had a different design configuration than those of Pioneers 10 and 11, it will be described in a later section of this chapter.

Pioneer 10 and 11's photopolarimeters were designed to operate in four modes and to produce several types of data. In the sky-mapping configuration, for example, the instrument was employed to detect and map the skyglow or the general brightness of the sky that is due to phenomena such as the zodiacal light and the light from the distant stars and galaxies.[13] The photopolarimeters also produced polarimetric and radiometric data, and what was pertinent to this study, two-color images of Jupiter, Saturn, and their satellites.

In its imaging mode, light from a scene a probe was scanning passed through a photopolarimeter's lens and a 0.043 millimeter aperture. The aperture defined the photopolarimeter's field of view and resolution. After passing through the aperture, the light was optically separated by a prism into two beams. The two beams then passed through filters that separated the light into its red and blue spectral components. Following this, two relay lenses channelled the red and blue beams to separate optical assemblies in the photopolarimeter. The relay lenses directed their respective light beams onto "channeltron" detectors. These sensors were spectrally responsive to the red and blue regions of light and thus to the red and blue beams.[14]

The Bendix channeltrons were photoelectric sensors. As the light beams were directed onto the channeltrons, the intensity of the light produced an electronic pulse. Like the Viking Landers, the Pioneers did not image a scene by activating a shutter and scanning a photoconductor to generate the video signal. Rather, the photopolarimeter scanned only a small section of a predetermined scene at a time. Consequently, the light from each section was directed to the sensors.

This created a signal that varied in strength in proportion to the intensity of the light from each scene. These signals were then digitized by an analog-to-digital converter and each picture element was coded into a six-bits word. Each binary word, in turn, represented black to white on a 0 through 63 scale in the transmitted photographs.[15]

The channeltrons were employed instead of a photomultiplier, which was another type of imaging sensor, or a slow scan vidicon, because of the constraints imposed by the Pioneer mission and space-craft. The channeltrons, for example, were smaller and less susceptible to the environmental conditions a Pioneer would encounter during its flight. This sensor's small size also contributed to its light weight, which was an important factor since a Pioneer spacecraft was severely weight limited. Finally, a channeltron also operated within the restricted parameters of a Pioneer's power supply produced by a probe's thermoelectric generator.[16]

The channeltrons generated their signals as a Pioneer progressively photographed one of the planetary bodies. As the spacecraft moved or rolled 360° as a function of its normal spinning motion, the lens pointed at and scanned only a segment of Jupiter, for example, for only a portion of the 360° revolution. The angle in which the photopolarimeter actually generated its data in each 360° roll was controlled by a command from the earth and was nominally set for a 14° arc. After a roll was completed, an automatic control repositioned the photopolarimeter's lens so it pointed at an adjacent section of the planet. The instrument then scanned another 14° swath during its roll, the lens was again repositioned, and the procedure was repeated until the desired area of Jupiter was imaged.[17] The repositioning of the lens was called a "step."

This process was analogous to the scanning sequence of a Viking Lander. The upward scan of a Lander's mirror and the azimuth step were equivalent to the Pioneer's 14° arc and lens movement. This process can also be illustrated by the procedure employed in the painting of a large cylindrical pipe, such as a water main, in single strokes. The paintbrush was placed at the desired starting point on the pipe and was moved in an upward direction. Even though the brush could have moved in a 360° circle in the pipe, the upward stroke was limited to a 14° arc. The paintbrush was then repositioned next to the completed stroke and was again moved in an upward motion. This procedure was repeated until a 14° wide section of the pipe was painted along its entire length. The 360° pipe section, the 14° upward stroke, and the repositioning of the brush were analogous to the Pioneer's rolling motion, the segment of the 360° roll on which the data were actually produced, and the repositioning of the lens respectively. In summation, the spacecraft's spinning motion provided the 14° arc movement while the photopolarimeter mechanically displaced the lens in a series of steps until the preselected area was fully scanned.

With this procedure, the photopolarimeter scanned a 8.14° × 14° swath of Jupiter every hour. Furthermore, as the distance decreased between the probe and a planet, it was no longer necessary to mechanically reposition the lens after every scan. The spacecraft's movement itself produced the steps at this close imaging range.[18]

Since the average scan area for one roll was only 14°, the imaging subsystem did not generate its photographic data throughout its 360° rotation. The data were produced during the 14° arc and were temporarily stored in a buffer device on the Pioneer. The digitized data, in turn, represented only a sample of all the picture elements created during the roll. The sample consisted of 508 blue and 507 red elements.[19] Therefore, when the Pioneer's photopolarimeter was completing its 14° scanning arc, the data were being digitized, sampled, and temporarily stored in the onboard buffer system. As the 14° arc was completed, the spacecraft continued its rolling motion. The data were transmitted at this time at a nominal rate of 1,024 bits per second.[20]

Picture Reconstruction

As the data were received on earth in nearly real time, some of the photographs were immediately reconstructed. This picture reception was real time in the sense that the data were transmitted and reconstructed as rapidly as they were produced and received on earth. The travel time for the signals, however, required additional time: it took over two hours for a transmission from Pioneer 11 to reach the earth during its Saturn encounter. Once the signals were intercepted by the Deep Space Network, they were channelled through a special reconstruction system called the Pioneer Image Converter System, or Pics. This assembly manipulated the Pioneer's photographic data to produce and display the mission's pictures.[21]

The reconstruction process of transforming a Pioneer's relayed pictorial information into photographs was complex. In one instance, the red and blue picture elements produced by the red and blue channeltrons were computer processed to synthesize a green signal. The green signal was then processed and mixed with the red and blue data to create a color composite of the planetary body. Prior to the processing, the red and blue channeltrons' data produced red and blue colored photographs. The photopolarimeter originally imaged in these two colors for scientific purposes. Yet, to depict a celestial object in its natural colors, the green signal was synthesized and mixed with the red and blue data.[22]

Another reconstruction process was the elimination of pictorial distortions. Unlike the immobile Viking Landers that imaged a stationary target, a Pioneer scanned Jupiter, for example, as the probe moved along its trajectory. Furthermore, Jupiter itself rotated during the scanning period and thus the cloud patterns on the planet were also in constant motion.

The scan paths a Pioneer produced with its photopolarimeter therefore were not uniform in size and shape, as the scan paths curved along the planet and with Jupiter's and the spacecraft's motion. It was the curved scan paths that created the geometric distortions.[23] In contrast, a Viking Lander's scan paths were uniform in shape and size since the probe linearly scanned the stationary Martian terrain.

The pictorial distortions were corrected in one of several ways. Using a scanning map, mission personnel were able to compute the coordinates of the photographic data for each scan swath as they would have appeared in a distortion-free photograph. The relayed picture elements were then repositioned or moved so it appeared that the scanning took place from one point in space at one instant in time. The picture elements were therefore displaced to match the coordinates of the undistorted photograph according to the map.[24]

In other instances, the data were processed to correct only some of the geometric distortions. This technique was employed throughout the mission, as it required less computer time to create these photographs than fully corrected ones. The uncorrected distortions, however, were only cosmetic in nature and did not affect the photograph's scientific value. A final correction was the replacement of complete scan swaths that were lost during transmission. Through computer processing and the interpolation of the existing pictorial information, the lost data were synthesized and employed to complete the photograph.[25]

Optics

The photopolarimeter's lens was a one-inch diameter telescope with a focal length of approximately 3.5 inches and a maximum aperture of F/3.4. Like all the optical systems carried by spacecraft, the Pioneer's telescope was thermally protected. Furthermore, the optical elements were produced from materials capable of withstanding the high radiation levels the spacecraft would encounter during the Jupiter flyby.[26]

The resolution of the lens changed with the distance from which it photographed a planetary body. From a distance of 130,000 kilometers, for example, planetary markings 200 kilometers in size were discernible. Hence, the photographs a photopolarimeter produced with this lens represented a three-fold increase in the resolution of Jupiter's cloud structure when compared with photographs taken from observatories on the earth.[27]

Pioneer Venus

Pioneers 10 and 11 photographed Jupiter and Saturn; a Pioneer also conducted a photographic reconnaissance of Venus. The mission itself was divided into two phases, with two different spacecraft. In one mission, a bus vehicle housed and transported four probes to Venus. The bus released the probes, which penetrated and relayed data about Venus as they plunged through the atmosphere. The bus followed shortly thereafter and transmitted its own information. It was during the second mission with the second Venus probe, the Pioneer Venus, that the planet was imaged with a photopolarimeter.[28] These two missions followed in the wake of NASA's Mariner 10 flyby and Russia's Venera 9 and 10 spacecraft that imaged the planet from its surface.

Pioneer Venus' photopolarimeter was a spin scan imaging device similar to those employed on the Pioneers 10 and 11 spacecraft. There were some technical differences between the two systems, however, including the sensor elements. The channeltrons on Pioneers 10 and 11 were replaced by ultraviolet silicon photodiodes. A photodiode was an imaging sensor similar to those employed on a Viking Lander. For the Pioneer Venus' photopolarimeter, the diodes were also sensitive to the ultraviolet region of light since the photographs from the earlier Mariner 10 mission demonstrated that ultraviolet imaging revealed Venus' cloud structure in the transmitted pictures.[29]

The Pioneer Venus spacecraft was also unique in an area other than its photopolarimeter's sensors. In contrast to Pioneer 10 and 11's flybys,

Pioneer Venus was inserted into an orbital position around Venus, and as of early 1983, the probe is still operational. The spacecraft's extended mission has permitted its photopolarimeter to photograph the planet extensively and chronicle the circulation of Venus' cloud cover. The collection of photographs has been correlated with information generated from the probe's other instruments, including a radar system that has penetrated Venus' clouds, to reveal the planet's surface features that remain hidden to the photopolarimeter.[30]

Since Venus is enveloped by a dense blanket of clouds, a visual imaging device such as a photopolarimeter cannot photograph the planet's surface. Thus, the radar generated these data. The only method by which a visual imaging device could survey the planet's surface features would be from or near the surface itself. This feat was accomplished by Russia's Veneras 9 and 10 spacecraft when they photographed Venus with a telephotometer, a form of an electro-optical device, after they landed on the planet's surface.[31] Veneras 13 and 14 subsequently landed on Venus during 1982 and photographed its surface with their television systems.

Since the Pioneer Venus spacecraft was restricted to only orbital views of Venus' clouds, the probe produced both partial and full disk views of the planet. The system's maximum resolution were cloud features 30 kilometers in size when the spacecraft was in one of its lower orbital positions.

When the probe produced its photographic data, it was usually received by one of the Deep Space Network's 64-meter antennas. The large antennas, vital components of the Pioneers 10 and 11 missions, were equally important for the Pioneer Venus mission when maneuvers or scientific experiments that required the use of the large antennas were conducted.[32]

Finally, the Pioneer Venus craft incorporated a data storage system. This device was employed by the spacecraft to store its data prior to its transmission and subsequent computer processing on earth. The data were usually stored when the probe or one of the Deep Space Network's antennas was not properly positioned to transmit and receive.[33]

Conclusion

While the Venus Pioneer revealed details of Venus' clouds, Pioneers 10 and 11 visually imaged, for the first time in human history, Jupiter and Saturn with electro-optical devices on unmanned outer space probes. The photopolarimeters that produced the photographs for all three spacecraft were also unique in that they generated a series of images while operating under severe power and transmission restrictions.

Pioneers 10 and 11 were followed by another series of twin probes, Voyagers 1 and 2. The Voyagers were Mariner class spacecraft with sophisticated and powerful transmission and television subsystems. Even though these probes produced technically superior photographs compared to those transmitted by their predecessors, nevertheless, the Pioneers' photopolarimeters provided scientists with the first close-up views of the outer planets and several of their satellites.

CHAPTER 6

Voyager Series

Introduction

The Voyagers 1 and 2 spacecraft that rendezvoused with Jupiter
and Saturn were the final outer space probes, up to the present time,
to employ visual imaging subsystems to explore the planetary bodies
in the solar system. The craft were powered by radioisotope thermoelectric generators as their operational distance from the sun precluded
the use of solar cells. Both probes had photographed Jupiter and Saturn
during their multiple flyby missions, and in 1986, with a gravitational
boost from Saturn, Voyager 2 is expected to fly by Uranus and then
Neptune in 1989. If Voyager's television subsystem remains operational
during these years, it cameras will produce the first moderate—and
possibly high—resolution photographs of these two worlds.[1]

Design Criteria

The primary design criterion that influenced the Voyagers' twin
television subsystems came from the mission objectives. Unlike a Pioneer
probe, a Voyager's design was based upon the Mariner configuration.
The craft incorporated a powerful transmission subsystem, a tape recorder, and television cameras with slow scan vidicons to produce technically superior photographs in comparison with those of Pioneers 10
and 11. The increased technical quality was a reflection of the Mariner
class spacecraft and the mission objective which, for the television subsystem, was an intensive photographic survey of Jupiter, Saturn, and
their satellites. This subsystem, therefore, was designed to produce a
large volume of high resolution photographs of these celestial bodies.[2]
The imaging survey included a plan to photograph Jupiter's Galilean
satellites, Io, Europa, Ganymede, and Callisto, in addition to Saturn's
ring system.

In order to fulfill the photographic objectives, a Voyager had to
carry a suitable visual imaging system. For reasons previously stated, the
Pioneers carried photopolarimeters. Even though their photographs

surpassed ground based images, nevertheless, a photopolarimeter was not specifically designed to produce pictures. It was a multipurpose instrument capable of measuring several different phenomena and, as such, it generated a variety of data, including the two-color images.[3] Hence, a Voyager was fitted with two television cameras that were specifically designed to produce both high and low resolution photographs. The spacecraft, however, did mount a photopolarimeter. In this instance, the instrument was designed to measure the brightness and polarization of light from the planetary bodies.[4]

In addition to its camera subsystem, a Voyager was also capable of producing high resolution images because of its transmission subsystem. It was the most powerful and advanced design ever carried by a probe that photographed planetary bodies. Like the Mariner 10 spacecraft, a Voyager transmitted its data at a rate of up to 115,200 bits per second. This speed permitted the probe to transmit real-time photographs.[5] In addition, as it was previously stated, each photograph was composed of bits which were picture information. Consequently, for a Voyager to transmit high resolution images that were composed of millions of bits, the transmission subsystem had to be able to handle this data flow. The Voyager's subsystem satisfied this requirement.

In summation, there were two design criteria that influenced a Voyager's imaging subsystem. The first was the Voyager's configuration as a Mariner class spacecraft. Its three-axis-stabilization system, in addition to its payload capacity to mount a heavier imaging subsystem, permitted the probe to carry a television subsystem and thus fulfill the second criterion. This was the objective of transmitting high resolution photographs which necessitated the use of a television camera and a powerful transmission subsystem.

Camera Design

The television subsystem itself consisted of two television cameras mounted on a moveable scan platform and the ancilliary camera electronics. The photographs the system produced consisted of 800 scan lines per frame with 800 picture elements per line. This was equal to 640,000 picture elements in one photograph. Furthermore, each picture element was coded into an eight digit binary word. Each binary word, in turn, represented black to white and graduations of gray in between in the transmitted photographs. The television system also employed an improved pre-amp that reduced noise or interference in a transmited signal in contrast with previous missions.[6] The pre-amp helped produce a technically superior photograph.

The cameras' shutter speeds ranged between 0.005 and 15.26 seconds

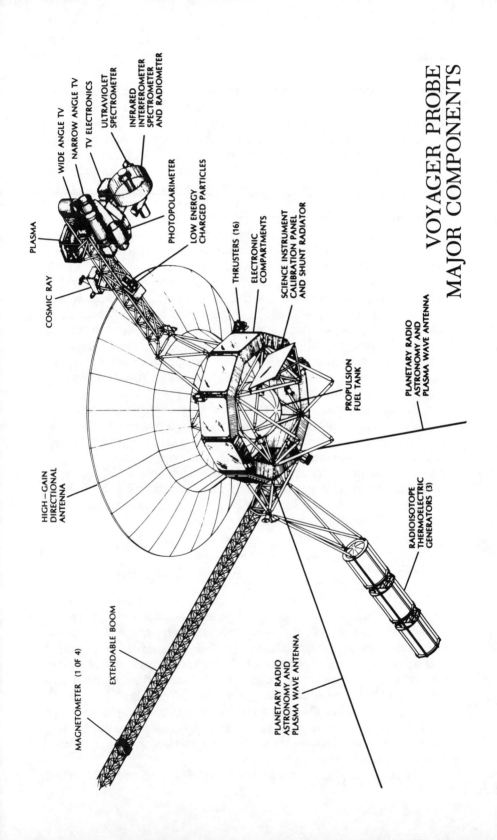

VOYAGER PROBE
MAJOR COMPONENTS

WIDE ANGLE TV
NARROW ANGLE TV
TV ELECTRONICS
ULTRAVIOLET SPECTROMETER
INFRARED INTERFEROMETER SPECTROMETER AND RADIOMETER

PLASMA

COSMIC RAY

PHOTOPOLARIMETER

LOW ENERGY CHARGED PARTICLES

THRUSTERS (16)
ELECTRONIC COMPARTMENTS
SCIENCE INSTRUMENT CALIBRATION PANEL AND SHUNT RADIATOR

PROPULSION FUEL TANK

PLANETARY RADIO ASTRONOMY AND PLASMA WAVE ANTENNA

RADIOISOTOPE THERMOELECTRIC GENERATORS (3)

HIGH-GAIN DIRECTIONAL ANTENNA

MAGNETOMETER (1 OF 4)

EXTENDABLE BOOM

PLANETARY RADIO ASTRONOMY AND PLASMA WAVE ANTENNA

during the system's nominal operation.[7] The wide range of speeds permitted a camera to adjust to the different light levels of the planetary bodies the Voyager would encounter during its flight. The camera was also capable of operating in an extended shutter speed range like the integration mode of a Surveyor probe. In this operation, the shutter remained open for an extended period of time while a faint object's light energy gradually accumulated on the vidicon's photoconductor thus photographing the object. In this mode, one camera produced an 11 minute exposure and recorded, for the first time, the faint ring that encircled Jupiter.[8]

After an object was imaged and the video signal was produced, the digitized data were either stored on a tape recorder or relayed in real time. With the first option, an onboard tape recorder was capable of storing approximately 100 photographs, equal to almost 500 million bits of information.[9] The recorder also served a function similar to those employed on previous missions. When the spacecraft was not able to transmit its data as rapidly as they were produced, the recorder operated as a buffer since the data were stored and retransmitted at a later time. The recorder was also used to store the photographic data when a Voyager was not properly positioned to transmit the pictures. This occurred throughout the mission, such as when the spacecraft's trajectory carried it behind Jupiter.[10] This blocked the probe's transmissions as effectively as Mercury prevented Mariner 10 from transmitting its data during its flight.

A Voyager also transmitted its data in real time at the rate of 115,220 bits per second. Even though this speed nearly matched Mariner 10's transmission, there was a difference in the distance each probe's signals had to travel. During a Jupiter flyby, for example, a Voyager's transmission distance was six times that of Mariner 10's. This distance increased during the subsequent Saturn rendezvous and will be even greater if Voyager 2 successfully encounters Uranus and Neptune. Consequently, in order to relay its photographic data over more than 300 million miles of space, a Voyager employed an X-band for its transmission frequency as well as the S-band channel.[11] The spacecraft was also equipped with a 3.7 meter antenna, which was the largest high gain antenna ever flown on a spacecraft. This helped to facilitate the Voyager's transmissions.

The 115,200 bits-per-second rate also was a reflection of the Voyager's maximum scanning rate for one of its cameras. At 48 seconds per scan per frame, a camera was capable of producing its data so they could be transmitted at this high real-time speed. The scanning time varied with the spacecraft's transmission rate. When a Voyager relayed its pictorial information from Saturn in real time, one frame was scanned in 144 seconds. The scanning time was increased 96 seconds during the Saturn encounter because the transmission rate dropped from 115,200 bits to 44,800 bits per second at this time.[12] This was due to the increased distance between the spacecraft and the earth which necessitated a reduction of the transmission rate. Consequently, the Voyager's cameras altered their scanning period to match the transmission subsystem's realtime picture rate.

The final link in the telecommunication circuit was the 64-meter Deep Space Network antennas. In order for a Voyager's data to be received, one of the antennas had to intercept the spacecraft's signals. The antennas were designed to receive both the X- and conventional S-band transmissions.[13] It was the use of the X-band and the 64-meter antennas which made it possible for a Voyager's photographs to be transmitted and received on earth.

The operational characteristics of a Voyager's television subsystem also produced the first high resolution "movies" or the first moving pictures of Jupiter's clouds. In this operation, Voyager 1 relayed one photograph of Jupiter every 96 seconds, which was equal to one color composite every four and three-quarters minutes. The transmission continued over a 100-hour period. This rapid production and accumulation of photographs over the extended period of time produced a photographic record of Jupiter that depicted the motion of the planet's clouds.[14]

When the data were received on earth, they were displayed on realtime monitors and recorded on magnetic tape. The picture information was then computer processed to correct any technical errors in the data in addition to the enhancement and production of color composites. The data were also manipulated to generate control networks for Jupiter's Galilean satellites.[15]

Camera Optics

The lenses that imaged these celestial bodies were 200mm F/3.5 wide and 1,500mm F/8.5 narrow angle optics. Each Voyager carried a wide and narrow angle lens combination. The original mission design called for the use of a 500mm telephoto similar to the one employed on the Mariner 9 probe.[16] The development of the 1,500mm lens for the Mariner 10 mission, however, provided the mission designers with this powerful telephoto capable of resolving smaller planetary features than the 500mm lens. The Voyager's lenses, like those carried by the Pioneers, were also designed and constructed of materials that could survive the Voyager's Jupiter encounter.[17]

The 200mm lens was extensively used throughout the near encounter phase of a mission when a Voyager made its closest approach to a planetary body. This lens not only yielded a wider field of view and thus imaged a greater surface area of a planetary body, but its photographs also exhibited less image smear than the photographs produced by the 1,500mm telephoto. This was due to the telephoto's higher magnification factor that emphasized the spacecraft's motion when it photographed a planetary body from these minimal distances during a near encounter phase.[18] The maximum resolution of the lens system was of one-kilometer planetary features with the 1,500mm telephoto from a distance of 50,000 kilometers.

The optical system's final component was a filter wheel. The 200mm lens was fitted with eight filters while the 1,500mm mounted six filters in the wheel. The filters were employed to create the color composites and to image the planetary bodies in different wavelengths of light. One filter on the wide angle camera, for example, was sensitive to sodium emissions. This filter was designed to detect sodium concentrations in the atmosphere and on the surface of Io, one of Jupiter's moons.[19] The camera's vidicon, therefore, was sensitive to the visible and other wavelengths of light.

Computer Command Subsystem

The control system for the filter wheels and for the television subsystem as a whole was a highly sophisticated onboard computer control (CCS). Because of a Voyager's operational distance from the earth, over 90 minutes were required for a command to reach a probe and for the craft to return a confirmation signal. Consequently, during the near encounter phases of the mission when a spacecraft made its closest approach to Jupiter, Saturn, or one of their satellites, it was vital that the television subsystem respond rapidly enough to image the predetermined targets. The 90 minute turnaround time for a radio command signal precluded the use of commands to control this subsystem. Thus, a Voyager employed a computer system that independently operated the craft with only a minimum of commands and instructions from earth.[20] This computer control made the Voyager the most autonomous probe that NASA ever launched to explore the solar system.

The control network was divided into a flight data system and an attitude and articulation control subsystem (AACS). At predetermined times during the mission, or upon the receipt of a command from the earth, the CCS signalled the AACS to maneuver the scan platform to reposition the television cameras and the other instruments the platform carried.[21]

Finally, as Voyager 2 journeyed past Jupiter to Saturn and hence toward Uranus and Neptune, the time delay for command signals increased—and will further increase as the probe travels away from the earth. Voyager 2's computer, therefore, was designed to store a sufficient quantity of commands so it could independently manipulate its television subsystem.[22] The Pioneer probes that similarly imaged Jupiter and Pioneer 11 which encountered Saturn did not possess this sophisticated control system. They were dependent upon command from the earth which were sent in a constant stream and were planned with the time delay factor. Thus, the command for an operation that had to take place in 45 minutes for example, was transmitted 45 minutes or more prior to the event in order for the Pioneer to receive and execute the command at the precise time.[23] This reliance upon earth commands was another reflection of the Pioneer series itself, which was a less sophisticated spacecraft.

Conclusion

Voyager 1 and 2's computer and television subsystems operated successfully throughout the Jupiter and Saturn encounters. The photographs the two probes transmitted revealed the surface features of Jupiter and Saturn's moons and the thousands of ringlets constituting the Saturnian ring system. These photographs were possible because of the technological evolution of the spacecraft's television and transmission subsystems and the increased sensitivity of the Deep Space Network's receiving antennas. A Voyager was capable of relaying its photographs in real time from Jupiter at a rate of 115,200 bits per second in contrast with the twenty-year-earlier Mariner 4's bits-per-second rate of only 8⅓.

The evolution of the spacecraft's subsystems was matched by the computer processing techniques on earth that manipulated a probe's photographic data to produce the final hard copy prints. These techniques were first employed with the Ranger series and were similarly employed when Voyager 2 transmitted its photographs. This final component of the visual imaging of the planetary bodies was as crucial to the success of the outer space probes' missions as the imaging subsystems themselves. Computer processing enabled scientists to maximize the data from the missions and in many instances, such as in the case with Pioneers 10 and 11, to reassemble the transmitted pictorial information into a photographic format.[24]

CHAPTER 7

Camera Calibration
and Image Processing

Introduction

Processing and enhancing of the visual imaging data consisted of a series of steps in which the data were manipulated to remove image distortions and defects. In other instances, photographs were enhanced to reveal specific characteristics of planetary bodies. This was illustrated during the Mariners 6 and 7 mission when both photometric and maximum-definition versions of the photographs were produced.[1] The first step in this processing, however, was the calibration of the imaging system carried by a spacecraft.

Calibration

A calibration procedure was one in which an imaging subsystem's components were tested and evaluated for their final operating characteristics. During the Voyager mission, for example, a calibration procedure was employed to precisely measure the lenses' focal lengths. The cameras photographed a star group, such as the Pleiades constellation, and through a series of tests, the transmitted photographs yielded the lenses' exact focal length.[2] This procedure was conducted to ensure that the television subsystem operated according to design specifications, as the launch phase and the space environment might have adversely affected the subsystem's characteristics.

The calibration procedure was especially important for television cameras that employed slow scan vidicons as their imaging sensors due to the vidicons' scanning process. When an image was stored on a photoconductor and the screen was scanned, the beam did not generate a uniform array.[3] Consequently, the scan lines were slightly distorted, which produced, in turn, geometrically distorted photographs.

To correct these errors, the television subsystem was calibrated. A pattern of metallic dots or squares called *reseau* marks were first deposited on the vidicon when it was manufactured. When the photographs were transmitted, the reseau pattern also appeared in the pictures. Consequently, the degree in which the pattern was distorted was equivalent to the degree in which the photographic information was distorted.[4]

Prior to the spacecraft's launch, a series of photographs were taken with the camera to measure and record the system's initial pictorial distortions. Other photographs were then taken throughout the flight to determine the effect of the launch and the environment on the cameras. The reseau marks on these transmitted images were then compared with those taken before the launch occurred.[5] The degree in which the inflight photographs were geometrically distorted and thus deviated from the pictures taken before the launch was discovered. Since the coordinates of the reseau marks in an undistorted image was known, the data were manipulated to match these markings. The reseau pattern, therefore, functioned as a map, much like the scan maps that were employed during the Pioneer 10 and 11 missions, to correct the photographs. However, before the pictorial information could be computer processed, it was necessary to determine the present status of the camera system. This was accomplished through the use of the calibration photographs taken prior to and during the flight.

Other components of the imaging system were also calibrated. A camera's photometric output was measured, for example, to determine the accuracy of its photometric data. If the information was not precise, the interpretations of the photographs, for example the relative brightness of a planetary body, would have been in error.[6] Furthermore, the spectral response of the vidicons, the shutter speeds, the focus point of a lens, and other functions were likewise calibrated.

These procedures yielded a standard set of measurements that defined an imaging subsystem's operational characteristics. The calibration process, therefore, was an important step in the production of photographs from space probes, because "the validity of the scientific measurements obtained from the television data is dependent upon the accuracy with which the operating characteristics of the television system are known at the time of operation."[7] Hence, for the accurate interpretation and production of photographs from the data, the instruments had to be calibrated.

Computer Processing

Once the calibration procedures were completed, the photographic data underwent computer processing. Image distortions or other forms of technical interference that impaired a photograph were first eliminated. This was called decalibration.[8]

The computer processing of photographs transmitted by outer space probes was employed initially during the various Ranger missions. Since these spacecraft transmitted their pictorial information in analog form, the data had to be digitized prior to processing. The analog data were translated into binary code whereby a six-bit word represented one picture element. Each word, in turn, was the equivalent of a step of gray on a 0 to 63 scale. Furthermore, since the original analog data were recorded on magnetic tape, there was only a minimal loss in the quality of the information when a digital tape was produced.[9]

After the data were digitized, they were processed as were all of the digital data from subsequent missions. An initial process was a geometric correction. By using the reseau marks as guides, the computer was run with a special program that eventually created a geometrically correct photograph.[10] The hard copy print, therefore, accurately reproduced the planetary body's surface as the camera initially imaged it without the distortions created by the vidicon.

Another decalibration process was employed during the Mariner 6 and 7 mission to remove extraneous noise in the transmitted video signal. This process yielded an improved signal-to-noise ratio.[11] Thus, when enhanced photographs were produced from these processed data, the improved signal-to-noise ratio generated superior photographs since the distorting noise was minimized. Additional decalibration procedures were also conducted with the data.

The second phase of the production of photographs from a spacecraft's visual imaging subsystem was the computer enhancement of the photographic data. This process was the method "to aid the human analyst in the extraction and interpretation of pictorial information."[12] With this procedure, the data were not manipulated to accurately reproduce the natural coloration, for example, of the imaged planetary body. Rather, depending upon the desired effect, the brightness variation of Mars' surface, for instance, was sacrificed in order to enhance the planet's geological features. This produced the maximum discriminability version of Mariner 6 and 7's photographs.[13] The opposite effect was achieved when Mars' photometric properties were enhanced instead of the planet's geological markings.

In other instances, the color of the photographs were improved. During the Viking Orbiter mission, for example, color composites were created. A technique was employed whereby the color components of the photograph—the hue, saturation, and intensity—were separated from each other.[14] These aspects of color were analogous to those of conventional television equipment in that the hue was the color, such as blue or green, saturation was the purity of this specific color or the level it was diluted, and intensity was the color's lightness or darkness.[15] During the final creation of the photographs from the Orbiter each of the three levels was capable of enhancement. Another color processing procedure was the creation of a color composite from the three photographs that were imaged through the three different filters. The color data were additionally manipulated during the Pioneer mission when the color green was synthesized from the red and blue signals to produce the final corrected color picture.[16]

The Vikings' photographic data were additionally processed in certain instances to yield stereo photogrammetric images, or those that revealed the contours, elevation, and other physical characteristics of a planetary body's surface. In this procedure, the data were first decalibrated to geometrically correct the photographs. Furthermore, the missing bits were replaced through the interpolation of the existing data, and the pictures were enhanced to maximize the definition of the geological features. The two photographs of the stereo pair were then projected to the same scale and orientation. Two photographs were employed since two images of the same surface region that were taken from different positions were required to produce a stereo image. Specific points of interest or geological formations in both the right and left pictures were then selected and their coordinates were correlated. The data was further manipulated and eventually the elevation of the stereopairs' selected features in addition to the contours of this region was produced.[17]

The data from the Viking Landers similarly underwent computer processing. In one instance, Lander 2 was positioned at approximately a 8° tilt relative to the horizon because of the nature of its landing site. Consequently, when the probe scanned the surrounding terrain, the tilt distorted the photographs. A technique called geometric projection, however, corrected this geometric displacement of the photographic data and produced distortion free pictures.[18]

Finally, selected frames from the Viking Landers and Orbiters were orthographically projected. In this procedure, the original photographs were altered to depict the surface area of Mars as though the spacecraft's camera was "looking straight down in the center of the image."[19] Thus, even though the probe might have photographed a surface feature at an angle, the orthographic projection displaced the image so it appeared that the camera was perpendicular to the center of the imaged region when the exposure was made.

Photographs that were subjected to this processing were used to create mosaics of Mars and other planetary bodies. These images were also overlaid, at times, with elevation contours. As it was previously described, select frames from the Viking Orbiter were used to create stereo pairs that generated photogrammetric data. The elevation contours that this process produced were overlaid on orthographically projected images. This produced an overhead or aerial view of specific regions of Mars, for example, with contour lines that revealed these areas' elevation.[20] The Viking Landers' data were similarly processed.

Conclusion

The preceding examples of data decalibration and enhancement were only a few of the computer processing techniques employed to improve the technical quality and to maximize the interperative value of the photographs transmitted by outer space probes. The technology for image processing evolved with each succeeding missions as did the spacecraft's imaging subsystems.

The first successful NASA outer space probe that employed a visual imaging subsystem, Ranger 7, transmitted data that were eventually digitized on earth. They were then processed to determine the photometric properties or the brightness variations and level of the lunar surface.[21] Because of the low contrast of the Martian surface, the photographs relayed by Mariner 4 in their raw state were virtually useless. Computer processing, however, replaced missing data and enhanced the photographs' contrast whereby Martian surface features that were hitherto obscured became visible to reveal the planet's geological formations.[22]

Subsequent missions such as Mariners 6 and 7 further refined the decalibration and enhancement techniques, and these procedures became more sophisticated with the later missions. In summation, the use of computer processing constituted the third and final stage in the production of photographs from spacecraft. The first step was the design and operation of the visual imaging and transmission subsystems carried by a probe. The second step was the design and ability of the Deep Space Network to receive the spacecrafts' transmissions. The final step was the decalibration and enhancement of the data to produce the final hard copy prints.

The next chapter describes some of the visual imaging subsystems' discoveries after the pictorial information was received and computer processed on the earth. These included the first detailed images of the planet Mercury, the mapping and observations of Venus' cloud structure, the intensive photographic survey of Mars that enabled scientists to map wide sections of the planet, the volcano on Io, one of Jupiter's moons, and the thousands of ringlets that constitute the Saturnian ring system.

CHAPTER 8

An Analysis of the Photographs

After Voyager 2 completed its Saturn flyby, the spacecraft was propelled toward its projected 1986 rendezvous with the planet Uranus. When the photographs transmitted by the probe were joined with those of previous missions, a body of data was collected that chronicled the physical characteristics of the planetary bodies.[1]

This photographic collection was used by scientists in a number of ways. In one instance, photographs taken in different spectral regions were employed to investigate the physical composition of the planets and satellites. Scientists also examined the pictures to trace a planetary body's geophysical history. Thus, the influence of physical forces, such as volcanism, that might have shaped a world's current physical state as was revealed in the photographs, was determined.[2]

In order to amass the necessary photographic data to provide scientists with sufficient information to initiate the aforementioned and other analytical and interpretative tasks, the planetary missions were designed to produce a variety of images highlighting different characteristics of the planets and satellites. Thus, in some missions, an outer space probe's trajectory was planned, as it was with the Ranger 8 Spacecraft, to relay photographs that had a three-dimensional effect.[3] The probe approached the lunar surface at a low angle of descent prior to its impact. This low angle produced photographs that highlighted the physical perspective of the lunar features and created the three-dimensional appearance.

The angle of the sun's light, or the angle of illumination of a planet and satellite, was another important criterion of the mission design. This was demonstrated during the Lunar Orbiter flights when the illumination qualities of the moon were correlated with other data to derive slope values of the lunar surface.[4] In this process, individual photographs were analyzed to produce quantitative data about select lunar features. The data were then used, in part, to create profiles of the lunar surface.

In another mission, as Voyager 2 departed from the Jovian system, the spacecraft photographed Jupiter's ring. Since the ring was backlit at the time, the ring's shape and features were highlighted in contrast with photographs taken at different lighting and imaging angles.[5]

Hence, through the compilation of photographs revealing those characteristics of planetary bodies that were accentuated, at times, by a spacecraft's trajectory or by the target's illumination, a photographic data base was created. By using this data base in conjunction with other information, scientists were then able to determine, in part, the bodies' structure and composition. In addition, they could develop hypotheses as to how these worlds and the entire solar system were created. Finally, the photographs relayed from the spacecraft that revealed physical activities on other worlds, such as Venus' atmospheric dynamics, were also employed to examine the earth's own such activities.

Mercury

The National Aeronautics and Space Administration's spacecraft missions to Mercury consisted solely of the Mariner 10 probe that rendezvoused with the planet three times. Prior to these encounters, scientists had never viewed Mercury's surface. Unlike the moon or a planet such as Jupiter, where scientists were able to examine photographs from earth observatories that resolved these bodies' respective surface and atmospheric markings (albeit to a limited degree), telescopic observations of Mercury did not reveal the planet's morphology or geological characteristics and formations.[6]

When Mariner 10 initiated its photographic transmission, however, the pictures revealed a world similar to the earth's moon in its general appearance. Craters dotted the landscape and smooth plains covered other surface regions. The photographs also highlighted a number of surface features that differentiated the planet from the moon, including Mercury's scarps—cliffs that were scattered throughout the photographed areas of the planet.[7] The formations' unique characteristic was that they appeared to have been formed by compressive forces within the planet. They were thrust, or reverse, faults in that Mercury contracted during its history, the original land mass was displaced and thrust upward to create the scarps.[8] Furthermore, since some scarps cut across craters in the Mariner 10 photographs, it appeared that the scarps were formed during or after Mercury's final heavy cratering period. If the scarps existed prior to this time, then the collisions between foreign materials and Mercury that formed the craters would also have obliterated a section of the scarp.[9]

Another prominent surface feature revealed by Mariner 10's photographs was a series of basins, including the Caloris with its 1,300 kilometer diameter. A basin was essentially a large and shallow depression formed by the impact of a foreign body. The Caloris basin was surrounded by a ring of mountains while some of Mercury's smaller basins were encircled by a double ring of mountains or walls.[10]

The photographs of Mercury were also used by scientists to analyze the planet's craters and to compare them with those of earth's moon. In terms of their general appearance, the craters on both worlds were similar. The youngest craters had sharp features and contours while the older craters, which were eroded from the bombardment of small particles for aeons, had rounded edges and were shallower in appearance.[11] There were also differences between the Mercurian and lunar craters that were due, in part, to the physical properties of each planetary body. The photographs of Mercury indicated, for example, that the length of a crater's ejecta was generally shorter than that of a comparably sized lunar crater. When a meteoroid or other foreign body collided with Mercury, the moon, or any other large planetary body, a crater was formed.[12] As this smaller body impacted with the larger body, the force and shock waves created by the collision evacuated a portion of the larger body's planetary material and thus produced a crater.[13] The evacuated material were called ejecta.

The distance the ejecta were propelled before they settled onto the surface of the parent body depended, in part, upon the strength of the planet's, or moon's, gravity. Since Mercury possessed a stronger gravitational field than the earth's moon, the ejecta's "ballistic range" was less than it was on the moon.[14] Hence, Mercury's gravity prevented the material from travelling as far as it did on the moon with its weaker gravitational field.

Mariner 10's photographs were also used to confirm the findings of earth radar in the determination of the length of Mercury's day. In this process, the shadows of selected surface features were measured in two sets of photographs produced during two of the planetary encounters. Since the time period between the encounters, the length of the shadows, and other criteria were known factors, scientists were able to compute and refine the radar's original determination of a Mercurian day.[15] This time period was the equivalent of 58.661 ± 0.017 earth days.

Finally, based upon the surface features depicted in the spacecraft's photographs, some scientists proposed that Mercury was volcanically active in the past. In some pictures, for example, it appeared that the plains and some of the depressions in the planet's surface were formed and filled respectively by a large volume of volcanic material.[16]

Mariner 10's photographs permitted scientists to view Mercury's surface for the first time. The images also constituted a data base since scientists were able to analyze and interpret the photographs to determine Mercury's past and present physical states. Furthermore, the pictures were also useful in comparing Mercury's geological formations with those of the other planetary bodies.

The Mariner 10 spacecraft that transmitted these images also rendezvoused with the planet Venus. This probe relayed high resolution photographs of the Venusian atmosphere and was subsequently followed by the Pioneer spacecraft which orbits the planet and was still in early 1983 transmitting images to earth. At the present time, the photographs from both probes have chronicled both the composition and dynamics of Venus' atmosphere.

Venus

The exploration of Venus prior to the space age was similar to that of Mercury in one respect. Scientists had never seen Venus' surface. Mercury's small size and distance from the earth precluded this examination; Venus' surface, however, could not be seen because of its dense atmospheric cover.[17] The atmosphere similarly prevented Mariner 10 and Pioneer Venus from photographing the planet's land masses.

In order to survey Venus, therefore, two different imaging methods were adopted. In one instance, earth based radar and a radar device aboard Pioneer Venus were used to map the planet's surface, since the atmosphere did not block radar signals. The second method employed the visual imaging devices carried by the two spacecraft. These cameras photographed Venus' atmosphere, its structure, and its circulation patterns.[18] In addition, as was mentioned in the two chapters that described the probes, based upon earth observations, the spacecraft were fitted with imaging systems that operated in the near ultraviolet region of light.

One of the initial discoveries of the Venusian spacecraft through their ultraviolet photographs was the distinct circulation patterns of the Venusian atmosphere. The patterns were revealed by photographic sequences taken over a period of time. The photographs chronicled the shifting atmospheric features and thus the circulation patterns.[19]

Based upon the pictures, it was computed that the circulation rate of Venus' upper atmosphere was approximately a time period of four days. Hence, specific atmospheric features would travel completely around or circumnavigate the planet in four days.[20] Venus, however, rotated around its axis only once in every 243 earth days. The atmosphere was therefore propelled around the planet at a speed that outstripped Venus' rotational period. Through an analysis of the photographs and by plotting the movement of the features, it was determined that winds circled the planet in the upper atmosphere at rates of up to 225 miles per hour.[21]

The photographs also revealed that Venus' atmosphere was vertically stratified into different regions. The wind speeds at the lower areas were less than those in the upper atmosphere. Scientists suggested that the upper atmosphere's higher speed was "due to the transfer of momentum from Venus' slow-moving, massive lower atmosphere to higher altitudes where the atmosphere was less massive, so the same momentum resulted in a much higher velocity."[22] The force of the momentum of the lower atmosphere as it circulated, therefore, helped propel the less dense higher atmosphere.

The stratification itself was discovered through the analysis of photographs taken at an angle and with an illumination that revealed the atmosphere's vertical structure.[23] This type of image, as will be explained in the next chapter, is called a limb photograph.

Recent photographs from the Pioneer Venus spacecraft also revealed a new atmospheric layer that enveloped the planet. It was an 18 mile thick haze layer that "appears and disappears over several year periods."[24] This periodicity of Venus' atmosphere was further revealed in photographs of the planet's general circulation patterns. Scientists discovered that the patterns themselves changed over a period of time and were not fixed.[25]

In addition to the changing patterns, the photographs also indicated that Venus exhibited a Hadley circulation pattern as a permanent atmospheric characteristic. Venus' Hadley system was a cell or a predominant wind flow pattern that stretched from the planet's equatorial to its pole regions. The atmospheric circulation followed this general route just as the trade winds on earth, in an analogous example, "correspond to the low level flow of the Hadley cell at the equator."[26]

Finally, the structure of the atmospheric features was also examined in Mariner 10's and Pioneer Venus' photographs. These features resembled dark bands, rays, and streaks that spread over the planet. In other instances, large and dark Y-shaped markings stretched across the planet whereby the "tail of the 'Y' extended eastward around the planet, and the arms [extended] westward."[27] The atmospheric features, therefore, exhibited a variety of shapes and sizes.

In conclusion, the Mariner 10 and Pioneer Venus spacecrafts' visual imaging subsystems permitted scientists to examine Venus' atmospheric features and circulation characteristics. Prior to these missions, the highest quality ultraviolet pictures that could be taken from the earth failed to reveal the atmosphere's intricate structure and patterns.[28]

Approximately one decade prior to Mariner 10's Venus encounter, however, the moon, which was the third planetary body in terms of its orbital position from the sun that was imaged by an outer space probe, was photographed by Ranger 7. This mission initiated the investigation of the lunar surface by unmanned spacecraft which ultimately concluded with the Apollo landings.

The Moon

Other than the earth, the moon was the most extensively explored planetary body in the solar system both prior to and after the unmanned and manned flights. This was due, in part, to the moon's close proximity to the earth and the absence of an atmosphere, which permitted earth observatories readily to view and photograph its surface. The earth observations, nevertheless, as were those for all of the planetary bodies, were limited by a number of factors. For example, the resolving power of telescopes meant that smaller lunar features were unobserved; the earth's atmosphere interfered with observations and blurred or reduced a telescope's resolution. A combination of these and other factors prevented small geological formations and the intricate characteristics of other lunar features from being depicted in earth based photographs.[29] These problems were of course alleviated in part with the photographs transmitted by the lunar spacecraft.

One of the primary contributions of the moon probes was the photographing of the moon's far side by the Lunar Orbiter series. The moon exhibits what is known as a synchronized rotation. The body's daily rotational period is equivalent to its orbital period around the earth.[30] These motions are analogous to the earth's 24 hour daily rotation and one year revolution around its axis and the sun respectively. Accordingly only one side, or hemisphere, of the moon, which is its near side, faces the earth. Its far side, or the hemisphere which never faces the earth, was therefore never explored until the advent of the lunar spacecraft.

The first outer space probe to transmit photographs of the moon's far side was the Soviet Lunar 3 probe in 1959. Yet, the pictures failed to resolve many of the lunar surface's features.[31] The photographs that were later relayed by the NASA Lunar Orbiter spacecraft, however, were of a high enough quality to resolve this hemisphere's morphology. The images depicted a surface that was different from the moon's near side in many respects. Unlike this hemisphere's variety of mare, for example, the far side was devoid of extensive mare regions and was heavily cratered.[32] To the naked eye, the mare appeared to be the smooth and bright sections of the moon. Prior to telescopic observations (which began more than 350 years ago), it was believed that the mare regions were physical bodies of water, hence, these areas were named *mare,* which was the Latin word for seas.[33] Later observations by telescope and the unmanned and manned spacecraft revealed that the mare were generally lightly cratered lava plains.

In addition to highlighting the different surface characteristics of the moon's near and far sides, the Lunar Orbiters' photographs also depicted the overall morphology of the lunar surface. The pictures revealed, for example, that the "level and gentle rolling terrain" of the moon, such as the mare regions, were peppered by a large number of small circular craters that ranged in size from 50 meters to the limit of the cameras' resolution.[34] High resolution photographs of these regions resolved many of these smaller craters that were not visible in earth observations. The photographs subsequently permitted scientists to calculate the crater's distribution frequency, which consisted of both random and nonrandom elements.[35]

The random distribution element consisted of primary craters or the original craters formed when the moon was struck by a foreign body. The nonrandom distribution pattern suggested, in turn, that some craters were secondary craters and craters formed by volcanic forces.[36] A secondary crater was one in which the crater was formed by the ejecta from a primary crater. When a meteoroid, for example, collided with the moon and created a primary crater, the displaced crater material was propelled in all directions. When portions of the ejecta eventually collided with the lunar surface at the conclusion of their flight, they created a series of small secondary craters.

The photographs from the Ranger, Surveyor, and Lunar Orbiter series also supported the hypothesis that the mare regions were created by volcanic activity and lava flows. The hypothesis was confirmed when the astronauts from the Apollo missions returned samples of these areas to earth. A series of tests subsequently revealed the samples' volcanic origins.[37]

In another instance, the lunar photographs resolved the fine structural details of the lunar craters and their floors. This was important for the investigation of the moon's geology since craters were the moon's predominant surface feature. The images were also analyzed by scientists in an attempt to determine the age of the craters and hence of the moon itself.[38]

The photographs from all three spacecraft series were also employed to determine the depth of the lunar regolith. The regolith was the dust and variably sized rubble layer that covered the lunar surface. It was generally formed from the craters' ejecta and the subsequent breakup of this material by micrometeorites and other physical phenomena.[39] Micrometeorites were extremely small foreign bodies or dust particles that constantly collided with and eroded the ejecta. The regolith itself was analogous, at least in terms of its physical location, to the earth's topsoil.

Scientists once believed that the lunar regolith was deep enough to completely envelop any spacecraft, be it unmanned or manned, that landed on the moon. The actual depth, however, was initially discovered through analysis of the lunar spacecraft's photographs and *in situ* examinations by the Surveyor spacecraft that soft-landed on the moon. The probes' photographs revealed that the regolith, at least at the Surveyor landing sites, ranged between one and over ten meters in depth.[40] The current consensus, which is based upon all of the spacecraft series' data and the Apollo landings, is that the regolith varies between one and twenty meters across the whole of the lunar surface.

The regolith, therefore, was a "topsoil" of material covering the moon's geological features. It was also determined that the layer possessed both compressive and cohesive properties. During several of the Surveyor missions, for example, after a craft had landed on the moon, its rocket was reignited and the Surveyor lifted off the surface, literally hopping to another landing site. This movement permitted a spacecraft's camera to photograph the depressions in the lunar surface produced by the Surveyor's footpads during the first landing.[41] The pictures of these initial imprints demonstrated that the lunar surface materials were "moderately compressible" and cohesive.[42] Additional photographs of other experiments supported this conclusion and the regolith's capacity to support a spacecraft.

In addition to revealing the lunar surface's characteristics, photographs were also produced to highlight different facets of these features. In one example, a Lunar Orbiter probe transmitted an overhead view of one of the moon's geological formations called a lunar dome. Another picture was taken of the same formation at an oblique angle. The overhead and oblique photographic angles depicted the dome's top and sides and its vertical structure and height respectively.[43] The views were analogous to an overhead and oblique side views of a dome or rounded hill-like formation on the earth. The overhead or aerial view would permit an observer to look down onto the dome and examine its top and sloping sides. The oblique view, on the other hand, would enable the observer to investigate the dome from an elevated side view and thus to examine the dome's vertical structure and scale.

A final consequence of the photographs transmitted by the outer space probes was that the images helped make the Apollo missions feasible. The photographs were used, in part, to locate and map suitable landing sites for the Lunar Modules that carried the astronauts to the lunar surface.[44] The Apollo missions, in turn, produced data that confirmed many of the photographic findings, such as the volcanic origin of the lunar mares.

In summation, the photographs from the lunar spacecraft chronicled the geological characteristics and physical history of the moon. Small craters and the details of geological formations that were not resolved by earth telescopes, for example, were revealed in the outer space probes' pictures. Furthermore, the photographs supported one scientific group's contention that the lunar landscape was molded by a number of physical processes. This included the formation of the craters by foreign bodies and volcanic activity and the fact that the moon's "seas" were, in fact, seas of lava.[45] The photographic data base for the moon surpasses that of any of the solar system's other planetary bodies. Only Mars, the next world after the moon in the orbital progression from the sun, approaches the quantity and quality of the lunar photographic data. The Mars' pictures were transmitted by Mariners 4, 6, 7, and 9, and the four Viking spacecraft.

Mars

Even though Mariner 4 was the first NASA spacecraft to photograph Mars, the planet was extensively surveyed by earth based instruments, including the telescope, prior to this flight. Unlike the moon, where many of the surface features were visible, much of the Martian terrain remained unresolved through earth telescopes. The instruments, however, did depict the planet's gross physical properties, such as red and green features that changed over time. What was believed to have been ice caps at Mars' poles were also identified as were a series of markings that some scientists had claimed were canals.[46]

The canal-like markings were first observed in the late 1800's by the Italian astronomer Schiaparelli, who called them *canali*, meaning "channels" but frequently mistranslated as "canals." The observations were later confirmed by the American astronomer Percival Lowell, who devoted his life to mapping what he believed was an extensive network of irrigation canals constructed by an intelligent race.[47] During Lowell's lifetime and after his death, a controversy arose within scientific circles as to the nature of the markings. Some scientists believed they were atmospheric anomalies and optical illusions, some – if not most – reserved judgment, while others thought the markings were channels. A few continued to consider them canals. Members of this latter group also suggested that the observed green regions of Mars that grew and receded in agreement with the planet's ice caps were areas of vegetation. As the Martian seasons progressed, the ice caps melted and the released water flowed through the canals to irrigate the vegetation. As winter approached, however, the water gradually receded to the poles where it was again frozen. Hence, without water, the green vegetation slowly died until all that remained was decayed matter, which was viewed by earth telescopes as brown regions.[48] This tantalizing vision of Mars as a world crisscrossed with irrigation canals and thriving native life forms was fairly well discredited, however, decades before the photographs from the outer space probes. Some scientists believe today that undetected Martian organisms may still exist.[49]

The photographs from the Mariner 4 spacecraft, which resolved a portion of Mars' surface, revealed a lunar-like world with a series of craters. Moreover, even though Mariner 4's picture swath "crossed several of the canallike markings sketched from time to time on maps," the photographs did not positively reveal any canal-like structures.[50]

The Mariners 6 and 7 spacecraft followed in the wake of Mariner 4 and transmitted photographs during their far and near encounters. Like the Mariner 4 images, the two spacecrafts' photographs revealed that craters were the predominant surface feature, and once again, canals were not observed.[51] Several years later, however, the view of Mars as a cratered world was radically altered after Mariner 9 relayed pictures during a prolonged orbital mission. Regions of Mars that were hitherto unobserved during the earlier missions were photographed for the first time. Mars' true morphology as a world of craters, as well as valleys, canyons, and volcanoes, thus emerged.[52]

After Mars' entire surface had been surveyed by Mariner 9 and the two Viking spacecraft, volcanoes were classified as the planet's largest surface feature. The volcanoes themselves were dominated by the Olympus Mons volcano with its 600 kilometer base and 26+ kilometer height. This can be compared with an average 120 kilometer base and nine kilometer height for the Hawaiian volcanoes, which were numbered among the largest of those on earth.[53]

The photographs also revealed that Olympus Mons' base was surrounded by a six kilometer high scarp. Based upon these images, scientists suggested that the scarp was possibly formed by internal geological forces or by wind and water erosion.[54] The latter interpretation, therefore, indicated that water may have flowed on Mars at one time in its past history. In addition, the volcano's height, which was determined, in part, by an analysis of the Viking Orbiters' photographs, permitted scientists to estimate the width of Mars' crust. In conjunction with the data from other instruments and Olympus Mons' height and physical mass, it was suggested that Mars' crust had to be at least 50 kilometers thick to support the weight of enormous volcanoes.[55]

Photographs of other formations, such as channels, provided additional support to the hypothesis that water had existed on Mars. Some scientists believed that the features were created through water or fluvial erosion, while others suggested that a channel, for example, may have been created by "sapping erosion associated with emanation of water from an underground water or ice table."[56] In this process, underground sources of water and ice caused the land above these areas to collapse and thus create the channels.

The shifting colors of the Martian landscape was also chronicled, in part, by the Viking Landers. Their photographs revealed that the surface color changed over a period of time and was partially a reflection of Martian dust storms. The probes depicted this role of the dust storms in addition to providing visual data as to the effect of wind and dust as one of Mars' erosion mechanisms.[57]

The spacecraft also photographed Phobos and Deimos, the two Martian moons. It was the first time that the satellites' gross and fine physical features were resolved. The photographs permitted scientists both to view the bodies' geological characteristics and, as will be described in the next chapter, to analyze Phobos and Deimos in an attempt to determine the surface morphologies of the asteroids.[58]

The photographs from the Mariner and Viking series, therefore, were examined to ascertain the present and past geological history of Mars and the forces that shaped the planet and its satellites. The exploration of Mars also demonstrated the necessity of investigating the entire planetary body to accurately depict its geological and physical characteristics. Hence, the initial impression of Mars as a heavily cratered planet was radically altered after Mariner 9 transmitted photographs of the entire planet and revealed the volcanoes and other surface features. This experience has influenced scientists to propose missions to planets that were only partially explored, such as Mercury, in order to accurately assess their physical states.[59]

Beyond the orbit of Mars lies the main asteroid belt with its thousands of small planetary bodies. As of early 1983 only four of NASA's outer space probes, namely, Pioneers 10 and 11 and Voyagers 1 and 2, have penetrated this region to explore the planets and the moons of the outer solar system.

Jupiter

The initial telescopic observations of Jupiter, the first of the so-called outer planets, were conducted by Galileo in the early 1600's. His instrument resolved the planetary disk and four of Jupiter's largest and brightest moons.[60] As earth observation techniques and instruments improved over the centuries, Jupiter's physical characteristics were gradually revealed.

Scientists determined, for example, that Jupiter's planetary core was enveloped by a dense atmosphere that limited visual observations of the planet to the atmosphere itself. The atmosphere was also physically "divided into alternating dark and light bands termed belts and zones, respectively," and there were also "irregularly distributed smaller features within the banded pattern consisting of an assortment of markings in the form of streaks, wisps, arches, and loops, as well as patches, lumps, or spots of either darker or lighter material."[61]

The Jovian satellites, however, were not obscured by dense atmospheres. Yet, their small size and distance from the earth prevented instruments from resolving their surface features. One of the primary photographic objectives of the outer space probes, therefore, was to visually survey the satellites. The other photographic objective was the imaging of Jupiter's atmosphere in order to enlarge and enhance the photographic data base originally created by the earth observations.

Consequently, the photographs transmitted from the Pioneer spacecraft, the first probes to explore Jupiter, were sufficiently resolved to reveal the intricate patterns of Jupiter's atmosphere that were not visible in earth observations. This included pictures of Jupiter's Great Red Spot and its internal structure.[62] This atmospheric feature was, as its name implied, a large red spot that has been observed on Jupiter for well over a hundred years. The Pioneer probes also photographed several of the moons. Because of the limited resolution of the spacecrafts' photopolarimeters and the distance from the satellites, however, only gross surface features and the surface coloration of these bodies were depicted in the photographs.[63]

The Voyager spacecrafts' television subsystems transmitted higher resolution photographs of the Jovian system because of their superior cameras, more powerful transmission subsystems, more stable shooting platform, and the Voyagers' trajectories, which brought them closer to their targets than their predecessors. The Voyagers' photographic sequences included the documentation of the motion of Jupiter's atmosphere. The initial photographs in the sequence identified both specific objects and their position in relation to other features and the planet itself. If the objects moved as time elapsed, their movement was recorded in subsequent photographs. This process generated a moving record or what was essentially a movie chronicling Jupiter's atmospheric dynamics.[64]

One of the measurements derived from these photographs was the directional flow of Jupiter's cloudbands. It was computed that the bands moved generally east to west at speeds from 150 to minus 50 meters per second.[65] The photographs also chronicled the Great Red Spot's counter-clockwise motion, including the movement of smaller objects that revolved around the Great Red Spot in a six day period.[66]

The Great Red Spot and several associated white oval-shaped features were also unique characteristics of Jupiter's atmosphere. Scientists used the spacecrafts' photographs to determine why and how these features survived in Jupiter's unstable atmosphere. Some scientists believed, for example, that the structures survived by "drawing energy from the zonal currents in which they sit."[67] Thus, the Great Red Spot and white ovals survived by literally drawing or "feeding" upon the energy flows that encompassed them. A determination of the probable cause for these objects also permitted scientists to postulate the internal structure and processes of the planet since the internal characteristics might have created these external atmospheric manifestations.[68]

Finally, the Voyagers' television cameras recorded two phenomena that were previously undetected. The first was a faint and narrow ring encircling Jupiter. Scientists estimated that the ring's maximum width was approximately 30 kilometers.[69] The second phenomenon occurred within Jupiter's atmosphere. When the spacecraft passed over the night-side of Jupiter, the cameras photographed atmospheric lightning discharges. This indicated that the atmospheric conditions on Jupiter, like those of the earth, generated electrical storms.[70]

In addition to Jupiter's atmosphere, the spacecraft also photographed the Jovian satellites. One of the most important finds of the missions was the detection of active volcanoes on the satellite Io. The first volcano was originally discovered through the detection of its 280 kilometer high plume. Further analyses of the photographs of Io revealed the presence of several additional active volcanoes.[71] Furthermore, the photographs also demonstrated that the "number and magnitude of these eruptions indicate that Io is the most volcanically active body so far discovered in the Solar System," even more so than the earth.[72]

The geologic variance of the Jovian moons was further highlighted by the satellite Ganymede. It was postulated, for example, that Ganymede's surface features were indicative of crustal movements similar to the earth's own crustal activity. Other than the earth and Ganymede, the outer space probes' photographs have not detected this physical phenomenon on any planetary body.[73]

In contrast with Io's active physical state and Ganymede's possible crustal movements, Callisto, another of Jupiter's moons, appeared to be the most inactive of the Jovian moons. If the body was or had been geologically active in its past, many of the craters that covered its surface would have been erased by the geological activity.[74] The photographs, therefore, depicted the satellite's surface morphology. Moreover, through the interpretation of the photographs, scientists constructed the hypothesis that Callisto was geologically inactive.

Jupiter's other so-called Galilean satellite, Europa, was also photographed. The pictures of this moon, in addition to those of Io, Callisto, and Ganymede, were employed to produce control networks of these bodies. Hence, identifiable structures and formations and their respective coordinates were indicated on a series of maps of the satellites.[75] The prominent features used in creating a control network for Io, for example, were its volcanoes, while Ganymede and Callisto's individual networks incorporated conspicuous craters. Europa's network, on the other hand, primarily employed the areas of the satellite where its "long linear features" intersected.[76] These linear features were characterized as a series of streaks that crisscrossed the entire surface of Europa. Scientists postulated that the streaks were possibly breaks in the satellite's thick ice crust created by an internal heat source.[77]

The photographs of the Jovian satellites revealed the wide variety of this system's geological characteristics as exemplified by Io's active and Callisto's inactive geological manifestations. The photographs of Jupiter itself confirmed earth based observations as to the dynamics of the planet's atmosphere. The photographs also resolved the structure of specific features within the atmosphere and Jupiter's ring.

As Pioneer 11 and Voyagers 1 and 2 sped away from the Jovian system, the spacecraft eventually rendezvoused with Saturn, the next planet out from the sun. This world and its moons were also the final planetary bodies photographed by outer space probes as of 1983.

Saturn

The photographs relayed by Pioneer 11 and the two Voyagers recorded the characteristics of Saturn's dense atmosphere, its satellites, and the ring system that encircled the planet. The rings had always fascinated scientists, for until the discovery of the faint rings that girded Jupiter and Uranus, the Saturnian ring system was believed to be a unique phenomenon.

The rings were initially discovered by Christian Huygens in the mid-1600's.[78] Since that time, scientists have surveyed this feature with telescopes, radio waves, and radar in an attempt to discover the ring's composition and structure. It was determined through telescopic observations, for example, that the rings were composed of four primary divisions, designated A, B, C, and D. A gap also separated the A and B rings and this region of apparently empty space was named Cassini's division after its discoverer, Jean Cassini.[79]

The rings depicted in the photographs, however, did not adhere to this now classical construct. With the Voyagers' television cameras the rings were resolved to a degree far surpassing earth observations. The probes' photographs revealed that the ring system was a highly complex structure in that the four major divisions were themselves composed of hundreds of rings or ringlets.[80] The photographs also demonstrated that there were also rings within the Cassini division.

Furthermore, on the basis of the photographs and other data, scientists postulated that many of the ringlets were formed and retained their shape, in part, through the action of small moons revolving around Saturn and embedded within the primary ring divisions. As these small moons revolved around the planet, the moons' gravitational torque exerted a force upon the ring material which was separated into the ringlets.[81]

This physical process can be likened to the following. The surface of a large circular and flat vessel is covered with a thin layer of positively charged iron particles or filings. A series of negatively charged pellets are then placed along a line representing the vessel's radius and are moved or made to revolve around the vessel's central axis. The pellets' negative charge would repel the positively charged iron filings that lay in the pellets' paths. As the pellets complete their motion around the vessel, and overhead view of the vessel would reveal that the once smooth surface of iron filings is now transformed. The pellets' paths would be cleared of the filings, while the space between two pellets would contain the displaced filings. The vessel, therefore, appears to consist of a series of gaps and ringlets.

In this analogy, the moon-like objects embedded within Saturn's rings and the material that composed the rings were represented by the pellets and iron filings respectively. Just as the pellets' negative charge helped form the ringlets as the pellets completed their revolution around the axis, so did the moons' gravitational torque possibly shape and create Saturn's ringlets.

A similar effect was observed in another photographic sequence of Saturn's newly discovered F-ring. The ring had a peculiar shape since it appeared to be braided at times, with another ring. Some scientists suggested that the gravitational torque of S13 and S14, the two moons that surrounded the ring, created both the ring and the braided effect.[82]

In addition to Saturn's ring system, the spacecraft also surveyed the planet's atmosphere. As with Jupiter, Saturn's atmosphere completely enveloped the planetary core in a dense and gaseous envelope. The atmosphere also exhibited a wide variety of structural features and a wind flow pattern that was computed to be four times stronger than that of Jupiter.[83] Scientists also determined that the wind flow, or zonal jets, were physically wider than those on Jupiter. Furthermore, the case with Jupiter in which its zonal jets apparently coincided with or matched the planet's atmospheric bands was not observed on Saturn.[84]

In addition to the higher wind speeds, photographs also revealed that Saturn's atmosphere lacked large oval features, such as Jupiter's Great Red Spot. The largest oval observed on Saturn was approximately one-tenth the size of the Great Red Spot.[85] Nevertheless, the planet exhibited a wide variety of markings. This included light and dark banding across sections of the planet and cloud-like features several hundred kilometers in size.[86]

Another facet of the Saturnian system photographed by the spacecraft was the planet's satellites. This included an investigation of Titan, the second largest and only satellite in the solar system to possess a "substantial atmosphere."[87] This enveloping layer prevented the spacecraft from photographing Titan's surface, as was the case with Venus, Jupiter and Saturn. Limb photographs, however, revealed the atmosphere's vertical stratification, including a 50 kilometer wide haze layer situated 100 kilometers above the atmosphere's aerosol layer.[88] Scientists believe the aerosol layer is composed of organic compounds and functions almost like a chemical smog cover since it obscures the lower atmosphere and the satellite's surface.

The spacecraft, however, did photograph the surface characteristics of other Saturnian satellites, since these bodies do not possess atmospheres. Mimas, Tethys, Rhea, and Dione, for example, were portrayed as worlds composed of ice. The satellites exhibited a variety of surface formations, including craters. Since Mimas, Tethys, Rhea, and Dione's average temperature was below 100° Kelvin, their structural strength was almost equal to that of rock. When a foreign body struck a satellite, the satellite reacted as though it was composed of rock.[89] Thus, the impact formed a crater instead of shattering the body.

Several of the Saturnian satellites, such as Dione and Tethys, were also scarred by trenches, and scientists offered two explanations for the formation of these markings. One was that the trenches and others markings were created by internal activity; if these bodies were once internally active, then they were not simply solid balls of ice. The second explanation, however, was that the surface markings — on Tethys, for example — came about from collisions between the satellite and foreign bodies, the impacts generating shock waves that created the markings.[90] In yet another example, some scientists suggested that Dione's bright streaks were created by internal activity and by the ejecta from impact craters.

Finally, the Voyager spacecraft also photographed the satellite Iapetus and revealed the distinct contrast between its light and dark hemispheres. After the photographs were analyzed, it was determined that the contrast was a reflection of the satellite's surface composition and was not created by lighting conditions.[91] As on Titan, scientists believe the dark hemisphere was created by organic materials that either fell upon Iapetus' surface or were produced by internal activity.

The photographs from the Voyager and Pioneer spacecraft have permitted scientists to examine Saturn's atmosphere and its satellites. Furthermore, the planet's rings, originally thought to have been composed of several divisions, were portrayed as a system of hundreds of ringlets and their corresponding moons.

Beyond Saturn lies the solar system's other two gas giants, Uranus and Neptune, and what is believed to be the final planet, the cold and icy world of Pluto.[92] At the present time, Voyager is tentatively scheduled to rendezvous with and photograph Uranus and Neptune in 1986 and 1989 respectively, while the reconnaissance of Pluto will have to be delayed until a later planetary mission.

Even though Uranus, Neptune, Pluto and their satellites, in addition to the solar system's smaller planetary bodies, such as comets and asteroids, have yet to be explored, nevertheless the photographic data base created from the Ranger through Voyager missions permitted scientists to compare the earth's present and past physical states with that of the other planetary bodies. This photographic data base has also been employed to investigate the evolution of the earth and the solar system.

The Earth in Relation to the Solar System

The photographs and other data transmitted by outer space probes have enhanced examination of the physical processes and characteristics of the earth. This was a reflection of the systematic exploration of the solar system in which the earth was no longer viewed as an isolated body. Rather, its past, present, and possible future were analyzed in relation to the other planetary bodies. As Carl Sagan stated, "exploring the Solar System gives us other worlds to compare our own with, to better understand and control our own planet."[93] Hence, in addition to generating data about other worlds, the reconnaissance of the solar system with a variety of scientific devices, including visual imaging ones, permitted scientists to compare the earth with other worlds in an attempt to better understand the earth.

In one instance, photographs of planetary atmospheres were analyzed to examine the physical composition and dynamics of the earth's atmosphere. Despite the fact that Jupiter's atmosphere was different from the earth's, a comparison between both planets was possible since "the laws that govern atmospheres must relate to each other."[94] Hence, the observations of the dynamics of Jupiter's atmosphere were analogous in certain ways to the earth's atmospheric dynamics.

One such Jovian phenomenon that was analyzed was Jupiter's Great Red Spot. In addition to the hypothesis that the Great Red Spot was created by the force of the currents in which it was embedded, it was also believed that the Spot could have been formed by convection.[95] The convection was the rising heat from Jupiter's interior and lower atmospheric regions.

In contrast with convection as a vehicle of atmospheric dynamics, the earth was primarily influenced by the sun, which functioned as an external heat source. Yet, a segment of the earth's atmosphere was affected by a form of convection. The corresponding land mass to this atmospheric region was the equatorial zone which was an area of "severe drought and famine" and "vicious tropical storms."[96]

Scientists who studied the interrelationship between Jupiter's convective phenomena and the earth's equatorial region believed, therefore, that there were "some interesting similarities between the superclusters of giant thunderstorms that plague the ITCZ (intertropical convergence zone) on earth and the big convective plumes in Jupiter's atmosphere."[97] Consequently, an analysis of Jupiter's convective plumes, such as the Great Red Spot, and how the vortices were formed and sustained, could possible be used to aid in exploring the operation of the earth's convective zone and the severe weather in the equatorial region.

In another study, the climatic changes that took place on the so-called terrestial planets through geological forces were investigated. On the basis of photographs of Mars, for example, some scientists suggested that the formation of specific geological features affected the planet in a similar way that the continental drift might have influenced the earth's climate.[98] The scientists believed that the formation of Mars' Tharsis complex, which was a series of volcanoes, ridges, and fractured terrain, altered Mars' normal physical position and the obliquity, or tilt, of its axis relative to the sun. This shift eventually affected Mars' climate. A tectonic or geologic activity on the earth that shaped the planet's surface, such as the continental drift, might have likewise influenced and altered the earth's climate in the past.

As a continent's physical position shifted, for example, a series of physical events were triggered that eventually altered the land masses' temperature and quantity of rain.[99] Photographs from Mars and the *in situ* examination of the earth, therefore, chronicled the possible tectonic activities that might have altered each planet's respective climate. Moreover, the observation of another planet through the use of photographs from space probes permitted scientists to compare the earth with Mars to better understand the interrelationship between the earth and the other planets. In addition, the analysis of Mars' tectonic activity and its possible effects provided scientists with a planetary model in which the earth's own physical processes could be compared with and possibly explained.

The photographs from the spacecraft and their subsequent analyses and interpretations were also employed to trace the evolutionary history of the solar system. By examining photographs of the planetary bodies, these worlds' current surface morphologies provided clues as to how they were formed. Thus, as it was previously described, Mercury's scarps led scientists to believe that the planet was subjected to compressive forces in the past.[100]

Like Mercury, the earth's geological history was revealed by its own geological formations. Scientists have suggested, for example, that the collision of the earth's continental plates, such as the European and African land masses, created features such as the Alps.[101] Thus, just as Mercury's scarps were examined to determine their origin, so was the earth investigated to reveal the forces that shaped its surface.

The outer space probes' photographs of the planetary bodies were also employed to chronicle the formation of the solar system. Some scientists believed that one stage of this creation consisted of the accretion of small dust particles and other materials. Through a series of collisions, several particles, for example, coalesced into a single body. This small body then collided with other particles and larger bodies, which led to the accretion of additional planetary material and the formation of yet a larger body. If this process continued for a long enough period, a planet-sized object was eventually formed.[102]

Based partially upon the photographs from the spacecraft, it was proposed in one instance that the earth might have once resembled, in both appearance and mass, the Martian moon Phobos. This resemblance would have occurred during one of the earth's early accretion stages.[103] Photographs of the Martian satellite apparently supported this contention. Phobos' surface was marked by a series of craters that indicated a number of collisions.[104] In the case of the earth, however, the collisions led to the accretion of the other bodies until the primordial earth was formed. Consequently, photographs of other worlds can be said to have been used to depict the earth during its own formative stages.

The photographs from spacecraft, therefore, were employed in a number of ways. The images revealed the surface morphologies of the solar system's planetary bodies, including features that were never viewed prior to the spacecraft missions. The subsequent examination of the photographs also permitted scientists possibly to determine the internal conditions of these worlds—hence, photographs of Olympus Mons indicated that Mars possessed a thick crust that could support this enormous mass.

The photographs also permitted scientists to explore other worlds and to employ their characteristics as models to examine the earth's present and past physical states. Finally, the pictures were also interpreted in an attempt to discover how the solar system itself was originally formed.

Even though the outer space probes have led to the compilation of a data base that has provided a number of significant revelations about the solar system, a new series of missions with spacecraft that mount cameras have been proposed. These probes would generate additional information about the planetary bodies that have already been explored and would also produce data about unexplored worlds, such as Neptune and the asteroids. These projected missions will be discussed in the next chapter.

CHAPTER 9

Proposed Outer Space Missions

Introduction

As was described in the previous chapter, the visual imaging subsystems on outer space probes transmitted thousands of photographs of the solar system's planetary bodies. The images revealed geological formations and atmospheric features of select planets and satellites. Moreover, through the use of filters, camera systems photographed planetary bodies in different spectral regions, such as Mariner 10's imaging of Venus in the ultraviolet region of light.[1] The photographic information was also employed to compare the earth with other worlds, as was the case with the geological features of Mars as viewed by the Viking Lander and the rocks of the earth's Western Egyptian Desert.[2]

At the present time, however, there are some planetary bodies that have not been surveyed by an unmanned spacecraft with a visual imaging subsystem. These include the planets Uranus, Neptune, and Pluto and their respective moons. Furthermore, neither the asteroids, the small planetary bodies with nominal orbital planes between Mars and Jupiter, nor the comets, with their orbits that may stretch from the sun to millions of miles beyond the outer regions of the solar system, have ever been photographed by an outer space probe. Hence, scientists have never viewed the surface features of an asteroid or seen a photograph revealing the detailed physical structure of a comet's nucleus.[3] In addition to these unexplored bodies, several of the planets and their satellites that were imaged by a space probe were subjected to only a preliminary survey whereby only large geological features or only a fraction of the planetary body was photographed.

Consequently, in order to complete the investigation of the solar system, NASA and various scientific organizations, such as the National Academy of Science's Space Science Board, have drafted a series of proposed outer space missions. The missions themselves fall into two categories. The first was an overall strategy for the investigation of all of the solar system's planetary bodies, while the second series of flights were designed to investigate specific planetary bodies. This chapter describes both sets of missions, the visual imaging subsystems the outer space probes might carry, and the criteria that influenced the design of the proposed spacecraft and their missions.

General Exploration Goals

The proposed spacecraft missions and their imaging subsystems were influenced by a general set of design criteria similarly affecting their predecessors. One was technological in nature. During the first decade of outer space exploration with probes that mounted cameras, for example, all of the spacecraft launched by the United States prior to 1972 other than the lunar probes were designed to rendezvous with Venus or Mars. These two planets of the inner solar system were selected as targets, in part, because of their proximity to the earth in contrast with the other planets. Furthermore, the conditions of space in these regions were less likely to damage a probe than in the vicinity of the outer planets.[4] Hence, up until the time of the Pioneer 10 and 11 spacecraft, it was technologically feasible and simpler to build a probe that could both survive a mission to Venus or Mars and communicate with the earth over these relatively short distances.

Similar technological factors also influenced the designs of projected spacecraft and their missions. This includes the proposed Jupiter Galileo atmospheric probe, for example, that has to survive Jupiter's powerful radiation field and its crushing atmospheric pressure. The designers of the probe had to possess the technological capability and tools to create a probe that would remain operational in a journey that would destroy a conventional probe.[5]

An additional technological criterion influencing the early Venus and Mars flights that will potentially affect the proposed missions are the probes' launch vehicles. Just as the Mariner spacecraft to Mars were built in accordance with weight specifications based upon the payload capacities of their launch vehicles, so were the later Jupiter and Saturn probes and would be the proposed spacecraft.[6]

A final example of a design criterion influencing all of the earlier missions through Voyagers 1 and 2 was the economic one. The original concept for the Voyager flights, for example, was an outer planets grand tour whereby four spacecraft would have explored Jupiter, Saturn, Uranus, Neptune, and Pluto. Fiscal support for the grand tour never materialized, however, and the project was scaled down to encompass the Voyager 1 and 2 missions.[7] Proposed flights have to operate under similar constraints, and this is exemplified by the projected Halley's Comet flyby spacecraft. This probe was initially designed to rendezvous with Halley's comet in 1985 and to investigate its chemical and structural compositions.[8] Because of subsequent budgetary constraints, the proposed mission is not scheduled for development and launching. Consequently, in the planning of projected missions, designers must consider not only available technology but fiscal support, just as their predecessors had to.

The criteria, in turn, have or will influence the spacecrafts' visual imaging subsystems. During the Pioneer 10 and 11 flights weight limitations and budgetary constraints dictated that a Pioneer would be a spin stabilized spacecraft with a photopolarimeter as the imaging device.[9] The apparent (in early 1983) cancellation of the proposed Halley's Comet flyby because of fiscal considerations will affect this spacecraft's imaging subsystem since it might never produce and transmit the photographs it was originally designed to create.

In addition to the effect of the design criteria, the overall strategy for the investigation of the planetary bodies by outer space probes with visual imaging subsystems was also influenced by two ideologies. The first school of thought was that NASA planetary missions should be narrowed and focused in that only a few selected bodies should be explored.[10] This concentrated reconnaissance, it was argued, would yield more scientific data and result in a greater understanding of a specific planet's physical properties.

Under this system, a planet, for example, would first be subjected to earth observations. This would be followed by flyby and orbital missions, and then by a soft-landing.[11] Thus, the first flyby mission would be based upon the knowledge generated by the preliminary earth observations, and the orbiter mission would benefit from the knowledge produced during the flyby mission and so on. This type of exploratory framework was employed during the Mars missions, for example, where initial flybys were eventually superseded by the Viking Orbiter and Lander spacecraft.[12]

The second ideology was the systematic investigation of all of the solar system's planetary members. The National Aeronautics and Space Administration's 1978 Authorization described this goal as the balanced exploration of the solar system. The Authorization stated that

> the flight missions concentrate on the exploration of many different objects in different parts of the Solar System. The need for balance stems from the requirements for comparative study of different planetary bodies in order to characterize and understand any one of them (including our own Earth).[13]

Within the guidelines established by this viewpoint, all of the planetary bodies and not just a few selected objects would be possible candidates for exploration.

This philosophy of a balanced investigation was exemplified by both past and proposed NASA missions. Intensive studies of specific planetary bodies and a systematic exploration of the solar system's members have been both carried out and further planned. This policy was reflected in a 1977 report by the members of the Terrestial Bodies Science Working Group, which met under the auspicies of NASA. The group recommended that the unexplored planetary bodies, such as comets and asteroids, should be investigated by spacecraft, while the inner planets that have already been visited by outer space probes should be subjected to further survey missions.[14] The Working Group also stressed the necessity of maintaining the balance between the goals of intensive and general exploratory missions.

Another strategy for the exploration of the solar system was proposed by the National Academy of Science's Space Science Board. This group studied the feasibility of missions to the outer planets, and the members suggested, in part, that the outer planets and their satellites should likewise be subjected to a balanced exploration by spacecraft.[15] This included the visual imaging of Jupiter, for example, where photographs would resolve the features and stratification of the planet's atmosphere.[16]

Finally, other groups also recommended that the exploration of both the inner and outer solar system should be conducted with different types of spacecraft. These included probes designed for flyby missions and spacecraft that would orbit a planet in follow-up missions. The orbital period would permit these probes to conduct extended surveys of a planet. Other types of probes included those that would plunge through a planet's atmosphere and spacecraft that would effect landings.[17] The latter mission proposal included a projected Mars flight in which a rover vehicle would soft-land on the planet.[18] The rover would not only image Mars from its surface, but it would also travel about and collect and chemically test samples of the Martian soil at different sites.

The mission proposals also stressed the necessity of incorporating a variety of scientific instruments on each spacecraft. A series of reports, for example, were prepared for NASA that examined the use of multiple science disciplines on a single outer space probe. An example of this was a proposal for a remotely piloted vehicle that would fly in a planet's atmosphere and conduct a number of experiments with different scientific devices.[19] These instruments may include a gamma ray spectrometer and an imaging subsystem to transmit high resolution photographs, of Mars for example, to earth. Furthermore, the same craft could be used to carry additional probes that would land on the planet's surface and conduct a series of experiments from the ground.[20] Thus, one spacecraft would generate a variety of scientific data in addition to functioning as a bus vehicle if it incorporated the landing probes.

In summary, the plan for the investigation of the planetary bodies for past and proposed missions was one in which spacecraft would incorporate a variety of scientific instruments and conduct both general surveys of the entire solar system and intensive studies of specific planetary bodies. It was a balanced exploratory framework. Each mission was also multidisciplinary in that,

> although one of the primary objectives of Viking [for example] was to search for life on Mars, the four Viking spacecraft investigated many aspects of Mars and its satellites that were not directly related to life detection experiments, including seismology, meteorology, atmospheric composition, and many other investigations.[21]

The proposed missions, therefore, would follow the pattern established by the Viking Landers and Orbiters. A spacecraft would systematically explore a planetary body with an array of scientific instruments that included visual imaging devices.

In addition to the accumulation of data from different experiments to determine the chemical and physical properties of a planet, various groups also called for the use of earth observations to complement those from a spacecraft. This includes the use of ground based radar, for example, to determine the rotational rate of a planet's satellite and the deployment of astronomical observations to generate spectrographic, photometric, and visual photographic data.[22] The dual use of radar was demonstrated during the Viking mission when the Orbiters' photographs and the radar data were correlated to profile possible landing sites.[23] The proposed imaging of a satellite with radar would be another function that earth-based radar could fulfill. In another instance, earth observations from Hawaii's Mauna Kea Observatory confirmed the findings of the Voyager spacecraft when a series of photographs from the probe revealed Jupiter's ring.[24] Visual observations could support future missions.

Besides the general strategies developed for the exploration of the planetary bodies, a series of general criteria were outlined for the reconnaissance of the outer planets' atmospheres and the types of photographs of these regions from a spacecraft that would permit scientists to map an atmosphere's structure, circulation patterns, and particle size and density.[25] One suggestion called for an imaging subsystem capable of producing a color movie of a planet's atmosphere in order to document its circulation pattern. This feat was accomplished during the Voyager mission when the spacecraft transmitted a series of photographs of Jupiter in rapid succession over a 100 hour period.[26] When the individual photographs were sequentially joined, they chronicled the movements of the Jovian atmosphere. This technique, therefore, could be employed to similarly photograph the atmospheres of Saturn, Uranus, and Neptune in future flights.

Another suggestion was the production of global observations of the outer planets in which photographs would depict the overall structure, markings, and atmospheric changes over an entire planetary disk. Other pictures could be limb photographs "if the limb can be imaged close to and just at the onset and end of solar occultation (180° phase angle)," and hence, "vertical structure [would] be particularly well evidenced."[27] The limb photographs would depict the limb or a segment of the rounded edge of a planet against the backdrop of space. The photographic angle and the illumination of the planet would highlight the planet's atmosphere's vertical features and structure.

Finally, before the proposed missions to specific planetary bodies can be described, there is one final general use of visual imaging subsystems for future missions that merits discussion. This plan calls for the deployment of electro-optical devices to function as the "eyes" of land roving vehicles on other planets.

One proposal described a rover that would explore Mars. A communication problem would develop, however, as the time period between the earth and Mars for the transmission of data from the vehicle and its subsequent reception of the response from mission controllers on earth could last up to 40 minutes. This delay would become more critical during the periods when the rover would be out of radio communication with the earth because of the revolution and orbital location of both planets.

The rover, therefore, essentially a robot vehicle, could not solely depend upon earth commands for its operation.[28] If the robot was autonomous and the cameras, or the rover's "eyes," and ultimately the onboard computer did not recognize potential danger areas, such as a steep wall, and this information could not be relayed to earth where observers could detect the danger, the vehicle could be damaged. Consequently, the proposed robot vehicle was designed to be semiautonomous. Based upon the images transmitted from the cameras, mission operators would plot a specific trajectory and series of operations for the rover. The robot would then complete these tasks without further earth commands.[29]

A research and development project was also conducted by the Jet Propulsion Laboratory to develop the rover's visual imaging subsystem. The proposed dual camera system would transmit photographs of the terrain the rover would traverse, monitor experiments and the manipulation of the rover's moveable arm, and generally provide detailed views of different regions of a planet.[30] The projected cameras would employ solid-state imaging sensors instead of vidicon tubes. A combination of a solid-state sensor and the image processing system would result in the production of pictures at a real-time rate of 1/30th of a second, like conventional television equipment used on earth. Furthermore, because of the operational characteristics of a solid-state array, the images produced would not be geometrically distorted to the extent of vidicon based pictures. The dual camera system would also yield stereo views of the planet's terrain and of the objects manipulated by the rover's moveable arm.[31]

In summation, the past and proposed outer space missions were guided, in part, by a policy issued by Dr. Robert A. Frosch, a former NASA administrator. He stated that in the exploration of planetary bodies,

> the first step is reconnaissance, that is to say, to take a first quick look at the major, and many of the minor, bodies in the solar system. Then we move on to systematic and more comprehensive exploration, and finally to intensive study. The intent is to build up in a systematic way a comprehensive understanding of the structure and characteristics of the various bodies, and to determine the way in which the whole system forms a pattern.[32]

Visual imaging subsystems would play a major role in this exploration whether they were on board a spacecraft or a land roving vehicle. The next section of this chapter describes proposed missions to specific planetary bodies and the imaging subsystems these craft may carry. It deviates, therefore, from the general description of the subsystems and the criteria that influenced their designs.

Specific Planetary Missions

Outlined in the following pages are proposed missions with spacecraft that would incorporate visual imaging subsystems. The missions include the Galileo project, which is a two-part spacecraft designed to survey the Jovian system in the 1980's, flights to investigate comets and asteroids, and a series of missions to both the outer and inner planets and satellites of the solar system.

Inner Planets

The first of the inner planets, Mercury, was initially investigated by the Mariner 10 spacecraft and both the Multiple Discipline Science

Assessment and the Terrestial Bodies Science Working Groups suggested that the next mission to this world should consist of an orbiter spacecraft. The probe would orbit Mercury and conduct an intensive and prolonged study of its geological features with cameras as major aspects of the spacecraft's scientific devices. The orbit itself could potentially be as low as 500 kilometers, which would permit the cameras to produce high resolution photographs of the planet's surface. Furthermore, the proposed probe would also photograph regions of Mercury not imaged by Mariner 10.[33] These new observations would enable scientists to better determine the planet's geophysical properties. They would also provide additional geophysical clues to the process that Mercury and the other planetary bodies underwent when they were first formed.[34]

The Mercury Orbiter could also serve as a platform for the visual observation of the sun. The planet's proximity to the sun would make it an ideal observation site. One of the probe's cameras would monitor the sun while another imaged Mercury.[35] The sun camera could also be fitted with special filters to photograph the sun in different spectral wavelengths just as a Voyager probe's wide angle camera was fitted with filters to image the planetary bodies within the sodium wavelength of light.[36] One spacecraft, therefore, would accomplish two photographic missions.

The second terrestial, or inner, planet is Venus. As with Mercury, scientists proposed a series of flights to further explore this world. One proposal called for an orbiting probe to generate more highly resolved photographs of Venus' atmosphere in a shorter period of time than those produced by the Pioneer Venus craft.[37] The observations of the atmosphere's composition and motion through these detailed pictures would lead to a better understanding of its dynamics and structure.

In another mission, a probe would physically land on Venus' surface and image the surrounding terrain much like the Russian Venera probes. Since a conventional visual imaging subsystem could not penetrate the atmosphere from an orbital position, Venus' surface would have to be photographed from either a landing site or, as has been suggested, from a carrier vehicle such as a balloon. This craft would fly over the planet's surface at an altitude low enough to minimize atmospheric interference, thus permitting the camera system to photograph the land masses.[38] The data produced from these photographs would depict the color, texture, and physical characteristics of the Venusian terrain.

Finally, a Venusian spacecraft has been designed and is tentatively scheduled for launch in the late 1980's. The probe is called VOIR (Venus Orbiting Imaging Radar) and would employ a special radar device to penetrate the cloud cover to reveal planetary features as small as 600 meters in size in addition to determining the altitude of selected regions.[39] Even though the data would not be in the form of photographs in the sense of pictures produced by a visual imaging subsystem, nevertheless the surface characteristics that the radar could reveal demonstrate the scientific value of the use of different imaging instruments in the exploration of the planetary bodies. The photographs from the Pioneer Venus and the proposed orbiter spacecraft would document Venus' atmospheric properties while VOIR would map the surface.

The complementary nature of data that different scientific devices produced would also be used in proposed Mars missions. In addition to the land roving vehicle, one suggestion featured a mission whereby Mars would be surveyed by probes from an orbital position and from its surface through the use of mobile and stationary bases.[40] The information from the probes would range from photographs through chemical and physical analyses of the soil.

One additional proposed mission is the use of the aforementioned remotely piloted vehicle (RPV). The RPV would essentially be a powered glider that could fly at altitudes as low as three kilometers from Mars' surface. This low level flight, in contrast with minimal orbital altitudes of several hundred miles for previous spacecraft, would enable the RPV's cameras to generate high resolution photographs of Mars.[41]

In summation, the spacecraft proposed to explore Mars and the other inner planets were multiple function craft. In addition to photographs, these spacecraft would also generate a variety of data constituting a systematic investigation of these worlds. Interpretations of the planets' geological features through the photographs, therefore, in tandem with the other information, would chronicle the evolutionary and geophysical history of not only these worlds, but as it was described in the previous chapter, of the solar system as a whole.

Comets and Asteroids

Besides those to the inner planets, missions have been planned to investigate comets that enter the solar system. The motivation for the study and photographing of these planetary bodies (in addition to the asteroids) is as follows:

> Missions to the comets in the solar system will contribute to the understanding of their role in the formation and evolution of the solar system and of the general laws of fragmentation and accretion. Comets, while offering a chance to study what is possibly primordial matter in a relatively undisturbed state, may provide the only way to learn of the early stages of the formation of larger celestial bodies in the solar system. Our ignorance of the accuracy of the various theories of cometary origin, composition and behavior will remain until automated spacecraft encounter and explore such a body.[42]

As the Jet Propulsion Laboratory report states, there was a theory that the planetary bodies were formed by a physical process known as fragmentation and accretion. The theory suggests that small planetary bodies such as comets and asteroids were formed prior to the existence of the planets. Over the millennia, however, the theory continues, these small bodies were subjected to a number of collisions that caused them to fragment into smaller pieces, or in some cases, to coalesce into a single mass. This process was repeated until a sufficient body of planetary material had combined to form a planet or major satellite.[43] The possible role of the comets, therefore, in the evolution of the solar system was important and a spacecraft would provide the first detailed view of these bodies.

The goal of the visual imaging subsystem on a cometary encounter spacecraft would be to photograph the comet's nucleus and tail. This would depict the physical characteristics, size, and composition of these components.[44] The members of a NASA colloquium held in 1976 also proposed that this photographic reconnaissance could best be accomplished through the use of a three-axis stabilized probe or a spin stabilized craft with a "despun" camera platform. In this instance, even though a probe would be rotating, as did the Pioneer 10 and 11 spin stabilized spacecraft, the camera would be mounted on a stationary or despun platform to permit the camera system to produce high resolution photographs.[45]

The mission criteria also dictated the cameras should be capable of resolving cometary features as small as 100 meters. During the actual close encounter phase of the mission when the spacecraft would produce these high resolution images, the data would be transmitted in real time in lieu of storing the information on a tape recorder. The scientists feared the comet's dust and particles could potentially damage the spacecraft and its recording subsystems. Hence, the real-time transmissions would eliminate this problem.[46]

A cometary mission was designed in conjunction with the European Space Agency to investigate both Halley's and the Tempel-2 Comets during their close approach to the earth in the mid-to-late 1980's. The spacecraft's trajectory would carry it past the comets whereby its cameras would initiate their photographic survey.[47] The mission would have provided NASA with its first opportunity to study a comet with one of its spacecraft. At the present time, however, the mission is not scheduled for development or launch, because of fiscal restraints.

Another series of missions proposed to explore the smaller and primitive bodies of the solar system other than the comets were those designed for the investigation of the asteroids. Unlike the comets, which have orbital periods that range from several to hundreds of years between the time a comet enters the solar system and its next trip, the majority of the asteroids are concentrated in the region of space between Mars and Jupiter and orbit the sun in somewhat fixed positions at fixed orbital rates. The diameters of these bodies range from smaller than one kilometer to 1,000 kilometers for Ceres, the largest asteroid.[48]

One reason for an asteroid mission was similar to that for a cometary mission. As a group, the asteroids represent what may have been the primordial building blocks of the solar system's major planetary bodies. As the Space Science Board's Committee on Planetary and Lunar Exploration wrote in a report on the investigation of asteroids,

> The primary scientific objectives for the exploration of asteroids are, in order of priority:
> 1. To determine their composition and bulk density;
> 2. To investigate the surface morphology, including evidence for endogenic and exogenic processes and evidence concerning interiors of precursor bodies.[49]

The visual observations of the asteroids, therefore, in conjunction with the data generated from other experiments, would help define the physical characteristics of these bodies and the other planetary bodies in the solar system since the larger bodies may have been formed, in part, through the accretion of the asteroids.

A series of missions, therefore, was proposed to investigate these bodies. One mission, for example, stressed the necessity of rendezvousing with more than one asteroid in a multiple flyby mission, as these bodies exhibit different physical characteristics.[50] The multiple flyby mission would permit scientists to examine a representative sample of the asteroids. A second proposal outlined a mission in which a spacecraft would land on an asteroid, collect a physical sample, and then either return the same to earth or conduct an immediate on-site analysis. The probe's cameras would reveal the physical characteristics of the body in addition to aiding mission controllers in locating a suitable landing site. Photographs from the Viking Orbiters were used to select a landing area for a Viking Lander; the pictures from the asteroid exploratory spacecraft's television cameras would serve a similar function.[51]

Mission designers also drafted what they considered to be the optimum imaging subsystem for an asteroid mission. In one instance, existing hardware such as the 1500mm and 200mm lenses employed on the Voyager craft were suggested as the subsystem's optical components. If the spacecraft orbited around an asteroid in an encounter, the system could potentially resolve surface features as small as 10 meters with the 1500mm lens in addition to providing color composite and multi-spectral images of the asteroid.[52] The transmitted photographs could also reveal an asteroid's "bulk measurements ... shape ... and volume."[53]

Furthermore, scientists have projected what the photographs of an asteroid might reveal. Based upon the Mariner spacecrafts' observations of Mars' two moons, Phobos and Deimos, it has been suggested that asteroids may resemble them. In the Mariner photographs, Phobos and Deimos were depicted as worlds marked with impact craters and grooves on their surfaces. The formation of these features was hypothesized as due to a series of collisions between the moons and other bodies. Consequently, since Phobos and Deimos may physically resemble asteroids, if indeed they were not originally asteroids captures by Mars' gravitational field, the same physical processes that molded these moons may have shaped the asteroids.[54]

As a spacecraft passes through and beyond the main asteroid belt, it enters the outer solar system encompassing Jupiter, Saturn, Uranus, Neptune, Pluto, and their satellites. Jupiter and Saturn have already been imaged by the Pioneer and Voyager probes, and proposed missions would further explore these and the other outer planetary bodies.

Outer Planets

The outer planets, with the exception of Pluto, are worlds enveloped by thick gaseous atmospheres. Accordingly, Jupiter, Saturn, Uranus, and Neptune are called the gas giants of the solar system. Like the planet Venus, the four planets' atmospheres prevent earth telescopes from imaging their surface features and they would similarly affect a spacecraft's visual imaging subsystem.[55] A flyby of these worlds, therefore, would photograph and survey their atmospheric structures and circulation patterns.

In addition to the planets' atmospheres, their satellites have also been designated as possible exploratory targets, and the absence of thick atmospheres on these worlds, with the possible exception of Titan, would permit the photographing of their surfaces. To achieve this goal, three possible types of photographs that a spacecraft's imaging system could produce was suggested: full disc, contiguous coverage, and high resolution photographs.[56]

The full disc images would reveal the entire surface of the satellite that faced the spacecraft at the time of the exposure. These pictures would chronicle any large scale changes that might occur over the satellite's surface. A color shift over time, for example, might indicate the presence of an atmosphere on the satellite. The contiguous coverage of the bodies could be used to create mosaics. These images would provide scientists with the necessary data to compare the geological features of the outer planets' satellites with those of Mars and the Earth. The contiguous imaging would also make it possible to construct control networks for the satellites.[57] Finally, the nested high resolution photographs would depict small geological formations and could possibly be used to create stereo views of the satellites. The highly resolved picture pairs would sharply define a moon's features in addition to aiding scientists in determining the altitude of selected geological formations.[58]

The spacecraft that would possibly explore the outer solar system would be Mariner and Pioneer class probes. As previously described, the Pioneer spacecraft with its spin stabilization system is an ideal platform for scientific instruments that have to scan large sections of the sky in order to generate their data. Furthermore, the craft would function as an inexpensive and lightweight vehicle that could deliver a series of probes to investigate an outer planet's atmosphere. The Mariner series with its three-axis stabilization design would also be used but as a stabilized base to produce high resolution photographs of these bodies.[59]

The projected mission to the outer planets, therefore, primarily consisted of two proposals. The first was the investigation of the outer planets' atmosphere and the second called for photographic reconnaissance of the planets' satellites. These projected missions may be transformed into an actual flight by the Galileo spacecraft, which is tentatively scheduled for launch in the late 1980's.

Galileo Project

The design and mission of the Galileo spacecraft were unique in the annals of space exploration. The craft was of a hybrid configuration and would become the first space probe to orbit one of the outer planets in addition to transporting and releasing a probe to investigate its atmosphere. The spacecraft, therefore, was essentially a synthesis of an orbiter and an atmospheric probe.[60] The craft would be carried by a space shuttle into an earth orbit. At this point, the Galileo probe would separate from the shuttle and a booster rocket would ignite and propel the craft toward Jupiter. After receiving a gravity assist from Mars, the spacecraft would approach Jupiter and at a predetermined time the atmospheric probe would be released. As the probe plunged through the atmosphere for the one hour time period scientists estimate the probe would survive Jupiter's atmospheric pressure, it would relay a stream of data to the Orbiter. The Orbiter would subsequently transmit this information to earth.[61] Once the probe ceased transmitting, the Orbiter mission would continue. The goal of the Galileo project was "to conduct comprehensive investigations of the Jupiter planetary system by making *in situ* and remote measurements of the planet, its environment, and its satellites."[62]

Once the atmospheric probe completed its mission, the Orbiter would initiate its primary mission goal, namely, the investigation of Jupiter's satellites. Galileo's trajectory was computed to complete a grand tour of the Jovian system. For a period of 20 months, the probe would orbit Jupiter in a series of irregularly shaped orbits. The orbits were devised to ensure that at least one of Jupiter's moons would be subjected to a close flyby during each orbital period. In order to conserve fuel during this extended mission, the gravity of the satellites would be employed to help shape the orbits and to propel the spacecraft.[63]

The Orbiter itself would incorporate both spinning and despun sections. As was described in the previous chapters, the Pioneer spacecraft's spin stabilization system made it an ideal platform for the investigation of certain astronomical phenomena. On the other hand, three-axis stabilization systems, such as the ones employed on a Mariner class spacecraft, provided the optimum stable imaging platform. Consequently, the Galileo probe is a hybrid craft that incorporates the best features of both spin and three-axis stabilization craft.[64] This form of an outer space probe for the exploration of the outer planets was suggested in 1969 by the National Academy of Sciences Space Science Board.[65]

The Galileo's television camera employs a unique imaging sensor. Instead of a slow scan vidicon, the camera would be fitted with a charge coupled device (CCD). A CCD is a light-sensitive sensor that creates a signal which is the equivalent of a scene a camera is photographing. It is superior to a vidicon in a number of ways, including the range of its sensitivity, spectral response, size and weight.[66] This type of sensor also produces technically superior photographs in that there is little geometric distortion, in contrast with a vidicon.

The CCD's high sensitivity would be especially critical for the Galileo mission. The projected trajectories would carry the probe close to a satellite's surface during its flyby in order to produce high resolution photographs of these bodies. The CCD's sensitivity would permit the camera to use a high shutter speed even if the satellite had a low light level reading. The high shutter speed, in turn, would reduce the image smear created by the spacecraft's motion and low imaging altitude.[67] The sensor's ability to register and record faint objects would also be used to photograph Jupiter's ring and the lightning discharges in the planet's atmosphere.

The camera's optical system is based upon the Voyager's 1500mm lens. It is a modified Cassegrain design with an F/8.5 aperture. Scientists estimate that the lens' nominal resolution of a satellite's geological features would be one kilometer, while the maximum resolution during a close flyby could approach 20 meters.[68]

In addition to employing the Voyager's lens design, the Galileo's camera also incorporates a similarly designed shutter mechanism and filter wheel assembly. The filters "were chosen to meet the various science objectives," and "the central wavelength of the filters are those best able to distinguish between the chemical composition of candidate surface materials on the Galilean satellites."[69] The filters' spectral characteristics and the CCD's complementary response would not only enable the camera to produce photographs revealing the satellites and Jupiter's respective geological and atmospheric structure but would also permit scientists to determine, in part, the physical composition of these bodies.

Finally, the shutter speed range for the camera varies between 4 1/6 milliseconds and 51.2 seconds. This wide shutter range is designed to accommodate the different light levels of the planetary bodies. After the shutter is activated, an analog signal is created. The signal then passes through a analog-to-digital converter whereby the signal is digitized and transformed into an eight bits binary code. The photographic information would then be transmitted to earth in real time or stored on an onboard tape recorder.[70] When the data reach earth, the binary code, which represents a scene the camera imaged, would be computer processed to produce a photograph.

The photographic output of the Galileo's camera could potentially reveal physical structures of the Jovian system that have never been viewed. Furthermore, due to the CCD's wide spectral response, Jupiter's atmosphere would be imaged to a depth hitherto impossible to attain. Thus, even more details of the planet's atmosphere would be revealed.[71]

Conclusion

Other than the Galileo project, the proposed missions to the planetary bodies remain proposals. If the missions are initiated, however, the data the spacecraft would transmit, including photographs, would greatly increase our knowledge of the solar system and how it was formed. It must also be noted that even though the Voyager mission to Jupiter and Saturn has been completed, nevertheless, it is also a future mission in that the spacecraft is scheduled to fly by Uranus and Neptune during the mid-to-late 1980's.

Finally, the CCD sensor that Galileo would employ has already been employed on earth in a number of instruments. This transfer of technology from an imaging system designed for use on an outer space probe to a terrestial application, however, was not unique. The slow scan vidicons first employed on the Ranger spacecraft and the digital techniques developed to process and enhance a spacecraft's photographic data, for example, were adopted by a number of institutions several years ago. The next chapter describes this transfer of space technology and its terrestial applications.

1. *Ranger Moon probe. 1964. Top — the television cameras are at A. Bottom — the camera subsystem had four partial- and two full-scan television cameras.*

2. *Lunar Orbiter Moon probe (model). 1966. Unique among NASA lunar craft, it employed a film subsystem. A pressurized metal shell (center) protected two cameras (see two shooting portholes).*

3. *Mock-up of the Surveyor (Moon soft-lander). 1966. The single television camera is located behind the post supporting the two solar panels.*

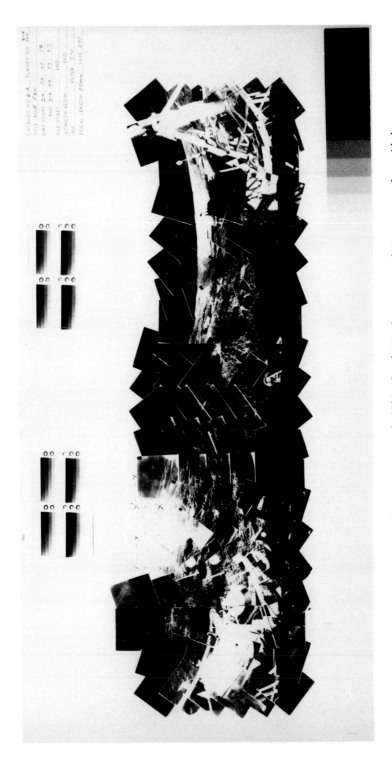

4. *Surveyor Moon probe mosaic photograph. 1966. In contrast to the Viking Lander single panorama, the Surveyor craft provided a mosaic that had to be pieced together.*

5. *The Moon photographed in high resolution by Lunar Orbiter 4. 1966.*

6. *Crater Alphonus on the Moon. 1965. Photograph by Ranger 9 from 426 kilometers out. White circle indicates where the spacecraft subsequently crashed. Black markings are the vidicon's* reseau *pattern.*

7. *Mariner 4, NASA's first Mars probe, launched November 28, 1964. Top — the single television camera is at the very bottom of the center octagonal structure. Bottom — the size of the all-digital camera (see ruler), which produced the first detailed view of Mars.*

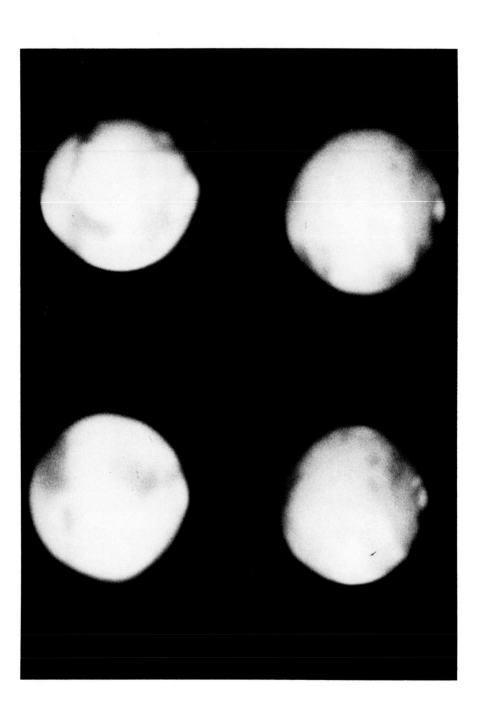

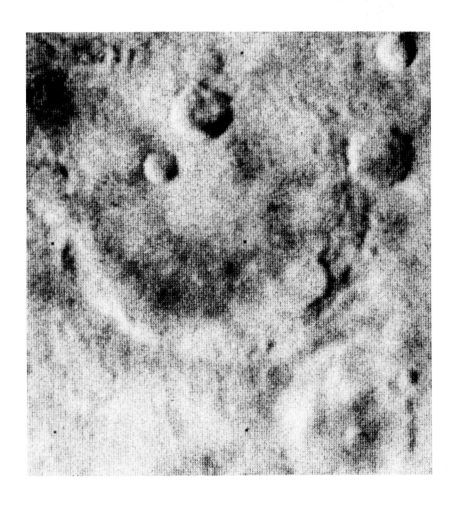

Photographs of Mars. Opposite: **8.** *By Earth-based 61-inch telescope. 1967. Reveals only gross features. Above:* **9.** *Mariner 4, 1964, the 11th of 22 photographs taken by this spacecraft. The craters led to the belief that Mars might have resembled the Moon and that craters were the planet's most distinctive feature. During the Mariner 9 flight, in 1971, an assortment of other features were discovered.*

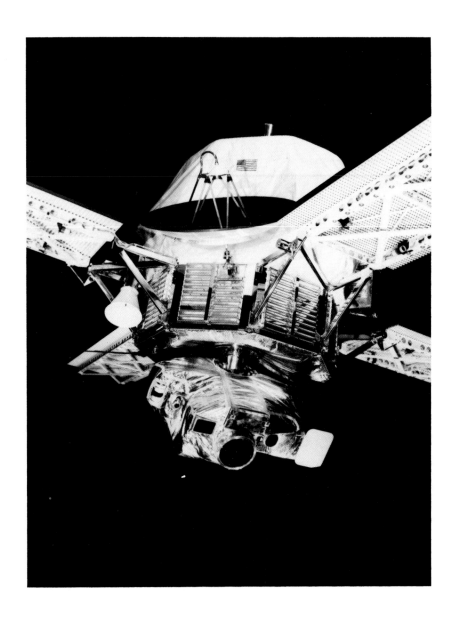

10. *Mariner 9 spacecraft. 1971. A 40-pound octagonal magnesium framework with eight electronic compartments. The television assembly is located at the very bottom.*

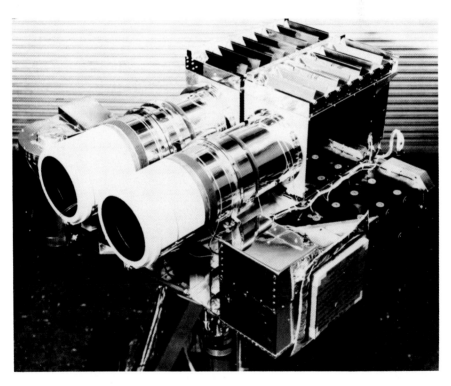

11. *Viking Orbiter Mars probe. 1975. The last spacecraft to orbit Mars. Top—a Viking Lander was housed in a protective bioshield (large assembly at bottom). The twin 475mm telephoto cameras are the light-colored assembly at left center. Bottom—a close-up view of the two telephoto television cameras. In addition to the cameras' normal thermal protection, a series of louvers (at rear top of assembly) dissipate excess heat.*

12. *Mars photographed by Viking Orbiter 1. 1975.*

13. *Mars photographed by Viking Orbiter 1. 1975. A mosaic.*

14. *Viking Lander Mars probe. 1975. Top—artist's rendering of Lander on Mars sur-face. Bottom— photograph of Mars by Viking Lander 1. The sampler scoop is at center (and see drawing, for scale). The Lander's cameras were used to monitor the function of various instruments as well as to produce photographs of the terrain.*

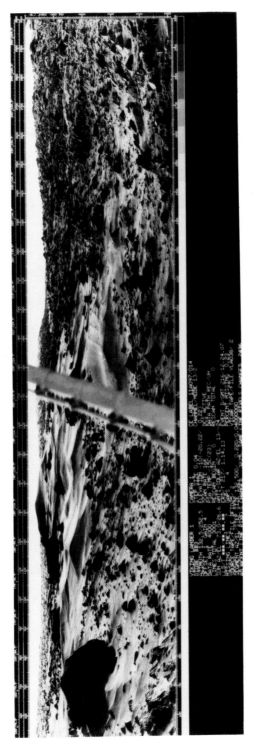

15. *Viking Lander 1 photograph of the Mars landing site in a 100° panorama revealing a variety of Martian formations including the 1 × 3 meter boulder at left. 1975.*

16. *Viking Lander 1: two photographs of the Mars landing site provide a stereoscopic view — which can be viewed with a standard stereo viewer. 1975.*

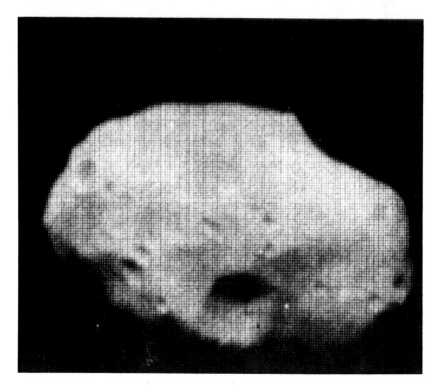

17. *Phobos photographed by Mariner 9. 1972. The two photographs of Mars' inner moon were taken during the spacecraft's 31st (top) and 34th orbits. The dark spot (at right in top image, bottom center in bottom image) is a crater about 6.8 kilometers (4.2 miles) across.*

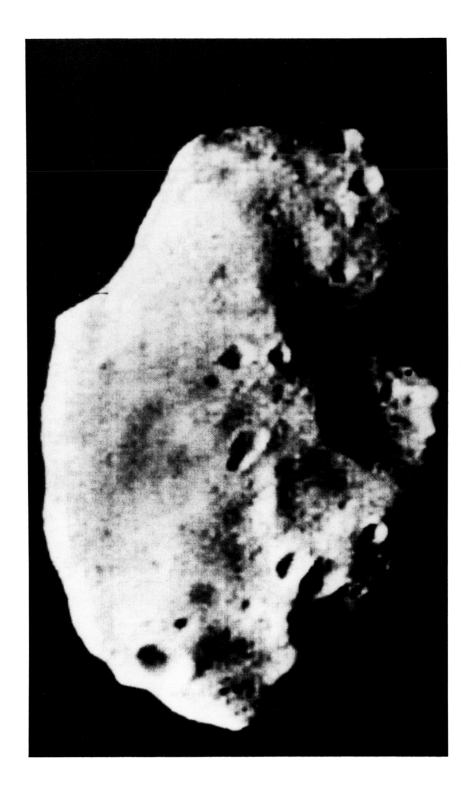

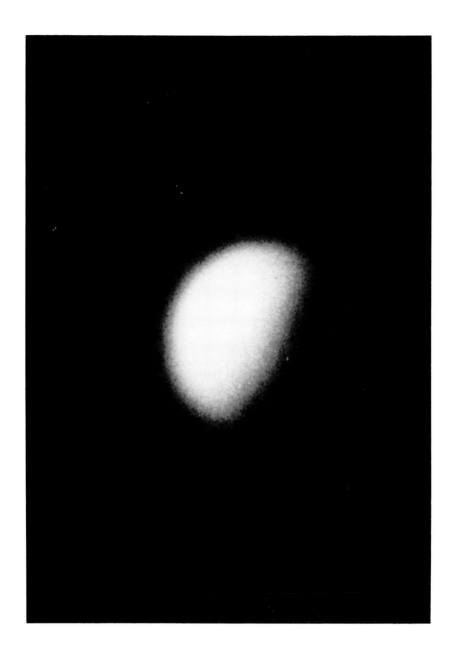

Opposite: **18.** *Phobos photographed by Mariner 9. 1972. Taken from 5440 kilometers away, this photograph has been computer enhanced (compare with unenhanced photograph on previous page). Computer enhancement reveals a wealth of geological features that were not resolved in the other image.*

Above: **19.** *Mercury photographed by a 61-inch Earth telescope (Catalina Observatory). 1970. Almost no surface features can be discerned. See next page.*

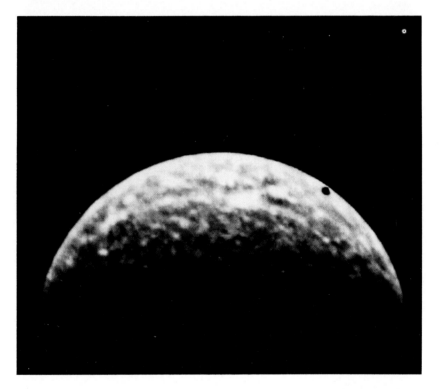

20. *Mercury photographed by Mariner 10. 1974. A real-time photograph from a distance of 2,750,000 kilometers (top picture). This photograph was then enlarged and computer enhanced to reveal surface characteristics (bottom picture). The dark spot along the upper right edge is one of the vidicon's calibration marks.*

21. *Mercury photographed by Mariner 10. 1974. A mosaic composed of 18 photographs, taken from a distance of 210,000 kilometers and computer enhanced.*

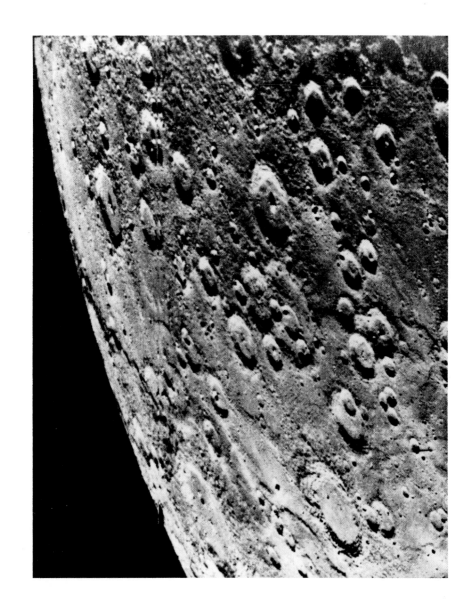

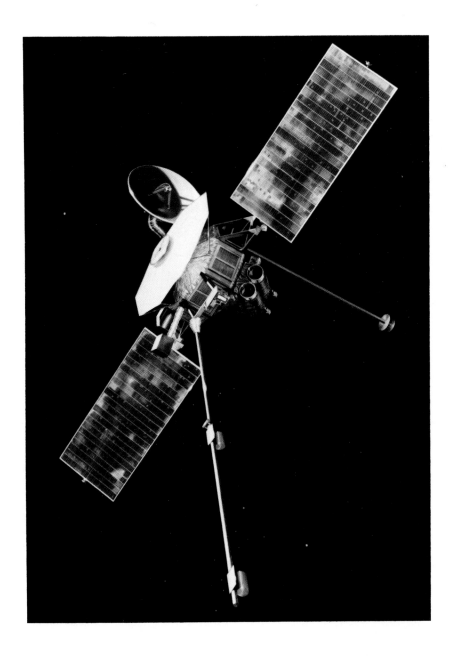

Opposite: **22.** *Mercury photographed by Mariner 10. 1974. In very strong contrast with the Earth-based view of Mercury (plate 19), Mariner 10 produced highly resolved images of the planet. This photograph was taken from a distance of 77,800 kilometers.*

Above: **23.** *Mariner 10 Venus/Mercury probe. 1973. This spacecraft photographed both Venus and Mercury with its twin 1500 telephoto cameras (see two large lenses at the right of the main assembly). The television subsystem was unique in that wide angle cameras (see two very small lenses mounted on the two large ones) were used in an auxiliary role.*

Opposite: **24.** *Top—Venus photographed by Pioneer Venus probe. 1978. The atmospheric structure was partly revealed in this full-disc picture. Bottom—Pioneer Venus Orbiter transmitted photographs of the planet's atmosphere through the use of a photopolarimeter. Unlike Pioneers 10 and 11, the Venus Pioneer was equipped with ultraviolet photodiodes to better record physical characteristics of the Venusian atmosphere.*

Above: **25.** *Jupiter photographed by Pioneer 10. 1974. Taken from a distance of 2,965,000 kilometers, this photograph shows the planet's cloud belts and the Great Red Spot (just below center).*

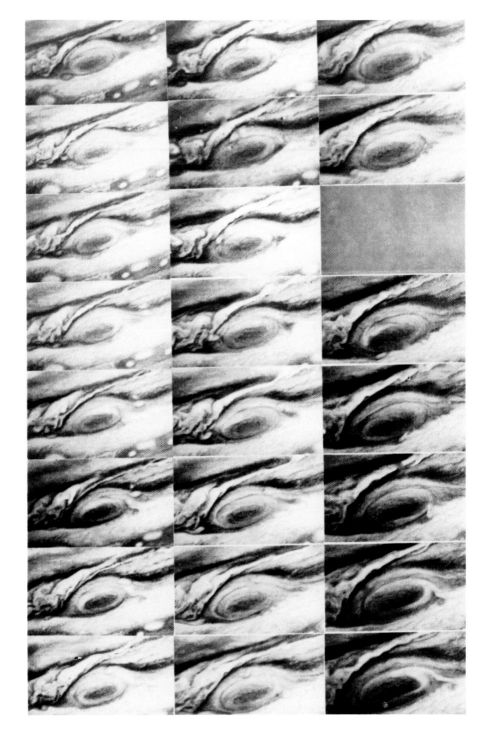

Jupiter photographed by Voyager 1. 1979. Opposite: **26.** *This sequence of photographs was produced by the spacecraft's television subsystem over an extended period of time. The time-lapse sequence reveals the flow of Jupiter's atmosphere. Above:* **27.** *This photograph taken from 32,700,000 kilometers away, has a higher resolution than that of the Pioneer image (plate 25), because of Voyager's television subsystem, its three-axis stabilization design, and its powerful transmission subsystem.*

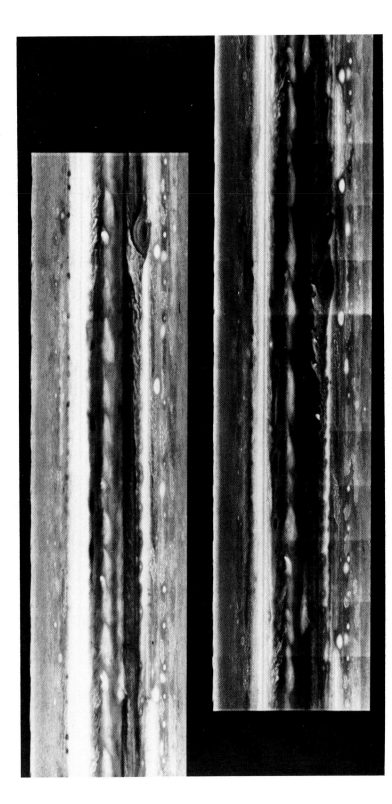

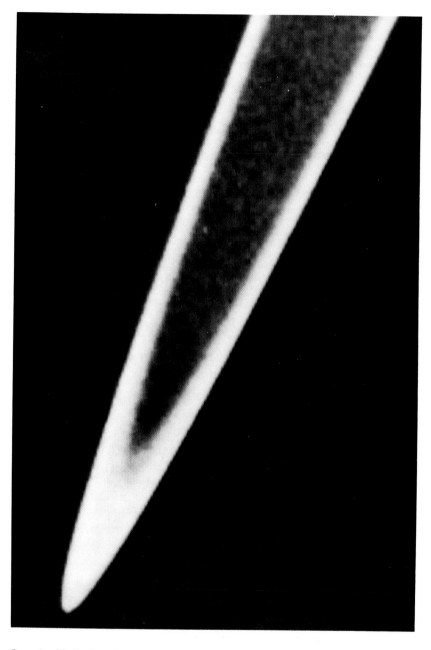

Opposite: **28.** *Jupiter photographed by Voyagers 1 and 2. 1979. The Voyager 1 (top — i.e., left) and 2 (bottom) images are cylindrical projections. The images are also aligned to match Jupiter's "longitude scale." Taken at different times, the two images afford a comparison of atmospheric conditions. Note, for example, the relative "westward" movement of the Great Red Spot.*

 Above: **29.** *Jupiter's ring photographed by Voyager 2. 1979. This image highlights a section of ring that, prior to the Voyager flights, was an undetected feature of the planet.*

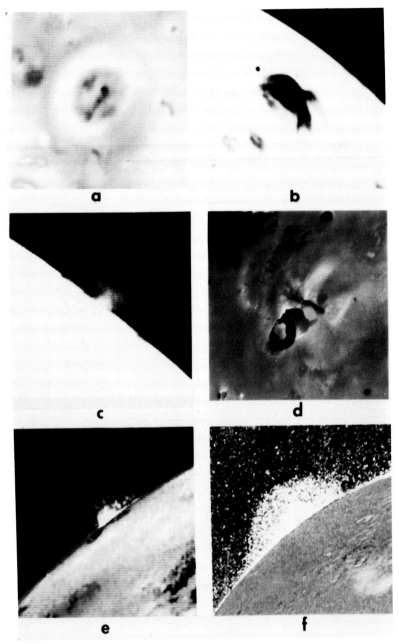

30. *Io photographed by Voyager 1. 1979. Photographs produced by the Voyager space-craft revealed another new phenomenon: a series of active volcanoes on Io. Prior to these photographs, the only active volcanoes known were on Earth. Images a, b and c are of the vent area (a) and eruptions over the disk (b) and bright limb (c) of a plume. Images d, e and f show the vent area (d) and two processed versions of the volcanic plume: e in visible light and f in ultraviolet. Image f reveals a second component of the plume visible only in the ultraviolet region.*

31. *Saturn photographed by Voyager 2. 1981. Taken from 21,000,000 kilometers out, this photograph reveals atmospheric characteristics including the bright and dark bands. Three of Saturn's moons are visible (white specks) as well as the shadow of Tethys (dark dot beneath ring).*

32. *Saturn's rings photographed by Voyager 2. 1981. This high resolution photograph reveals the hundreds of "ringlets" that compose the ring. The Voyagers' cameras revealed the complexity of the ring, which was formerly thought to be composed of only several major ring divisions.*

CHAPTER 10

Terrestrial Applications
of Spacecraft Cameras

Introduction

The electro-optical subsystems and the image processing techniques developed for outer space probes were not limited to the sole use of the National Aeronautics and Space Administration. There was a transfer of technology from the space program to the business and private sectors, which employed these instruments and techniques in a variety of ways. This chapter describes the use of spacecraft technology on earth. The chapter is organized into three major areas where the transfer of technology has taken place: the communication industry, medical and health services, and the discipline of astronomy with both earth-based and space telescopes.

Communication Industry

The communication field in both the broadcast and nonbroadcast sectors adopted the equipment and techniques used by NASA in its unmanned spacecraft missions. This included the industry's use of slow scan transmission systems, the computer manipulation of pictorial data, and the employment of solid-state sensors in a variety of electro-optical devices.

The slow scan vidicon was not originally created by NASA. The Administration did, however, pioneer the development of slow scan equipment and its use as a communication system.[1] This refinement of both the equipment and the techniques for the transmission of pictorial information over the years helped make the slow scan system a practical terrestial communication conduit.

In its most common terrestrial form, the slow scan system does not employ a slow scan vidicon tube as did the outer space probes. Rather, standard video (television) cameras that are commercially available are employed. This slow scan system operates in the following manner. The camera produces its pictorial data, the video signal, during its 1/30th of a second scanning time. The camera's output is then channelled into a device that compresses the video signal's bandwidth prior to its transmission.[2] This device is analogous to a spacecraft's slow scan vidicon tube since one of the device's functions is to reduce the transmission rate of the pictorial data so they can be accommodated on a compressed transmission bandwidth.

The versatility and commercial value of the terrestrial slow scan system lies in its compatability with a wide range of commercially available cameras and, more importantly, its ability to relay visual images over standard telephone lines. Instead of broadcasting a picture over the air or relaying it by cable, the slow scan systems compress the video bandwidth to a narrower range. The compressed data can then be relayed over a traditional conduit, namely a telephone line.[3]

The actual field operation of the slow scan system can be illustrated by the following example. A company with a branch office located in a different state must exchange information, including visual illustrations and photographs, on a daily basis. To initiate communications, a phone call is placed to the branch office to establish a telephone link between both locations. A line drawing, for example, is then imaged or scanned by the television camera at the headquarters and the camera's video signal is channelled to a video compressor. This device converts the camera's normal scan and frame rate to a slow scan rate by processing only one frame instead of all of the frames produced during the camera's 1/30th of a second scanning time. Furthermore, instead of processing all of the picture elements that compose this one frame, only selected picture elements through a sampling process are eventually relayed. The sampling stage, therefore, is employed to help compress the video bandwidth.

The compressed signal is then relayed over the telephone wire to the branch office. The information is received by a video expander that stores the information as it is received. The video expander then reconverts the data into the original picture, which is then displayed and viewed on a television set.[4] The branch office must also of course be equipped with a television camera and the necessary slow-scan transmission equipment if pictorial information is to be relayed from this site to the headquarters.

In order for the data to be accommodated on a telephone line, they are also sent at a reduced rate, which, in addition to the sampling technique, helps to compress the bandwidth. Accordingly, the relay time for one picture (frame) for one company's slow-scan system varies between 8 and 256 seconds for images with 128×128 and $512 \times 1,024$ picture elements per frame respectively.[5] The factor that influences the time frame is the information content of each picture. Hence, since the $512 \times 1,024$ frame is composed of a greater number of picture elements (and thus is more highly resolved), it requires a longer time period to relay a picture than at the 128 × 128 frame transmission.[6] In essence, the more information a picture contains, which is dictated by the number of picture elements, the longer it takes to relay it.

The slow scan process, therefore, relays visual information over standard telephone lines or in some cases via a radio transmission. The system's disadvantage is its inability to relay video and audio information simultaneously on the same telephone channel. In order to continue a two-way conversation while a picture is transmitted via a telephone line, another audio channel must be employed.[7] Furthermore, slow scan transmissions are limited to stationary (and not moving) pictures.

Even with these disadvantages, the slow scan system has been adopted by a number of institutions. United Press International, for example, employed a slow scan system for the transmission of its news program. The program was a sequence of still photographs and the corresponding audio narration for each picture. A video tape of still photographs was initially produced on standard television equipment. The tape's video signal was then channelled to a video compressor that compressed the bandwidth and the compressed video was linked with the audio commentary for the photographic sequence.[8]

At this stage, both signals were transmitted to a satellite and were subsequently rebroadcast. The signals were received by earth stations equipped with a converter that separated the video and audio signals and converted the compressed video into its original bandwidth — the equivalent of the photographs that U.P.I. transmitted. The picture and audio components were then recorded on standard video tape and broadcast, or relayed on cable by the earth station.[9] Thus, because of the slow scan system, a complete audio and visual news program was transmitted via satellite while employing only a fraction of the bandwidth that a standard television or video signal would have required.

Another application of the slow scan system as a communication conduit is its transmission of visual materials in support of the audio sequences of instructional programs. The advantage of the system is that the pictorial information can be relayed over substantial distances to many locations via the telephone lines.[10] This form of communication is more cost efficient than both cable and over-the-air broadcasts.

The slow scan system has also been operated in conjunction with digital equipment. Just as a spacecraft converted its photographic information into a digital code, so too have terrestrial systems employed digital techniques. Furthermore, the signals from the terrestrial slow scan systems which used digital equipment, such as U.P.I.'s news program, enjoyed the same benefits as did the outer space probes' digital transmissions. The data were accurate, less distorted by interfering noise, and generally produced technically superior signals and thus technically superior pictures.[11]

The field of digital communication is yet another area NASA helped pioneer and develop. In one instance, digital techniques originally employed to process and enhance the spacecrafts' photographs may eventually be used by the film industry.[12] A device called a composite printer, currently under development, would "take two pieces of photographic film, read them digitally, store them in computer memory as very high resolution color images, and then combine them into one image."[13] Digital techniques would therefore permit filmmakers to manipulate images, combine them, and alter specific characteristics of a film, such as its tonal gradations and color. These operations would be analogous to NASA's image processing and enhancing techniques when a photograph's contrast or photometric qualities, for example, are manipulated.[14]

This innovation in digital communication has also influenced the design of commercial television equipment. As was described in Chapter 4, the first all digital television camera was incorporated on the Mariner 4 spacecraft. At the present time, digital television equipment for both broadcast and nonbroadcast applications are being developed and used.[15] This includes devices such as digital video–tape recorders and special effect consoles.

A digital special effect console can manipulate the video data to freeze a frame, for example, whereby a stationary frame or image remains on the television screen for an extended period of time.[16] In another example, a console can also create a zoom effect where a small image grows larger or "zooms in" to fill the entire television screen.[17]

The transfer of technology from outer space probes to terrestrial applications also influenced the development of imaging sensors for the communication field, including those used in picturephone systems. As described above, slow scan systems were employed for teleconferences. Slow scan technology was also used in an early version of the picturephone, a telephone that relayed both audio and video signals on a telephone line.[18]

The first commercially available picturephone units, however, did not employ a slow scan system and used a wide bandwidth for their transmission. Yet, the wide bandwidth proved to be expensive both in terms of bandwidth economy and the financial costs to use and operate the system. Consequently, engineers attempted to reduce the bandwidth and thus the operational costs by lowering the system's data requirements. A charge-coupled-device (CCD) sensor, whose development was pioneered by NASA for its inner and outer space probes, was therefore incorporated in the picturephone.[19]

In this new configuration, the picturephone's camera visually imaged a person, for example, and channelled the video data to the CCD element at the camera's standard 1/30th of a second scanning rate. The camera's first frame was initially stored on the CCD. As each new frame was generated during the scanning time, it was likewise fed to the CCD and replaced the previously stored frame. Both the new and original frames were also channelled to a comparator device. The comparator compared and detected any discrepancies between the new and original frames. If a portion of the two sequential frames were different, the comparator would detect this change. Consequently, when the pictorial information was finally relayed by the picturephone, only the segment of the two frames that had changed was transmitted at this time.[20]

This process is analogous to the following situation. If an individual using the picturephone raises his or her hand while talking, only the picture information or bits that change over time would be transmitted, that is, bits that constitute the moving hand. Thus, the picturephone with the CCD element can employ a narrow bandwidth because an entire frame does not have to be transmitted every 1/30th of a second. In addition, since less information is relayed, a smaller bandwidth can accommodate the reduced data load. The reduced bandwidth, in turn, would lower the picturephone's operational cost.[21]

The CCD's special properties which would improve the picturephone are also being used in commercial cameras. The Sony Corporation, for example, has designed a small and lightweight camera with a CCD sensor to photograph and record still pictures on a magnetic disk.[22] Also RCA initially employed a CCD sensor in an experimental camera the size of a pack of cigarettes. The camera produced pictures with 525 lines to equal the output of standard sized video cameras.[23]

The CCD and other solid state sensors incorporated in Sony's Mavica, RCA's experimental, and the portable video cameras currently being introduced in the commercial market are also superior to other electronic sensors in several ways. Just as the Galileo spacecraft's CCD sensor, for example, is lighter, more sensitive and rugged, and smaller than a conventional slow scan vidicon tube, so too are the solid state sensors employed in terrestrial cameras when compared with their counterparts.[24]

The NASA development of solid state sensor elements, digital equipment and picture processing techniques, and slow scan systems for its spacecraft helped spur the design and use of these devices and techniques on earth, but not solely by the communication industry: they were also employed by both the medical and astronomical fields.

Medicine and Astronomy

One innovation introduced into the medical field was the use of slow scan systems for the relay of medical information. Rural areas, such as northwestern Ontario, lacked advanced medical facilities. Consequently, to enhance the region's medical care, a slow scan system was employed. Photographs of patients, X-rays, and other visual data were relayed from the rural settings to advanced medical facilities by the slow scan system. This operation permitted medical personnel in a rural area to consult with others at a distant hospital, for example, where the pictures or X-rays could be properly diagnosed.[25]

The same system was also used, in one instance, to enhance the education and skills of the rural personnel. An illustrated dialogue about plastic surgery care techniques, for example, was relayed to rural regions. Consequently, the medical staff was able to improve its own skills in this area through the use of the slow scan system.[26] Finally, the cost effectiveness of relaying visual data over standard telephone lines made the slow scan system a viable communication conduit for the rural medical facilities.

In addition to these benefits due to the slow scan's compression of visual data, a complete medical consultation could be stored on a single audio cassette. The stored information can then be reconverted into the original photographs by channelling the cassette's output to the slow scan equipment.[27] The use of audio cassettes to record and store data is a cost effective method of preserving medical records of this type, compared with storing the data on standard video tape cassettes. The audio tapes also require less storage space than the video tapes.

The digital techniques developed to correct and enhance pictorial information from outer space probes were also applied to the medical field. In one instance, X-rays were converted to digital information and computer enhanced. The enhanced X-rays then permitted doctors and technicians to detect previously undetected lesions.[28] Digital techniques were also employed to produce technically superior medical images.

The techniques used in the medical field were similarly employed by astronomical observatories on earth. Large telescopes, for example, were subject to image degradation due to admospheric turbulence. Digital processing techniques were therefore employed to enhance photographs taken through the telescopes. The processing helped restore some of the resolution lost because of interference.[29]

Color photographs taken through the telescopes were also enhanced. Images of celestial objects were computer processed in some instances to "exaggerate and display small spectral differences in the same way contrast enhancement is used to exaggerate and display small intensity differences."[30] Even though the processed photographs did not reveal the object's true spectral characteristics, the "exaggerated differences" that might have remained undetected in the true color photographs were revealed.[31] In another example, telescopic photographs were processed to highlight the gross structural properties of celestial objects, such as galaxies, that might have remained hidden on unprocessed images.[32]

Charge-coupled-devices were also employed in astronomical observations. Because of the CCD's increased sensitivity compared to other sensors, details of the planetary bodies hitherto undetected were revealed. This included atmospheric details, for example, of the planet Uranus.[33] Finally, CCDs were also designed to operate in an integration mode. In this process, an exposure lasted for an extended period of time to record a faint celestial object.[34]

The CCD's ability to operate in an integration mode in addition to its other characteristics and broad spectral response, made it an ideal imaging sensor for a proposed orbiting astronomical observatory called the space telescope. The observatory is a satellite that would be locked in an earth orbit to explore the solar system and distant celestial objects with its telescope.[35]

The space telescope's orbit would place it above the earth's atmosphere, to produce an unobstructed view of the heavens. When the absence of atmospheric interference is combined with the CCD sensors in the satellite's wide field planetary camera, the space telescope's potential resolution in both visible and nonvisible spectral regions would exceed any earth based telescope's. The satellite's observations would include the planetary bodies and their atmospheres.[36] Other projected uses are extended observations of Jupiter's atmosphere and celestial objects beyond the solar system's boundaries.[37] This encompasses galaxies, star clusters, nebulae, and other phenomena. Some scientists also plan to use the space telescope to search for other planetary systems that may revolve around distant stars.[38]

CHAPTER 11

Implications and Conclusion

Terrestrial applications of various spacecrafts' visual imaging systems was only one facet of the use of these devices and the photographs they transmitted. The spacecraft themselves were developed over a period of years and were influenced by a peculiar set of design criteria. Thus, the Pioneer 10 and 11 probes, for example, were spin-stabilized spacecraft, in part because of fiscal constraints. As described, the spacecrafts' spin-stabilization configuration in turn dictated the use of a photopolarimeter as the Pioneers' imaging device.

The photographic data base produced by the Pioneer and other spacecraft was subsequently analyzed by scientists to examine a planetary body's surface characteristics and in some instances, its atmosphere. The data base was also used in conjunction with the information from other instruments in an attempt to determine the physical processes that might have molded a body's current physical state as was revealed in the photographs. Furthermore, after computer processing and enhancement, the pictures enabled scientists to compare the earth's physical activities, such as its atmospheric dynamics, with similar activities on other worlds.

In addition to these past missions, a series of future flights with a new generation of visual imaging subsystems incorporating solid-state sensors, such as CCDs, are being planned. These missions could produce additional information about explored worlds and also enable us to view the surface of a comet or an asteroid for the first time in recorded history. The development of the imaging systems on these probes may even lead to a new series of terrestrial applications.

Photographs from the spacecraft have also enabled us to view an active volcano on another world, the hundreds of ringlets that encircle Saturn, and the plains, craters, and scarps of Mercury. Furthermore, Voyager 2 may permit us to stretch this vision to Uranus and Neptune within a few years, while the space telescope promises to extend our vision to hitherto unimaginable depths of outer space.

In conclusion, the human race has always explored its environment. This is reflected in the earliest documents of Western literature — classical heroes such as Odysseus searched the world in the quest of knowledge. At the present time, we possess the technology to explore new worlds and fulfill a dream that stretches back to the dawn of history when humans first looked up at the heavens. This aeons-old dream was carried through the age of Galileo, who first turned his telescope to the sky, to the present time, when spacecraft are exploring the planetary bodies up close. The next step is manned flights to these worlds. The Apollo missions, plotted in part through the Ranger, Surveyor, and Lunar Orbiter photographs, may have only been the beginning.

Chapter Notes

Chapter 2 Notes

1. National Aeronautics and Space Administration, *NASA Day* (Washington, DC: U.S. Gov. Printing Office, 1962), p. 2.

2. United Nations, Department of Economic and Social Affairs, *The Application of Space Technology to Development* (E.72.II.A.12), 1973, p. 1.

3. *Ibid.*, p. 26.

4. *Ibid.*

5. NASA, *NASA Day*, p. 27.

6. Arthur C. Clarke, *The Promise of Space* (New York: Pyramid Books, 1968), p. 105.

7. United Nations, *The Application of Space Technology to Development,* p. 14.

8. Clarke, *The Promise of Space*, p. 123.

9. *Ibid.*, p. 163.

10 R. Cargill Hall, *Lunar Impact: A History of Project Ranger* (Washington, DC: U.S. Gov. Printing Office, 1977), p. 264.

11. Barton Kreuzer, "Electronic and Motion-Picture Systems in the Space Age," *Journal of the Society of Motion Picture and Television Engineers*, 70 (December 1961): 962.

12. *Ibid.*, p. 963.

13. Max H. Mesner, "Television's Toughest Challenge," *Electronics* (17 May 1965): 86.

14. Kreuzer, "Electronic and Motion-Picture Systems in the Space Age," *Journal of SMPTE,* p. 963.

15. *Ibid.*

16. Hall, *Lunar Impact*, p. 78.

17. *Ibid.*, p. 222.

18. *Ibid.*, p. 219.

19. *Ibid.*, p. 261.

20. *Ibid.*, p. 219.

21. National Aeronautics and Space Administration, *Spacecraft Sterilization Technology* (Washington, DC: U.S. Gov. Printing Office, 1966), p. 402.

22. *Ibid.*, p. 560.

23. *Ibid.*, p. 3.

24. William R. Corliss, *The Viking Mission to Mars* (Washington, DC: NASA, p. 33.

25. Advances in Electronic and Electron Physics, *Proceedings of the Third Symposium* (Imperial College, London: Academic Press): "The Mariner 4 Spacecraft Television System," by J. Denton Allen, p. 853.

26. The Society of Photo-Optical Instrumentation Engineers, *Effective Systems Integration and Optical Design,* Vol. 54 (Palos Verdes Estates, CA: SPIE, 1975): "Reconciling the Requirements of the Science Team and the Spacecraft Engineering Team with a Realizable Optical System," by Dr. Leonard Larks, p. 53.

Chapter 3 Notes

1. R. L. Heacock, et al., *Ranger 7, Part 2. Experimenters' Analyses and Interpretations* (Pasadena, CA: Jet Propulsion Laboratory, 1965), p. 3.

2. *Ibid.*

3. American Astronautical Society, *Proceedings of the Tenth Annual Meeting of the American Astronautical Society, 4-7 May, 1964, Lunar Flight Programs*, Vol. 18 (North Hollywood, CA: Western Periodicals Co., 1964): "Ranger TV Subsystem," by Bernard P. Miller, p. 115.

4. R. E. Hoffman, "Vidicon for Space Applications," *Journal of the Society of Motion Picture and Television Engineers*, 76 (August 1967):780.

5. Jet Propulsion Laboratory, *Ranger 7, Part 1. Mission Description and Performance*, Technical Report No. 32-700 (Pasadena, CA: Jet Propulsion Laboratory, 1964), p. 37.

6. Gerald Millerson, *The Technique of Television Production* (New York: Hastings House, 1975), p. 19.

7. Jet Propulsion Laboratory, *Ranger 7, Part 1*, p. 37.

8. Leonard R. Malling, "Space Astronomy and the Slow Scan Vidicon," *Journal of the Society of Motion Picture and Television Engineers*, 72 (November 1963):872.

9. Donald H. Kinct and Joseph R. Staniszewski, *The Design of the Ranger Television System to Obtain High Resolution Photographs of the Lunar Surface*, Technical Report No. 32-717 (Pasadena, CA: Jet Propulsion Laboratory, 1965), p. 9.

10. M. H. Mesner, "Television's Toughest Challenge," *Electronics* (17 May 1965):83.

11. E. P. Martz, Jr., "Optical Problems of Television Recording of the Moon and Planets from Approaching Spacecraft," *Applied Optics*, 2 (January 1963):48.

12. Kinct and Staniszewski, *The Design of the Ranger Television System*, p. 10.

13. American Astronautical Society, *Lunar Flight Programs*: Miller, p. 120.

14. Jet Propulsion Laboratory, *Ranger 7, Part 1*, p. 38.

15. American Astronautical Society, *Lunar Flight Programs:* Miller, "Ranger TV Subsystem," p. 125.

16. Jet Propulsion Laboratory, *Ranger 7. Part 1*, p. 37.

17. *Ibid.*

18. Kinct and Staniszewski, *The Design of the Ranger Television System*, p. 11.

19. *Ibid.*

20. *Ibid.*

21. American Astronautical Society, *Lunar Flight Programs:* Miller, "Ranger TV Subsystem," p. 124.

22. National Aeronautics and Space Administration, *Mars 1964: Final Project Report* (Washington, DC: U.S. Gov. Printing Office, 1967), p. 65.

23. American Astronautical Society, *Lunar Flight Programs*: Miller, "Ranger TV Subsystem," p. 121.

24. *Ibid.*, p. 125.

25. R. Cargill Hall, *Lunar Impact: A History of Project Ranger* (Washington, DC: U.S. Gov. Printing Office, 1977), p. 195.

26. Kinct and Staniszewski, *The Design of the Ranger Television System*, p. 5.

27. Jet Propulsion Laboratory, *Ranger 7. Part 1*, p. 35.

28. *Ibid.*, p. 40.

29. Jet Propulsion Laboratory, *The Deep Space Network Progress Report 42−55* (Pasadena, CA: Jet Propulsion Laboratory, 1980): "Network Functions and Facilities," by N. A. Renzetti, p. 1.

30. Jet Propulsion Laboratory, *Ranger 7. Part 1*, p. 43.

31. *Ibid.*, p. 28.

32. Hall, *Lunar Impact*, p. 326.

33. National Aeronautics and Space Administration, *Surveyor: Program Results* (Washington, DC: U.S. Gov. Printing Office, 1969): "Television Observations from Surveyor," by E. M. Shoemaker, et al., p. 19.

34. Leonard D. Jaffe, "The Surveyor Lunar Landings," *Science*, 164 (16 May 1969): 780.

35. *Ibid.*

36. NASA, *Surveyor:* E. M. Shoemaker, "Television Observations from Surveyor," p. 22.

37. Donald T. Heckel and Ronald L. Quandt, "Environmental and Thermal Effects on Surveyor Vidicon Performance," *Journal of the Society of Motion Picture and Television Engineers,* 77 (April 1968):324.

38. *Ibid.*, p. 328.

39. *Ibid.*, p. 329.

40. Harold W. Krueger and James W. Williams, "Surveyor Television Power Conditioning," *Journal of the Society of Motion Picture and Television Engineers,* 77 (April 1968): 337.

41. NASA, *Surveyor:* E. M. Shoemaker, "Television Observations from Surveyor," p. 132.

42. *Ibid.*

43. NASA, *Surveyor*, p. iii.

44. *Ibid.*

45. Donald T. Heckel, "Unit and System Design of a Lunar Operating Camera," *Journal of the Society of Motion Picture and Television Engineers,* 76 (August 1967): 774.

46. National Aeronautics and Space Administration, *Optical Telescope Technology* (Washington, DC: U.S. Gov. Printing Office, 1970): "Surveyor Spacecraft Real-Time Payload Operations" by Jack N. Lindsley, p. 622.

47. NASA, *Surveyor:* L. D. Jaffe and R. H. Steinbacher, "Introduction," p. 3.

48. NASA, *Optical Telescope Technology:* Lindsley, "Surveyor Spacecraft Real-Time Payload Operations," p. 622.

49. E. M. Shoemaker, et al., "Television Observations from Surveyor 3," *Journal of Geophysical Research*, 73 (15 June 1968):3990.

50. NASA, *Surveyor:* Shoemaker, "Television Observations from Surveyor," p. 22.

51. Gerald Millerson, *The Technique of Television Production* (New York: Hastings House, 1975), p. 42.

52. *Ibid.*, p. 21.

53. NASA, *Surveyor:* Shoemaker, "Television Observations from Surveyor," p. 22.

54. Shoemaker, et al., "Television Observations from Surveyor 3," *Journal of Geophysical Research*, p. 3991.

55. *Ibid.*

56. Lewis H. Allen and P. M. Salomon, "Operation of the Surveyor Television System in the Photo-Integration Mode," *Journal of the Society of Motion Picture and Television Engineers*, 79 (July 1970):615.

57. L. E. Blanchard, "The Design of the Postlanding Television System Photometric Charts for the Surveyor Spacecraft," *Journal of the Society of Motion Picture and Television Engineers*, 79 (March 1970):228.

58. Heckel, "Unit and System Design of a Lunar Operating TV Camera," *Journal of SMPTE, p. 775.*

59. Millerson, *The Technique of Television Production*, p. 413.

60. Blanchard, "The Design of Postlanding Television System Photometric Charts for the Surveyor Spacecraft," *Journal of SMPTE*, p. 228.

61. NASA, *Surveyor:* Shoemaker, "Television Observations from Surveyor," p. 20.

62. *Ibid.*

63. Carvyn Ellman, "The Surveyor Variable and Fixed Focal-Length Lenses." *Journal of the Society of Motion Picture and Television Engineers*, 77 (April 1968):334.

64. Shoemaker, et al., "Television Observations from Surveyor 3," *Journal of Geophysical Research*, p. 3990.

65. American Astronautical Society, *Proceedings of the Tenth Annual Meeting of the American Astronautical Society, 4–7 May, 1964, Lunar Flight Programs,* Vol. 18

(North Hollywood, CA: Western Periodicals Co., 1964): "Surveyor Lander Mission and Capabilities," by Milton Beilock, p. 166.

66. NASA, *Optical Telescope Technology:* Lindsley, "Surveyor Spacecraft Real-Time Payload Operations," p. 615.

67. Heckel, "Unit and System Design of a Lunar Operating TV Camera," *Journal of SMPTE*, p. 775.

68. NASA, *Optical Telescope Technology:* Lindsley, "Surveyor Spacecraft Real-Time Payload Operations," p. 624.

69. Heckel, "Unit and System Design of a Lunar Operating TV Camera," *Journal of SMPTE*, p. 775.

70. *Ibid.*

71. NASA, *Optical Telescope Technology:* Lindsley, "Surveyor Spacecraft Real-Time Payload Operations," p. 622.

72. *Ibid.*, p. 624.

73. NASA, *Surveyor,* Jaffe and Steinbacher, "Introduction," p. 4.

74. *Ibid.*

75. Jaffe, "The Surveyor Lunar Landings," *Science*, p. 774.

76. Edgar M. Cortright, ed., *Exploring Space with a Camera* (Washington, DC: U.S. Gov. Printing Office, 1968), p. 42.

77. A. Jensen, et al., "Lunar Orbiter Readout," *Journal of the Society of Motion Picture and Television Engineers*, 76 (August 1967):757.

78. Cortright, *Exploring Space with a Camera*, p. 42.

79. Merton E. Davies and Bruce C. Murray, *The View from Space: Photographic Exploration of the Planets* (New York: Columbia University Press, 1971), p. 135.

80. *Ibid.*, p. 36.

81. *Ibid.*

82. Leon J. Kosofsky and G. Calvin Broome, "Lunar Orbiter: A Photographic Satellite," *Journal of the Society of Motion Picture and Television Engineers*, 74 (September 1965):775.

83. *Ibid.*

84. H. K. Heen, et al., "Lunar Orbiter Camera," *Journal of the Society of Motion Picture and Television Engineers*, 76 (August 1967):744.

85. B. L. Elle, et al., "The Lunar Orbiter Photographic System," *Journal of the Society of Motion Picture and Television Engineers,* 76 (August 1967):734.

86. Davies and Murray, *The View from Space*, p. 42.

87. American Astronautical Society, *Proceedings of the Tenth Annual Meeting of the American Astronautical Society, 4-7 May, 1964: Lunar Flight Programs*, Vol. 18 (North Hollywood, CA: Western Periodicals Co., 1964): "Lunar Orbiter—Its Mission and Capabilities," by Israel Taback, p. 154.

88. Elle, "The Lunar Orbiter Photographic System," *The Journal of SMPTE*, p. 734.

89. American Astronautical Society, *Lunar Flight Programs:* Taback, "Lunar Orbiter—Its Mission and Capabilities," p. 153.

90. Heen, "Lunar Orbiter Camera," *Journal of SMPTE*, p. 744.

91. American Astronautical Society, *Lunar Flight Programs:* Taback, "Lunar Orbiter—Its Mission and Capabilities," p. 154.

92. Michael Langford, *Visual Aids and Photography in Education* (New York: Hasting House, 1973), p. 93.

93. American Astronautical Society, *Lunar Flight Programs:* Taback, "Lunar Orbiter—Its Mission and Capabilities," p. 154.

94. J. J. Meyers, D. Endter, and R. F. Limoges, "Film Processor—Dryer for Lunar Orbiter Photo System," *Journal of the Society of Motion Picture and Television Engineers,* 76 (August 1967):750.

95. American Astronautical Society, *Proceedings of an AAS Symposium held on May 25-27, 1967, Use of Space Systems for Planetary Geology and Geophysics*, Vol. 17, (Tarzana, CA: American Astronautical Association, 1967): "A Photometric Technique for Deriving Slopes from Lunar Orbiter Photography," by J. J. Lambiotte and G. R. Taylor, p. 207.

96. Davies and Murray, *The View from Space*, p. 43.

97. Kosofsky and Broome, "Lunar Orbiter: A Photographic Satellite," *Journal of SMPTE,* p. 776.

98. R. E. Kinzly, M. J. Mazurowski, and T. M. Holladay, "Image Evaluation and Its Application to Lunar Orbiter," *Applied Optics,* 7 (August 1968):1579.

99. Kosofsky and Broome, "Lunar Orbiter: A Photographic Satellite," *Journal of SMPTE,* p. 776.

100. A. Jensen, et al. "Lunar Orbiter Readout," *Journal of SMPTE,* p. 761.

101. *Ibid.*

102. American Astronautical Society, *Lunar Flight Programs:* Taback, "Lunar Orbiter — Its Mission and Capabilities," p. 154.

103. *Ibid.*, p. 147.

104. A. Jensen, et al., "Lunar Orbiter Readout," *Journal of SMPTE,* p. 761.

105. Kinzly, Mazurowski, and Holladay, "Image Evaluation and Its Application to Lunar Orbiter," *Applied Optics,* p. 1579.

106. R. A. Grammer, Jr., et al., "Ground Reconstruction of Lunar Orbiter Photography," *Journal of the Society of Motion Picture and Television Engineers,* 76 (August 1967):769.

107. American Astronautical Society, *Use of Space Systems for Planetary Geology and Geophysics*, Lambiotte and Taylor, "A Photometric Technique for Deriving Slopes from Lunar Orbiter Photography," p. 208.

108. R. A. Grammer, Jr., et al., "Ground Reconstruction of Lunar Orbiter Photography," *Journal of SMPTE,* p. 771.

109. *Ibid.*, p. 770.

110. American Astronautical Society, *Use of Space Systems for Planetary Geology and Geophysics,* Lambiotte and Taylor, "A Photometric Technique for Deriving Slopes from Lunar Orbiter Photography," p. 208.

111. Cortright, *Exploring Space with a Camera,* p. 88.

112. H. K. Heen, et al., "Lunar Orbiter Camera," *Journal of SMPTE,* p. 740.

113. Kinzly, Mazurowski, Holladay, "Image Evaluation and Its Application to Lunar Orbiter," p. 746.

114. H. K. Heen, et al., "Lunar Orbiter Camera," *Journal of SMPTE,* p. 746.

115. *Ibid.*

116. B. L. Elle, et al., "The Lunar Orbiter Photographic System," *Journal of SMPTE,* p. 739.

117. Davies and Murray, *The View from Space,* p. 143.

118. B. L. Elle, et al., "The Lunar Orbiter Photographic System," *Journal of SMPTE,* p. 736.

119. American Astronautical Society, *Proceedings of an AAS/AAAS Symposium, 29 December, 1966, Physics of the Moon* (Tarzana, CA: American Astronautical Society, 1966): "Orbiter Observations of the Lunar Surface," by L. C. Rowan, p. 3.

120. Newell J. Trask and Lawerence C. Rowan, "Lunar Orbiter Photographs: Some Fundamental Observations," *Science,* 158 (22 December 1967):1529.

121. Bruce C. Murray, "The Mariner 10 Pictures of Mercury: An Overview, *Journal of Geophysical Research,* 80 (10 June 1975): p. 2343.

122. Kosofsky and Broome, "Lunar Orbiter: A Photographic Satellite," *Journal of SMPTE,* p. 775.

123. National Aeronautics and Space Administration, *Voyage to Jupiter* (Washington, DC: U.S. Gov. Printing Office, 1980), p. 31.

124. John S. Carroll, *Photographic Lab Handbook* (Garden City, NY: American Photographic Book Publishing Co., Inc., 1977), p. 100.

125. H. K. Heen, et al., "Lunar Orbiter Camera," *Journal of SMPTE,* p. 744.

126. NASA, *Voyage to Jupiter,* p. 75.

127. D. Herman, J. Moore, and P. Tarver, "Mission Building Blocks for Outer Solar System Exploration," *Space Science Reviews,* 14 (1973):376.

128. B. L. Elle, et al., "The Lunar Orbiter Photographic System," *Journal of SMPTE,* p. 739.

129. G. Edward Danielson Jr., Kenneth P. Klassen, and James L. Anderson, "Acquisition and Description of Mariner 10 Television Science Data at Mercury," *Journal of Geophysical Research,* 80 (10 June 1975):2357.

130. Davies and Murray, *The View from Space*, p. 81.
131. Stewart A. Collins, *The Mariner 6 and 7 Pictures of Mars* (Washington, DC: U.S. Gov. Printing Office, 1971), p. 15.

Chapter 4 Notes

1. Edgar M. Cortright, ed., *Exploring Space with a Camera* (Washington, DC: U.S. Gov. Printing Office, 1968), p. 129.
2. William R. Corliss, *Space Probes and Planetary Exploration* (Princeton, NJ: D. Van Nostrand Company, Inc., 1965), p. 264.
3. Merton E. Davies and Bruce C. Murray, *The View from Space: Photographic Exploration of the Planets* (New York: Columbia University Press, 1971), p. 71.
4. E. C. Stone and A. L. Lane, "Voyager 1 Encounter with the Jovian System," *Science*, 204 (1 June 1979):945.
5. National Aeronautical and Space Administration, *Mariner-Mars 1964: Final Project Report* (Washington, DC: U.S. Gov. Printing Office, 1967), p. 48.
6. *Ibid.*, p. 140.
7. *Ibid.*, p. 83.
8. Bruce C. Murray, "Imaging of the Outer Planets and Satellites," *Space Science Reviews*, 14 (1973):475.
9. E. E. Russell, et al., *Study of Spin-Scan Imaging for Outer Planets Missions* (Santa Barbara, CA: Santa Barbara Research Center, 1974), p. 1–2.
10. James H. Wilson, *Two Over Mars* (Washington, DC: U.S. Gov. Printing Office, 1973), p. 6.
11. Samuel Glasstone, *The Book of Mars* (Washington, DC: U.S. Gov. Printing Office, 1968), p. 289.
12. R. A. Becker, *Design and Test Performance of Mariner 4 Television Optical System*, Technical Report No. 32–773 (Pasadena, CA: Jet Propulsion Laboratory, 1965), p. 2.
13. Aaron C. Waters, *Moon Craters and Oregon Volcanoes* (Eugene, Oregon: Oregon State System of Higher Education, 1967), p. i.
14. NASA, *Mariner-Mars 1964*, p. 6.
15. *Ibid.*
16. Henry Canvel, "A Slow-Scan Television Film Recorder," *Journal of the Society of Motion Picture and Television Engineers*, 74 (September 1965):770.
17. Davies and Murray, *The View from Space*, p. 78.
18. Robert Nathan, *Digital Video-Data Handling*, Technical Report No. 32-877 (Pasadena, CA: Jet Propulsion Laboratory, 1966), p. 2.
19. NASA, *Mariner-Mars 1964*, p. 262.
20. *Ibid.*
21. Richard O. Fimmel, William Swindell, and Eric Burgess, *Pioneer Odyssey* (Washington, DC: U.S. Gov. Printing Office, 1977), p. 132.
22. P. M. Salomon, "Applications of Slow-Scan Television Systems to Planetary Exploration," *Journal of the Society of Motion Picture and Television Engineers,* 79 (July 1970):612.
23. *Ibid.*
24. Advances in Electronics and Electron Physics, *Proceedings of the Third Symposium held at Imperial College, London, September 20–24, 1965 Photo-Electronic Image Devices*, Vol. 22B (London: Academic Press, 1966): The Mariner 4 Spacecraft Television System," by J. Denton Allen, p. 853.
25. Becker, *Design and Test Performance of Mariner 4 Television*, p. 6.
26. *Ibid.*
27. Advances in Electronics and Electron Physics, *Proceedings of the Third Symposium Held at Imperial College, London, September 20–24, Photo-Electronic Image Devices,* Vol. 22B (London: Academic Press, 1966): "The Slow-Scan Vidicon as an Interplanetary Imaging Device," by L. R. Malling and Denton Allen, p. 837.

28. *Ibid.*, p. 845.

29. *Ibid.*, p. 837.

30. NASA, *Mariner–Mars 1964*, p. 262.

31. *Ibid.*

32. *Ibid.*

33. Advances in Electronics and Electron Physics, *Photo-Electronic Image Devices*, Malling and Denton, "The Slow-Scan Vidicon as an Interplanetary Imaging Device," p. 841.

34. Gerald Millerson, *The Technique of Television Production* (New York: Hastings House, 1975), p. 21.

35. Salomon, "Applications of Slow-Scan Television Systems to Planetary Exploration," *Journal of SMPTE*, p. 608.

36. NASA, *Mariner–Mars 1964*, p. 65.

37. American Astronautical Society, *Proceedings of the American Astronautical Society Symposium on Unmanned Exploration of the Solar System, February 8–10, 1965, Unmanned Exploration of the Solar System*, Vol. 19 (North Hollywood, CA: Periodicals Co., 1965): "Some Possible Means of Acquiring Increased Information Return from Mars," by Philip K. Eckman, p. 177.

38. NASA, *Mariner–Mars 1964*, p. 263.

39. *Ibid.*, p. 48.

40. *Ibid.*, p. 233.

41. *Ibid.*, p. 241.

42. Davies and Murray, *The View from Space*, p. 76.

43. Becker, *Design and Test Performance of Mariner 4 Television Optical System*, p. 3.

44. *Ibid.*

45. *Ibid.*, p. 7.

46. NASA, *Mariner–Mars 1964*, p. 263.

47. Becker, *Design and Test Performance of Mariner 4 Television Optical System*, p. 8.

48. *Ibid.*

49. NASA, *Mariner–Mars 1964*, p. 151.

50. *Ibid.*, p. 71.

51. Samuel Glasstone, *The Book of Mars* (Washington, DC: U.S. Gov. Printing Office, 1968), p. 289.

52. NASA, *Mariner–Mars 1964*, p. 111.

53. *Ibid.*, p. 149.

54. Glasstone, *The Book of Mars*, p. 290.

55. *Ibid.*, p. 150.

56. Davies and Murray, *The View from Space*, p. 142.

57. Glasstone, *The Book of Mars*, p. 292.

58. *Ibid.*, p. 293.

59. Wilson, *Two Over Mars*, p. 12.

60. G. Edward Danielson, Jr., and D. T. Montgomery, "Calibration of the Mariner Mars 1969 Television Cameras," *Journal of Geophysical Research*, 76 (10 January 1971):418.

61. Davies and Murray, *The View from Space*, p. 79.

62. NASA, *Mariner–Mars 1964*, p. 50.

63. Davies and Murray, *The View from Space*, p. 78.

64. D. R. Montgomery and L. A. Adams, "Optics and the Mariner Imaging Instrument," *Applied Optics*, 9 (February 1970):278.

65. *Ibid.*

66. *Ibid.*

67. Salomon, "Applications of Slow-Scan Television Systems to Planetary Exploration," *Journal of SMPTE*, p. 613.

68. B. C. Murray and M. E. Davies, "Space Photography and the Exploration of Mars," *Applied Optics*, 9 (June 1970):1,276.

69. Stewart A. Collins, *The Mariner 6 and 7 Pictures of Mars* (Washington, DC: U.S. Gov. Printing Office, 1971), p. 12.

70. Danielson and Montgomery, "Calibration of the 1969 Mariner Mars Television Cameras," *Journal of Geophysical Research*, p. 418.
71. L. B. Leighton, "Mariner 6 and 7 Television Pictures: Preliminary Analysis," *Science*, 166 (3 October 1969):51.
72. Wilson, *Two Over Mars*, p. 11.
73. Montgomery and Adams, "Optics and the Mariner Imaging," p. 281.
74. *Ibid.*
75. Davies and Murray, *The View from Space*, p. 142.
76. Collins, *The Mariner 6 and 7 Pictures of Mars*, p. 12.
77. Salomon, "Applications of Slow-Scan Television Systems to Planetary Exploration," *Journal of SMPTE*, p. 611.
78. Collins, *The Mariner 6 and 7 Pictures of Mars*, p. 17.
79. A. T. Young and S. A. Collins, "Photometric Properties of the Mariner Cameras and of Selected Regions on Mars," *Journal of Geophysical Research*, 76 (10 January 1971):432.
80. Collins, *The Mariner 6 and 7 Pictures of Mars*, p. 17.
81. Davies and Murray, *The View from Space*, p. 142.
82. Collins, *The Mariner 6 and 7 Pictures of Mars*, p. 12.
83. L. B. Leighton, et al., "Mariner 6 and 7 Television Pictures: Preliminary Analysis." *Science*, p. 49.
84. *Ibid.*
85. *Ibid.*
86. Collins, *The Mariner 6 and 7 Pictures of Mars*, p. i.
87. Wilson, *Two Over Mars*, p. 10.
88. L. B. Leighton, et al., "Mariner 6 and 7 Television Pictures: Preliminary Analysis," *Science*, p. 51.
89. Wilson, *Two Over Mars*, p. 25.
90. L. B. Leighton, et al., "Mariner 6 and 7 Television Pictures: Preliminary Analysis," *Science*, p. 51.
91. Davies and Murray, *The View from Space*, p. 142.
92. Eric Burgess, *To the Red Planet* (New York: Columbia Univ. Press, 1978), p. 28.
93. *Space World*, "Mariner 9 Mission Summary," J-2-110 (February 1973):47.
94. Jet Propulsion Laboratory, *Development and Testing of the Television Instrument for the Mariner Mars 1971 Spacecraft,* Technical Memorandum 33-505 (Pasadena, CA: Jet Propulsion Laboratory, 1971), p. 4.
95. *Ibid.*
96. Murray and Davies, "Space Photography and the Exploration of Mars," *Applied Optics*, p. 1275.
97. *Ibid.*
98. *Ibid.*
99. Harold Masursky, et al. "Mariner 9 Television Reconnaissance of Mars and Its Satellites: Preliminary Results," *Science*, 175 (21 January 1972):297.
100. JPL, *Development and Testing of the Television Instrument for the Mariner Mars 1971 Spacecraft*, p. 28.
101. *Space World*, n.t., Vol. I-2-98 (Fall 1972):22.
102. G. Edward Danielson, Jr., Kenneth P. Klaasen, and James L. Anderson, "Acquisition and Description of Mariner 10 Television Science Data at Mercury," *Journal of Geophysical Research*, 80 (10 June 1975):2358.
103. Owen Gingerich, ed., *New Frontiers in Astronomy* (San Francisco: W. H. Freeman and Company, 1975): "Mars from Mariner 9," by Bruce C. Murray, p. 20.
104. JPL, *Development and Testing of the Television Instrument for the Mariner Mars 1971 Spacecraft*, p. 6.
105. *Ibid.*
106. Davies and Arthur, "Martian Surface Coordinates," *Journal of Geophysical Research*, 78 (10 July 1973):4356.
107. Harold Masursky, "An Overview of Geological Results from Mariner 9," *Journal of Geophysical Research*, 78 (10 July 1973):4010.
108. Davies and Arthur, "Martian Surface Coordinates," *Journal of Geophysical Research*, p. 4356.

109. Montgomery, "Optics and the Mariner Imaging Instrument," *Applied Optics*, p. 283.

110. JPL, *Development and Testing of the Television Instrument for the Mariner Mars 1971 Spacecraft*, p. 17.

111. Montgomery, "Optics and the Mariner Imaging Instrument," *Applied Optics*, p. 283.

112. Harold Masursky, et al., "Mariner 9 Television Reconnaissance of Mars and Its Satellites: Preliminary Results," *Science*, p. 294.

113. *Space World*, "Mariner 9 Mission Survey," p. 47.

114. JPL, *Development and Testing of the Television Instrument for the Mariner Mars 1971 Spacecraft*, p. 1.

115. Becker, *Design and Test Performance of Mariner 4 Television*, p. 75.

116. Carl Sagan, "The Lost Pictures of Mars," *Astronomy*, 2 (May 1974):15.

117. Gerald A. Soffen, "The Viking Project," *Journal of Geophysical Research*, 82 (30 September 1977):3963.

118. Conway W. Snyder, "The Extended Mission of Viking," *Journal of Geophysical Research*, 84 (30 December 1979):7920.

119. William R. Corliss, *The Viking Mission to Mars* (Washington, DC: U.S. Gov. Printing Office, 1974), p. 35.

120. Cary R. Spitzer, ed., *Viking Orbiter Views of Mars* (Washington, DC: U.S. Gov. Printing Office, 1980), p. 5.

121. M. H. Carr, et al. "Imaging Experiment: The Viking Mars Orbiter," *Icarus*, 16 (1972):19.

122. *Ibid.*

123. Conway W. Snyder, "The Mission of the Viking Orbiters," *Journal of Geophysical Research*, 82 (30 September 1977):3983.

124. Davies and Murray, *The View from Space*, p. 142.

125. Snyder, "The Mission of the Viking Orbiters," *Journal of Geophysical Research*, p. 3979.

126. Spitzer, ed., *Viking Orbiter Views of Mars*, p. 177.

127. *Ibid.*

128. Kenneth P. Klassen, Thomas E. Thorpe, and Linda A. Morabito, "Inflight Performance of the Viking Visual Imaging Subsystem," *Applied Optics*, 16 (December 1977):3168.

129. Danielson, Jr., Klaasen, and Anderson, "Acquisition and Description of Mariner 10 Television Science Data at Mercury," *Journal of Geophysical Research*, p. 2357.

130. Snyder, "The Mission of the Viking Orbiters, *Journal of Geophysical Research*, p. 3971.

131. Soffen, "The Viking Project," *Journal of Geophysical Research*, p. 3963.

132. Snyder, "The Mission of the Viking Orbiters," *Journal of Geophysical Research*, p. 3979.

133. Klaasen, Thorpe, and Morabito, "Inflight Performance of the Viking Visual Imaging Subsystem," *Applied Optics*, p. 3979.

134. *Ibid.*

135. L. T. Seaman and V. Klemas, "Comparison of Visual Imaging Systems for a Mars Orbiter," *Journal of the Society of Motion Picture and Television Engineers*, 79 (January 1970):7.

136. Corliss, *The Viking Mission to Mars*, p. 28.

137. Snyder, "The Mission of the Viking Orbiters," *Journal of Geophysical Research*, p. 3977.

138. Society of Photo-Optical Instrumentation Engineers, *Proceedings of the Society of Photo-Optical Instrumentation Engineers, January 29–February 1, 1979. Instrumentation in Astronomy III*, Vol. 172 (Bellingham, Washington: Society of Photo-Optical Instrumentation Engineers, 1979): "Optical System of the Visual Imaging Subsystem on the Viking Orbiter Spacecraft," by Leonard Larks, p. 388.

139. Corliss, *The Viking Mission to Mars*, p. 43.

140. *Ibid.*

141. Michael H. Carr, et al., "Preliminary Results from the Viking Orbiter Imaging Experiment," *Science*, 193 (27 August 1976):766.

142. *Ibid.*
143. *Ibid.*
144. Soffen, "The Viking Project," *Journal of Geophysical Research*, p. 3963.
145. Snyder, "The Mission of the Viking Orbiters," *Journal of Geophysical Research*, p. 3982.
146. *Ibid.*, p. 3976.
147. Snyder, "The Extended Mission of Viking," *Journal of Geophysical Research*, p. 7930.
148. *Ibid.*
149. Corliss, *The Viking Mission to Mars*, p. 33.
150. Snyder, "The Extended Mission of Viking," *Journal of Geophysical Research*, p. 7919.
151. *Ibid.*, p. 7933.
152. F. O. Huck, et al., "The Viking Mars Lander Camera," *Space Science Instrumentation*, 1 (May 1975):210.
153. Raymond M. Batson, "Photogrammetry with Surface-Based Images," *Applied Optics*, 8 (July 1969):1321.
154. P. M. Salomon, "Applications of Slow-Scan Systems to Planetary Exploration," *Journal of the Society of Motion Picture and Television Engineers*, p. 614.
155. *Ibid.*
156. National Aeronautical and Space Administration, *Optical Telescope Technology* (Washington, DC: U.S. Gov. Printing Office, 1970): "Surveyor Spacecraft Real-Time Payload Operations," by Jack L. Lindsley, p. 626.
157. *Ibid.*, p. 624.
158. Batson, "Photogrammetry with Surface-Based Images," *Applied Optics*, p. 1317.
159. Sidney Liebes, Jr., and Arnold A. Schwartz, "Viking 1975 Mars Lander Interactive Computerized Video Stereophotogrammetry," *Journal of Geophysical Research*, 82 (10 September 1977):4421.
160. Huck, et al., "The Viking Mars Lander Camera," *Space Science Instrumentation*, p. 189.
161. Corliss, *The Viking Mission to Mars*, p. 35.
162. *Ibid.*, p. 33.
163. Huck, et al., "The Viking Mars Lander Camera," *Space Science Instrumentation*, p. 199.
164. Liebes, Jr., and Schwartz, "Viking 1975 Mars Lander Interactive Computerized Video Stereophotogrammetry," *Journal of Geophysical Research*, p. 4421.
165. Huck, et al., "The Viking Mars Lander Camera," *Space Science Instrumentation*, p. 190.
166. *Ibid.*
167. T. A. Mutch, "Imaging Experiment: The Viking Lander," *Icarus*, 16 (1972):95.
168. Society of Photo-Optical Instrumentation Engineers, *Proceedings of the International Optical Computing Conference 1977, Applications of Digital Image Processing*, Vol. 119 (Bellingham, Washington: Society of Photo-Optical Instrumentation Engineers, 1979): "Viking Image Processing," by William B. Green, p. 2.
169. Huck, et al., "The Viking Mars Lander Camera," *Space Science Instrumentation*, p. 200.
170. *Ibid.*
171. Corliss, *The Viking Mission to Mars*, p. 35.
172. Huck, et al., "The Viking Mars Lander Camera," *Space Science Instrumentation*, p. 179.
173. Mutch, et al., "Imaging Experiment: The Viking Lander," *Icarus*, p. 95.
174. Huck, et al., "The Viking Mars Lander Camera," *Space Science Instrumentation*, p. 209.
175. *Ibid.*, p. 216.
176. Mutch, et al., "Imaging Experiment: The Viking Lander," *Icarus*, p. 98.
177. *Ibid.*
178. Huck, et al., "The Viking Mars Lander Camera," *Space Science Instrumentation*, p. 238.

179. U.S. Congress, House, Committee on Science and Technology, *Briefing on Mars Exploration, Hearing before the Subcommittee on Space Science and Applications*, 94th Cong., 2nd sess., 1976, p. 10.

180. Jet Propulsion Laboratory, *Mariner Venus–Mercury 1973 Project Final Report*, Vol. 1, Technical Memorandum 33-734 (Pasadena, CA: Jet Propulsion Laboratory, 1976), p. iii.

181. Society of Photo-Optical Instrumentation Engineers, *Proceedings of the Society of Photo-Optical Instrumentation Engineers, Effective Systems Integration and Optical Design*, Vol. 54 (Palos Verdes Estates, CA: Society of Photo-Optical Instrumentation Engineers, 1975): "The MVM Imaging System and Its Spacecraft Interactions," by Fred E. Vescelus, p. 123.

182. Bruce Hapke, et al., "Photometric Observations of Mercury from Mariner 10," *Journal of Geophysical Research*, 80 (10 June 1975):2341.

183. *Ibid.*

184. SPIE, *Effective Systems Integration and Optical Design*, Vescelus, "The MVM Imaging System and Its Spacecraft Interaction," p. 127.

185. JPL, *Mariner Venus–Mercury 1973 Project Final Report*, Vol. 1, p. 5.

186. SPIE, *Effective Systems Integration and Optical Design,* Vescelus, "The MVM Imaging System and Its Spacecraft Interaction," p. 128.

187. *Ibid.*

188. Danielson, Klaasen, and Anderson, "Acquisition and Description of Mariner 10 Television Science Data at Mercury," *Journal of Geophysical Research*, p. 2357.

189. *Ibid.*, p. 2358.

190. *Ibid.*, p. 2359.

191. JPL, *Mariner Venus–Mercury 1973 Project Final Report*, Vol. 1, p. 5.

192. James M. Soha, "JPL Processing of the Mariner 10 Images of Mercury," *Journal of Geophysical Research*, 80 (10 June 1975):2399.

193. *Ibid.*, p. 2395.

194. Danielson, Klaasen, and Anderson, "Acquisition and Description of Mariner 10 Television Science Data at Mercury," *Journal of Geophysical Research,* p. 2359.

195. SPIE, *Effective Systems Integration and Optical Design*, Vescelus, "The MVM Imaging System and Its Spacecraft Interaction," p. 128.

196. Jet Propulsion Laboratory, *Mariner Venus–Mercury 1973 Final Project Report*, Vol 2, Technical Memorandum 33-734 (Pasadena, CA: Jet Propulsion Laboratory, 1975), p. 9.

197. Danielson, Klaasen, and Anderson, "Acquisition and Description of Mariner 10 Television Science Data at Mercury," *Journal of Geophysical Research,* p. 2359.

198. *Ibid.*

199. JPL, *Mariner Venus–Mercury 1973 Final Project Report*, Vol. 2, p. iii.

200. Danielson, Klaasen, and Anderson, "Acquisition and Description of Mariner 10 Television Science Data at Mercury," *Journal of Geophysical Research*, p. 2359.

Chapter 5 Notes

1. Richard O. Fimmel, William Swindell, and Eric Burgess, *Pioneer Odyssey* (Washington, DC: U.S. Gov. Printing Office, 1977), p. 70.

2. Charles Redmond and Peter Waller, *NASA News: Venus Cloud Studies Show Changes in Long-Term Wind Pattern*, No. 81-33 (9 March 1981):1.

3. L. Ralph Baker, "Pioneer 11 Saturn Display System," *Journal of the Society of Motion Picture and Television Engineers*, 89 (August 1980):557.

4. D. Herman, J. Moore, and P. Tarver, "Mission Building Blocks for Outer Solar System Exploration," *Space Science Reviews*, 14 (1973):373.

5. Fimmel, Swindell, Burgess, *Pioneer Odyssey*, p. 45.

6. David Morrison and Jane Samz, *Voyage to Jupiter* (Washington, DC: U.S. Gov. Printing Office, 1980), p. 12.

7. E. E. Russell, et al., *Study of Spin-Scan Imaging for Outer Planets Imaging* (Santa Barbara, CA: Santa Barbara Research Center, 1974), p. 2.

8. Morrison and Samz, *Voyage to Jupiter*, p. 12.

9. Fimmel, Swindell, Burgess, *Pioneer Odyssey*, p. 188.

10. William Swindell and Lyn R. Doose, "The Imaging Experiment on Pioneer 10," *Journal of Geophysical Research*, 79 (1 September 1974):3634.

11. Dr. Thomas A. Mutch, Fred D. Kochendorfer, and Dr. John Wolfe, *Pioneer Saturn Encounter News Briefing* (21 August 1979):6.

12. National Aeronautics and Space Administration, *The Planet Jupiter (1970): NASA Space Vehicle Design Criteria* (Washington, DC: National Aeronautical and Space Administration, 1971), p. 1.

13. M. S. Hanner and J. L. Weinberg, "Gegenschein Observations from Pioneer 10," *Sky and Telescope*, 45 (April 1973):217.

14. S. F. Pellicori, E. E. Russell, and L. A. Watts, "Pioneer Imaging Photopolarimeter Optical System," *Applied Optics*, 12 (June 1973):1251.

15. J. J. Burke, T. Gehrels, and R. N. Strickland, "Cloud Forms on Saturn," *Journal of Geophysical Research*, 85 (1 November 1980):5883.

16. Pellicori, Russell, Watts, "Pioneer Imaging Photopolarimeter Optical System, *Applied Optics*, p. 1252.

17. Swindell and Doose, "Imaging Experiment on Pioneer 10," *Journal of Geophysical Research*, p. 3634.

18. Fimmel, Swindell, Burgess, *Pioneer Odyssey*, p. 188.

19. L. Ralph Baker, "Pioneer/Jupiter Real-Time Display System," *Journal of the Society of Motion Picture and Television Engineers*, 84 (June 1975):482.

20. Fimmel, Swindell, Burgess, *Pioneer Odyssey*, p. 188.

21. Baker, "Pioneer 11 Saturn Display System," *Journal of SMPTE*, p. 557.

22. Baker, "Pioneer/Jupiter Real-Time Display System," *Journal of SMPTE* p. 485.

23. Fimmel, Swindell, Burgess, *Pioneer Odyssey*, p. 127.

24. *Ibid.*, p. 131.

25. Swindell and Doose, "The Imaging Experiment on Pioneer 10," *Journal of Geophysical Research*, p. 3635.

26. Pellicori, Russell, Watts, "Pioneer Imaging Photopolarimeter Optical System," *Applied Optics*, p. 1248.

27. Morrison and Samz, *Voyage to Jupiter*, p. 14.

28. Lawrence Colin and Charles F. Hall, "The Pioneer Venus Program," *Space Science Reviews*, 20 (1977):283.

29. L. Colin and D. M. Hunten, eds., "Pioneer Venus Experiment Descriptions," *Space Science Reviews,* 20 (1977): "Orbiter Cloud Photopolarimeter," by J. Hansen, p. 504.

30. Peter Waller, NASA News: *Pioneer Venus 1 Completes Two Years in Orbit, Mission Planned Through 1986* (1 December 1980):1.

31. M. V. Keldysh, "Venus Exploration with the Venera 9 and Venera 10 Spacecraft," *Icarus*, 30 (1977):613.

32. "Pioneer Venus," *Telecommunication Journal*, 45 (September 1978):480.

33. *Ibid.*, p. 472.

Chapter 6 Notes

1. ABC, "Nightline," 25 August 1981, p. 8.

2. B. A. Smith, et al., "Voyager Imaging Experiment," *Space Science Reviews*, 21 (1977):103.

3. L. Ralph Baker, "Pioneer 11 Saturn Display System," *Journal of the Society of Motion Picture and Television Engineers*, 89 (August 1980):557.

4. David Morrison and Jane Samz, *Voyage to Jupiter* (Washington, DC: U.S. Gov. Printing Office, 1980), p. 39.

5. *Telecommunication Journal,* 44 (December 1977):583.

6. B. A. Smith, et al., "Voyager Imaging Experiment," *Space Science Reviews,* p. 124.

7. Donald M. Hunten, et al., *The Saturn System* (Pasadena, CA: Jet Propulsion Laboratory, 1978), p. 303.

8. Morrison and Samz, *Voyage to Jupiter,* p. 84.

9. *Ibid.,* p. 27.

10. *Ibid.,* p. 75.

11. Robert E. Edelson, et al., "Voyager Telecommunications: The Broadcast from Jupiter," *Science,* 204 (1 June 1979):918.

12. "Voyager," *Telecommunication Journal,* p. 586.

13. Edelson, et al., "Voyager Telecommunications: The Broadcast from Jupiter," *Science,* p. 919.

14. Morrison and Samz, *Voyage to Jupiter,* p. 58.

15. Merton E. Davies, et al., *Control Networks for the Galilean Satellites: November 1979* (Santa Monica, CA: Rand Corporation, 1979), p. 2.

16. Jet Propulsion Laboratory, *Proceedings of the Saturn's Rings Workshop, July 31–August 1, 1973, The Rings of Saturn* (Washington, DC: U.S. Gov. Printing Office, 1974): "The Mariner/Jupiter Visual Imaging System," by Bradford A. Smith.

17. Society of Photo-Optical Instrumentation Engineers, *Proceedings of the Society of Photo-Optical Instrumentation Engineers, January 29–February 1, 1979, Instrumentation in Astronomy III,* Vol 172, "Visual Imaging Optical Systems of the Mariner to Jupiter and Saturn Spacecraft," by Leonard Larks, p. 383.

18. Davies, et al., *Control Networks for the Galilean Satellites: November 1979,* p. 2.

19. B. A. Smith, et al., "Voyager Imaging Experiment," *Space Science Reviews,* p. 117.

20. E. C. Stone and A. L. Lane, "Voyager 1 Encounter with the Jovian System," *Science,* 204 (1 June 1979):945.

21. *Ibid.*

22. *Ibid.*

23. Richard O. Fimmel, William Swindell, and Eric Burgess, *Pioneer Odyssey* (Washington, DC: U.S. Gov. Printing Office, 1977), p. 127.

24. *Ibid.*

Chapter 7 Notes

1. Stewart A. Collins, *The Mariner 6 and 7 Pictures of Mars* (Washington, DC: U.S. Gov. Printing Office, 1971), p. 17.

2. Merton E. Davies, et al., *Control Networks for the Galilean Satellites: November 1979* (Santa Monica, CA: Rand Corporation, 1979), p. 4.

3. Douglas A. O'Handley and William B. Green, "Recent Developments in Digital Image Processing at the Image Processing Laboratory at the Jet Propulsion Laboratory," *Proceedings of the IEEE,* 60 (July 1972):821.

4. P. M. Salomon, "Applications of Slow-Scan Television Systems to Planetary Exploration," *Journal of the Society of Motion Picture and Television Engineers,* 79 (July 1970):613.

5. Kenneth P. Klaasen, Thomas E. Thorpe, and Linda A. Morabito, "Inflight Performance on the Viking Visual Imaging Subsystem," *Applied Optics,* 16 (December 1977):3167.

6. T. E. Thorpe, "Verification of Performance of the Mariner 9 Television Cameras," *Applied Optics,* 12 (August 1973):1779.

7. Salomon, "Applications of Slow-Scan Television Systems to Planetary Exploration," *Journal of SMPTE,* p. 613.

8. Reuben M. Ruiz, "JPL Processing of the Viking Orbiter Images of Mars," *Journal of Geophysical Research,* 82 (30 September 1977):4189.

9. Robert Nathan, *Digital Video-Data Handling* (Pasadena, CA: Jet Propulsion Laboratory, 1966), p. 2.

10. O'Handley and Green, "Recent Developments in Digital Image Processing at the Image Processing Laboratory at the Jet Propulsion Laboratory," p. 822.

11. T. C. Rindfleisch, "Digital Processing of the Mariner 6 and 7 Pictures," *Journal of Geophysical Research*, 76 (10 January 1971):398.

12. Johannes G. Moik, *Digital Processing of Remotely Sensed Images* (Washington, DC: U.S. Gov. Printing Office, 1980), p. 127.

13. J. A. Dunne, et al., "Maximum Discriminability Versions of the Near-Encounter Pictures," *Journal of Geophysical Research*, 76 (10 January 1971):438.

14. Ruiz, et al., "JPL Processing of the Viking Orbiter Images of Mars," *Journal of Geophysical Research*, p. 4199.

15. Gerald Millerson, *The Technique of Television Production* (New York: Hastings House, 1975), p. 414.

16. L. Ralph Baker, "Pioneer/Jupiter Real-Time Display System," *Journal of the Society of Motion Picture and Television Engineers*, 84 (June 1975):841.

17. Ruiz, et al., "JPL Processing of the Viking Orbiter Images of Mars," *Journal of Geophysical Research*, p. 4191.

18. Society of Photo-Optical Instrumentation Engineers, *Proceedings of the International Optical Computing Conference '77, August 25–26, 1977, Applications of Digital Image Processing,* Vol. 119 (Bellingham, Washington: Society of Photo-Optical Instrumentation Engineers, 1979): "Viking Image Processing," by William B. Green, p. 3.

19. *Ibid.*

20. *Ibid.*, p. 7.

21. Jet Propulsion Laboratory, *Ranger 7. Part 1. Mission Description and Performance,* Technical Report No. 32-700 (Pasadena, CA: Jet Propulsion Laboratory, 1964), p. 61.

22. National Aeronautical and Space Administration, *Mariner–Mars 1964: Final Project Report* (Washington, DC: U.S. Gov. Printing Office, 1967), p. 267.

Chapter 8 Notes

1. Bruce Murray, Michael C. Malin, and Ronald Greeley, *Earthlike Planets* (San Francisco: W. H. Freeman and Company, 1981), p. 2.

2. *Ibid.*, p. 4.

3. William B. Wallace, "Beefing Up Moon Photos," *Electronics* (8 March 1965): 130.

4. American Astronautical Society, *Proceedings of an AAS Symposium held on May 25–27, 1967, Use of Space Systems for Planetary Geology and Geophysics,* Vol. 17 (Tarzana, CA: American Astronautical Association, 1967): "A Photometric Technique for Deriving Slopes from Lunar Orbiter Photography," by J. J. Lambiotte and G. R. Taylor, p. 205.

5. J. Kelly Beatty, Brian O'Leary, and Andrew Chaikin, eds., *The New Solar System* (New York: Cambridge University Press, 1981): "The Voyager Encounters," by Bradford A. Smith, p. 109.

6. Robert G. Strom, "Mercury: A Post Mariner 10 Assessment," *Space Science Reviews*, 24 (1979):4.

7. *Ibid.*, p. 19.

8. John H. Pomeroy and Norman J. Hubbard, eds., *The Soviet-American Conference on Cosmochemistry of the Moon and Planets* (Washington, DC: U.S. Gov. Printing Office, 1977): "Television Observations of Mercury by Mariner 10," by Bruce C. Murray, et al., p. 881.

9. *Ibid.*

10. Murray, Malin, and Greeley, *Earthlike Planets*, p. 247.

11. Donald E. Gault, et al., "Some Comparisons of Impact Craters on Mercury and the Moon," *Journal of Geophysical Research*, 80 (10 June 1975):2444.

12. Pomeroy and Hubbard, eds., *The Soviet-American Conference on Geochemistry:* "Television Observations of Mercury by Mariner 10," by Murray, p. 871.

13. Murray, Malin, and Greeley, *Earthlike Planets*, p. 13.

14. Pomeroy and Hubbard, eds., *The Soviet-American Conference on Geochemistry:* "Television Observations of Mercury by Mariner 10," by Murray, p. 871.

15. Kenneth P. Klaasen, "Mercury Rotation Period Determined from Mariner 10 Photography," *Journal of Geophysical Research*, 80 (10 June 1975):2415.

16. Robert G. Strom, Newell J. Trask, and John E. Guest, "Tectonism and Volcanism on Mercury," *Journal of Geophysical Research*, 80 (10 June 1975):2507.

17. R. G. Knollenberg, et al., "The Clouds of Venus," *Space Science Reviews*, 20 (1977):329.

18. Beatty, O'Leary, and Chaikin, eds., *The New Solar System:* "Atmospheres of the Terrestrial Planets," by James B. Pollack, p. 63.

19. G. Schubert, et al., "Dynamics, Winds, Circulation, and Turbulence in the Atmosphere of Venus," *Space Science Reviews*, 20 (1977):364.

20. *Ibid.*, p. 360.

21. National Aeronautics and Space Administration, *NASA News: Venus Cloud Studies Show Changes in Long Term Wind Patterns,* No. 81-33, p. 2.

22. *Ibid.*, p. 3.

23. "Venus Observed by Mariner," *Sky and Telescope*, 47 (April 1974):237.

24. NASA, *NASA News: Venus Cloud Studies*, p. 2.

25. *Ibid.*

26. Beatty, O'Leary, and Chaikin, eds., *The New Solar System*, "Atmospheres of the Terrestrial Planets," by James B. Pollack, p. 61.

27. NASA, *NASA News: Venus Cloud Studies*, p. 5.

28. "Planetary Bonanza," *Astronomy*, 2 (June 1974):18.

29. E. P. Martz, Jr., "Optical Problems of Television Recording of the Moon and Planets from Approaching Spacecraft," *Applied Optics*, 2 (January 1963):41.

30. Murray, Malin, and Greeley, *Earthlike Planets*, p. 27.

31. Merton E. Davies and Bruce C. Murray, *The View from Space* (New York: Columbia University Press, 1971), p. 37.

32. *Ibid.*, p. 39.

33. B. C. Taylor and K. E. Prentice, *Selected Latin Readings* (Canada: J. M. Dent and Sons, Limited, 1965), p. 366.

34. Newell E. Trask and Lawrence C. Rowan, "Lunar Orbiter Photographs: Some Fundamental Observations," *Science*, 158 (22 December 1967):1529.

35. *Ibid.*

36. *Ibid.*

37. Murray, Malin, and Greeley, *Earthlike Planets*, p. 219.

38. Peter H. Schultz, *Moon Morphology* (Austin, Texas: University of Texas Press, 1976), p. 7.

39. J. Kelly Beatty, Brian O'Leary, and Andrew Chaikin, eds., *The New Solar System* (New York: Cambridge University Press, 1981): "The Moon," by Bevan M. French, p. 72.

40. National Aeronautics and Space Administration, *Surveyor: Program Results* (Washington, DC: U.S. Gov. Printing Office, 1969), p. 96.

41. *Ibid.,* p. 135.

42. E. M. Shoemaker, et al., "Television Observations from Surveyor 3," *Journal of Geophysical Research,* 73 (15 June 1968):4022.

43. Schultz, *Moon Morphology*, p. 291.

44. American Astronautical Society, *Proceedings of the Tenth Annual Meeting of the American Astronautical Society 4-7, May, 1967,* Vol. 18 (North Hollywood, CA: Western Periodicals Co., 1967): "Lunar Orbiter — Its Mission and Capabilities," by Israel Taback, p. 138.

45. Murray, Malin, and Greeley, *Earthlike Planets*, p. 223.

46. Samuel Glasstone, *The Book of Mars* (Washington, DC: U.S. Gov. Printing Office, 1968), p. 22.

47. *Ibid.*, p. 24.

48. Eric Burgess, *To the Red Planet* (New York: Columbia Univ. Press, 1978), p. 7.

49. *Ibid.*, p. 9.

50. National Aeronautics and Space Administration, *Mariner-Mars 1964: Final Project Report* (Washington, DC: U.S. Gov. Printing Office, 1967), p. 315.

51. Burgess, *To the Red Planet*, p. 25.

52. *Ibid.*, p. 33.

53. M. H. Carr, et al., *Viking Orbiter Views of Mars* (Washington, DC: U.S. Gov. Printing Office, 1980), p. 47.

54. John S. King and James R. Riehle, "A Proposed Origin of the Olympus Mons Escarpment," *Icarus*, 23 (1974):309.

55. Conway W. Snyder, "The Planet Mars as Seen at the End of the Viking Mission," *Journal of Geophysical Research*, 84 (30 December 1979):8488.

56. Murray, Malin, and Greeley, *Earthlike Planets*, p. 290.

57. James B. Pollack, et al., "Properties and Effects of Dust Particles Suspended in the Martian Atmosphere," *Journal of Geophysical Research*, 84 (10 June 1979):2944.

58. P. Thomas and J. Veverka, "Grooves on Asteroids: A Prediction," *Icarus*, 40 (1979):394.

59. Murray, Malin, and Greeley, *Earthlike Planets*, p. 268.

60. David Morrison and Jane Samz, *Voyage to Jupiter* (Washington, DC: U.S. Gov. Printing Office, 1980), p. 7.

61. C. M. Michaux, et al., *Handbook of the Physical Properties of the Planet Jupiter* (Washington, DC: U.S. Gov. Printing Office, 1967), p. 69.

62. Richard O. Fimmel, William Swindell, and Eric Burgess, *Pioneer Odyssey* (Washington, DC: U.S. Gov. Printing Office, 1977), p. 171.

63. *Ibid.*, p. 181.

64. Morrison and Samz, *Voyage to Jupiter*, p. 58.

65. Bradford A. Smith, et al., "The Jupiter System Through the Eyes of Voyager 1," *Science* (1 June 1979):952.

66. J. Kelly Beatty, Brian O'Leary, and Andrew Chaikin, eds., *The New Solar System* (New York: Cambridge University Press, 1981): "Jupiter and Saturn," by Andrew Ingersoll, p. 124.

67. *Ibid.*, p. 125.

68. Andrew P. Ingersoll, "Jupiter and Saturn," *Scientific American,* 245 (December 1981):108.

69. Smith, et al., "The Jupiter System...," *Science,* p. 955.

70. A. F. Cook II, T. C. Duxbury, and G. E. Hunt, "First Results on Jovian Lightning," *Nature*, 280 (August 1979):794.

71. M. H. Carr, et al., "Volcanic Features of Io," *Nature*, 280 (30 Aug. 1979):729.

72. Robert G. Strom, et al., "Volcanic Eruption Plumes on Io," *Nature*, 280 (30 August 1979):733.

73. Morrison and Samz, *Voyage to Jupiter*, p. 148.

74. *Ibid.*, p. 144.

75. Merton E. Davies, et al., *Control Networks for the Galilean Satellites: November 1979* (Santa Monica, CA: The Rand Corporation, 1975), p. 15.

76. *Ibid.*

77. Morrison and Samz, *Voyage to Jupiter*, p. 148.

78. J. Kelly Beatty, "Rendezvous with a Ringed Giant," *Sky and Telescope*, 61 (January 1981):7.

79. W. H. Ip, "Physical Studies of the Planetary Rings," *Space Science Reviews,* 26 (1980):42.

80. Bradford A. Smith, et al., "Encounter with Saturn: Voyager 1 Imaging Science Results," *Science*, 212 (10 April 1981):212.

81. Edward C. Stone, "How Voyager 2 Has Been Reprogrammed," *Nature*, 292 (20 August 1981):675.

82. Stanley F. Dermott, "The 'Braided' F-Ring of Saturn," *Nature*, 290 (9 April 1981):454.

83. Smith, et al., "Encounter with Saturn: Voyager 1 Imaging Science Results," *Science*, p. 163.

84. *Ibid.*, p. 166.

85. *Ibid.*, p. 163.

86. Beatty, "Rendezvous with a Ringed Giant," *Sky and Telescope*, p. 8.

87. Smith, et al., "Encounter with Saturn: Voyager 1 Imaging Science Results," *Science*, p. 122.

88. *Ibid.*, p. 167.

89. J. Kelly Beatty, Brian O'Leary, and Andrew Chaikin, eds., *The New Solar System* (New York, Cambridge University Press, 1981): "The Outer Solar System," by David Morrison and Dale P. Cruikshank, p. 175.

90. Beatty, "Rendezvous with a Ringed Giant," *Sky and Telescope*, p. 16.

91. ABC, "Nightline," 24 August 1981, "Voyager 2," p. 6.

92. Beatty, O'Leary, and Chaikin, *The New Solar System*: "The Outer Solar System," by Morrison and Cruikshank, p. 172.

93. ABC, "Nightline," 25 August 1981, "Voyager 2," p. 5.

94. William Hoffer, "Looking Up to Know Ourselves," *Mosaic* (September/October):39.

95. *Ibid.*, p. 43.

96. *Ibid.*

97. *Ibid.*

98. James B. Pollack, "Climate Change on the Terrestrial Planets," *Icarus*, 37 (1979):550.

99. *Ibid.*, p. 509.

100. Murray, Malin, and Greeley, *Earthlike Planets*, p. 187.

101. *Ibid.*, p. 136.

102. *Ibid.*, p. 6.

103. S. F. Dermott, ed., *The Origin of the Solar System* (New York: John Wiley and Sons, 1976): "Origin of the Solar System," by H. Alfven, p. 30.

104. *Ibid.*, p. 31.

Chapter 9 Notes

1. G. Edward Danielson, Jr., Kenneth P. Klaasen, and James L. Anderson, "Acquisition and Description of Mariner 10 Television Science Data," *Journal of Geophysical Research*, 80 (10 June, 1975):2359.

2. J. F. McCauley, et al., "Pitted and Fluted Rocks in the Western Desert of Egypt: Viking Comparisons," *Journal of Geophysical Research*, 84 (30 December 1979): 8222.

3. Space Science Board, *Strategy for the Exploration of Primitive Solar System Bodies—Asteroids, Comets, and Meteoroids: 1980-1990* (Washington, DC: National Academy of Sciences, 1980), p. 37.

4. Science Advisory Group, "A Strategy for Investigation of the Outer Solar System," *Space Science Reviews*, 14 (1973):348.

5. Jet Propulsion Laboratory, *Galileo to Jupiter* (Pasadena, CA: Jet Propulsion Laboratory, 1979), p. 12.

6. Science Advisory Group, "A Strategy for Investigation of the Outer Solar System," *Space Science Reviews*, p. 357.

7. David Morrison and Jane Samz, *Voyage to Jupiter* (Washington, DC: U.S. Gov. Printing Office, 1980), p. 24.

8. Jet Propulsion Laboratory, *Mission Summary: Halley Flyby/Tempel-2 Rendezvous* (Pasadena, CA: Jet Propulsion Laboratory, 1979), p. iii.

9. Richard O. Fimmel, William Swindell, and Eric Burgess, *Pioneer Odyssey* (Washington, DC: U.S. Gov. Printing Office, 1977), p. 123.

10. Science Advisory Group, "A Strategy for Investigation of the Outer Solar System," *Space Science Reviews*, p. 359.

11. International Astronomical Union, *Symposium No. 65 Held on 5-8 September, 1973, Exploration of the Planetary System* (Dordrecht, Holland: D. Reidel Publishing Company, 1974): I. Rasool, et al., "Rationale for NASA Planetary Exploration Program," p. 549.

12. Science Advisory Group, "A Strategy for Investigation of the Outer Solar System," *Space Science Reviews*, p. 359.

13. U.S. Congress, House, Committee on Science and Technology, *1978 NASA Authorization, Hearings before a Subcommittee on Space Science and Technology*, 95th Cong., 1st sess., 1977, p. 894.

14. Jet Propulsion Laboratory, *Report of the Terrestrial Bodies Science Working Group: Executive Summary*, Vol. 1 (Pasadena, CA: Jet Propulsion Laboratory, 1977) p. 5.

15. Space Science Board, *The Outer Solar System* (Washington, DC, National Academy of Sciences, 1969), p. 10.

16. *Ibid.*, p. 34.

17. D. Herman, J. Moore, and P. Tarver, "Mission Building Blocks for Outer Solar System Exploration," *Space Science Reviews*, 14 (1973):375.

18. JPL, *Report of the Terrestrial Bodies Science Working Group: Executive Summary*, p. 7.

19. Dr. William C. Wells, *Multiple Discipline Science Assessment* (Schaumburg, IL: Science Applications, Inc., 1978), p. 76.

20. *Ibid.*, p. 77.

21. U.S. Congress, House, *1978 NASA Authorization*, p. 894.

22. Space Science Board, *The Outer Solar System*, p. 39.

23. Gerald A. Soffen, "The Viking Project," *Journal of Geophysical Research,* 82 (30 September 1977):3963.

24. Morrison and Samz, *Voyage to Jupiter*, p. 85.

25. Bruce C. Murray, "Imaging of the Outer Planets and Satellites," *Space Science Reviews*, 14 (1973):481.

26. Morrison and Samz, *Voyage to Jupiter*, p. 58.

27. Murray, "Imaging of the Outer Planets and Satellites," *Space Science Reviews*, p. 484.

28. National Aeronautics and Space Administration, *Machine Intelligence and Robotics: Report of the NASA Study Group, Final Report* (Washington, DC: U.S. Gov. Printing Office, 1980), p. 24.

29. *Ibid.*, p. 29.

30. Society of Photo-Optical Instrumentation Engineers, *Proceedings of the International Optical Computing Conference '77, August 25–26, 1977, Vol. 119, Applications of Digital Image Processing* (Bellingham, WA: Society of Photo-Optical Instrumentation Engineers, 1979): "The Robot's Eyes: Stereo Vision for Automated Scene Analysis," by Donald S. Williams, p. 16.

31. *Ibid.*, p. 17.

32. Speech given by Dr. Robert A. Frosch, National Aeronautics and Space Administration, to Commonwealth Club on 14 September, 1979, p. 5.

33. Jet Propulsion Laboratory, *Report of the Terrestrial Bodies Science Working Group: Mercury*, Vol. 2 (Pasadena, CA: Jet Propulsion Laboratory, 1977), p. 12.

34. *Ibid.*, p. 6.

35. Wells, *Multiple Discipline Science Assessment*, p. 35.

36. Morrison and Samz, *Voyage to Jupiter*, p. 37.

37. Jet Propulsion Laboratory, *Report of the Terrestrial Bodies Science Working Group: Venus*, Vol. 3 (Pasadena, CA: Jet Propulsion Laboratory, 1977), p. 19.

38. *Ibid.*, p. 12.

39. Warren James, "Unveiling Venus with Voir," *Sky and Telescope*, 63 (February 1982):142.

40. JPL, *Report of the Terrestrial Bodies Science Working Group: Executive Summary*, p. 13.

41. Wells, *Multiple Discipline Science Assessment*, p. 16.

42. Jet Propulsion Laboratory, *Halley Flyby/Tempel-2*, p. 4.

43. Space Science Board, *Strategy for the Exploration of Primitive Solar System Bodies—Asteroids, Comets, and Meteoroids: 1980–1990* (Washington, DC: National Academy of Science, 1980), p. 19.

44. National Aeronautics and Space Administration, *Proceedings of IAU Colloquium No. 25, October 28–November 1, 1974, Part 2, The Study of Comets* (Washington,

DC: U.S. Gov. Printing Office, 1976): "Science Aspects of 1980 Ballistic Missions to Comet Encke, Using Mariner and Pioneer Spacecraft," by L. D. Jaffe, et al., p. 1059.

45. *Ibid.*

46. *Ibid.*, p. 1065.

47. JPL, *Halley Flyby/Tempel-2*, p. 4.

48. Space Science Board, *Strategy for the Exploration of Primitive Solar System Bodies*, p. 41.

49. *Ibid.*, p. 47.

50. A. Brahic, et al., "Feasibility Study of a Multiple Flyby Mission of Main Belt Asteroids," *Icarus*, 40 (1979):424.

51. National Aeronautics and Space Administration, *Physical Studies of Minor Planets,* Ed. T. Gehrels (Washington, DC: U.S. Gov. Printing Office, 1971): "Design and Science Instrumentation of an Unmanned Vehicle for Sample Return from the Asteroid Eros," by H. F. Meissinger and E. W. Greenstadt, p. 553.

52. Tom Gehrels, ed., *Asteroids* (Tucson, AZ: The University of Arizona Press, 1979): "Future Exploration of the Asteroids," by David Morrison and John Niehoff, p. 240.

53. *Ibid.*

54. P. Thomas and J. Veverka, "Grooves on Asteroids: A Prediction," *Icarus*, 40 (1979):394.

55. J. Kelly Beatty, Brian O'Leary, and Andrew Chaikan, eds., *The New Solar System* (New York: Cambridge University Press, 1981): "The Outer Solar System," by David Morrison and Dale P. Cruikshank, p. 171.

56. Murray, "Imaging of the Outer Planets," *Space Science Reviews,* p. 489.

57. *Ibid.*, p. 491.

58. *Ibid.*, p. 492.

59. Science Advisory Group, "A Strategy for Investigation of the Outer Solar System," *Space Science Reviews*, p. 357.

60. Clayne M. Yeates and Theodore C. Clarke, "Galileo Mission to Jupiter, *Astronomy*, 10 (February 1982):10.

61. Morrison and Samz, *Voyage to Jupiter*, p. 170.

62. U.S. Congress, House, Committee on Science and Technology, *1978 NASA Authorization*, p. 2074.

63. Yeates and Clarke, "Galileo Mission to Jupiter," *Astronomy*, p. 16.

64. National Aeronautics and Space Administration, *The Saturn System,* eds., Hunten and Morrison (Washington, DC: U.S. Gov. Printing Office, 1978): "Galileo Orbiter Instrumentation and Spacecraft," by David Morrison, p. 380.

65. Space Science Board, *The Outer Solar System*, p. 17.

66. Jet Propulsion Laboratory, *Proceedings Symposium on Charge-Coupled Device Technology for Science and Imaging Applications, June 15, 1975* (Pasadena, CA: Jet Propulsion Laboratory, 1975): "Introduction," by G. M. Smith, p. 3.

67. Morrison and Samz, *Voyage to Jupiter*, p. 171.

68. Kenneth P. Klaasen, Maurice C. Clary, and James R. Janesick, "The CCD Television Camera for NASA's Galileo Mission to Jupiter," Paper, p. 1.

69. *Ibid.*, p. 3.

70. *Ibid.*, p. 4.

71. *Ibid.*, p. 11.

Chapter 10 Notes

1. Bernard C. Embrey, Jr., and Glen R. Southworth, "Application of Narrow-Band Television to Industrial and Commercial Communications," p. 3.

2. *Ibid.*, p. 6.

3. Glen O. Robinson, ed., *Communications for Tomorrow* (New York: Praeger Publishers, 1978): "Telecommunications Technologies and Services," by William A. Lucas, p. 263.

4. Colorado Video Incorporated, "Narrow Band Video Systems," Brochure.

5. Glen Southworth, "Slow Scan TV Teleconferencing," Colorado Video, Inc., Brochure.

6. *Ibid.*

7. *Ibid.*

8. Carla Selby, "UPI Newstime Uses Satellites and Slow-Scan TV to Distribute News," *Communication News* (March 1979):60.

9. *Ibid.*, p. 61.

10. Glen R. Southworth, "Instructional Television over Phone Lines," *Audio Visual Instruction* (April 1970):32.

11. Selby, "UPI Newstime," *Communication News*, p. 61.

12. Robert Nathan, *Digital Video-Data Handling* (Pasadena, CA: Jet Propulsion Laboratory, 1966), p. 1.

13. Dennis Meredith, "Special Effects in the Movies," *Technology Review* (February/March 1982):63.

14. Nathan, *Digital Video-Data Handling*, p. 5.

15. Frederick M. Remley, "Factors Leading to the Choice of a Digital Television System," *Journal of the Society of Motion Picture and Television Engineers*, 90 (November 1981):1056.

16. *Ibid.*, p. 1057.

17. *Ibid.*

18. Harold E. Ennes, "Slow-Sweep TV for Closed-Circuit Use," *Electronics* (November 1956):140.

19. Glen O. Robinson, ed., *Communications for Tomorrow* (New York: Praeger Publishers, 1978): "Telecommunications Technology in the 1980's," by Walter S. Baer, p. 81.

20. "Bandwidth Economy," *Electronics* (17 August 1970):39.

21. Robinson, ed., *Communications for Tomorrow:* "Telecommunications Technology for the 1980's," by Baer, p. 82.

22. Sony Corporation of America, "Revolutionary Video Still Camera Called Mavica Disclosed by Sony," 24 August, 1981 Press Release.

23. R. L. Rodgers III, "Charge-Coupled Imager for 525 Line Television," Presented at IEEE Intercon, N.Y., N.Y. on March, 1974.

24. National Aeronautics and Space Administration, *Optics and Lasers — Technology Utilization* (Washington, DC: U.S. Gov. Printing Office, 1976), p. 20.

25. Earl V. Dunn, M.D., et al., "The Use of Slow-Scan Video for CME in a Remote Area," *Journal of Medical Education*, 6 (June 1980):494.

26. *Ibid.*, p. 495.

27. Glen Southworth, "Slow-Scan TV Telemedicine," Colorado Video, Inc., Brochure.

28. Douglas A. O'Handley and William B. Green, "Recent Developments in Digital Image Processing at the Image Processing Laboratory at the Jet Propulsion Laboratory," *Proceedings of the IEEE*, 60 (July 1972):824.

29. *Ibid.*, p. 827.

30. Jean J. Lorre and Donald J. Lynn, *Application of Digital Image Processing Techniques to Astronomical Imagery 1977* (Pasadena, CA: Jet Propulsion Laboratory, 1978), p. 13.

31. *Ibid.*, p. 7.

32. *Ibid.*, p. 12.

33. U.S. Congress, House, Committee on Science and Technology, *1979 NASA Authorization (Program Review), Hearings before a Subcommittee of the House Committee on Space Science and Applications*, 95th Cong., 1st sess., 1979, p. 8.

34. Jet Propulsion Laboratory, *Proceedings Symposium on Charge-Coupled Device Technology for Scientific Imaging Applications* (Pasadena, CA: Jet Propulsion Laboratory, 1975): "Cooled Slow-Scan Performance of a 512 X 320 Element Charge-Coupled Imager," by R. L. Rodgers III and D. L. Giovachino, p. 119.

35. COSPAR, *Proceedings of a Symposium of the Twentieth Plenary Meeting of COSPAR, 7-18 June 1977, New Instrumentation for Space Astronomy* (New York: Pergamon Press, 1977): "The Space Telescope," by C. R. Dell, p. 19.

36. International Astronomical Union, *International Astronomical Union Colloquium Number 54 Co-sponsored by COSPAR, August 8–11 1979, Scientific Research with the Space Telescope* (Washington, DC: U.S. Gov. Printing Office, 1979): "Planetary Astronomy with the Space Telescope," by J. S. Belton, p. 57.

37. *Ibid.*, p. 80.
38. *Ibid.*, p. 89.

Bibliography

NASA Documents

Athey, Skipwith W. *Magnetic Tape Recording*. Washington, DC: U.S. Gov. Printing Office, 1966.

Burgess, Eric. *To the Red Planet*. New York: Columbia University Press, 1978.

Cargill, R., ed. *Essays on the History of Rocketry and Astronautics: Proceedings of the Third Through the Sixth Symposium of the International Academy of Astronautics*. Vols. 1 and 2. Washington, DC: U.S. Gov. Printing Office, 1977.

Carr, M. H.; Baum, W. A.; Blasius, K. R.; Briggs, G. A.; Cutts, J. A.; Duxbury, T. C.; Greeley, R.; Guest, J.; Marursky, H.; Smith, B. A.; Soderblom, L. A.; Veverka, J.; and Wellman, J. B. *Viking Orbiter Views of Mars*. Spitzer, Cary R., ed. Washington, DC: U.S. Gov. Printing Office, 1980.

_____, and Greeley, R. *Volcanic Features of Hawaii: A Basis for Comparison with Mars*. Washington, DC: U.S. Gov. Printing Office, 1980.

Collins, Stewart A. *The Mariner 6 and 7 Pictures of Mars*. Washington, DC: U.S. Gov. Printing Office, 1971.

Corliss, William R. *The Interplanetary Pioneers*. Vol. 2. Washington, DC: U.S. Gov. Printing Office, 1972.

Cortright, Edgar M., ed. *Exploring Space with a Camera*. Washington, DC: U.S. Gov. Printing Office, 1968.

Donn, B.; Mumma, M.; Jackson, W.; Hearn, M. A.; and Harrington, R., eds. *The Study of Comets. The Proceedings of an IAU Colloquium No. 25 held at Goddard Space Flight Center on October 28-November 1, 1978*. Part 2. Washington, DC: U.S. Gov. Printing Office, 1976.

Fimmel, Richard O.; Swindell, William; and Burgess, Eric. *Pioneer Odyssey*. Washington, DC: U.S. Gov. Printing Office, 1977.

Gehrels, T., ed. *Physical Studies of Minor Planets*. Washington, DC: U.S. Gov. Printing Office, 1971.

Glasstone, Samuel. *The Book of Mars*. Washington, DC: U.S. Gov. Printing Office, 1968.

Hall, R. Cargill. *Lunar Impact: A History of Project Ranger*. Washington, DC: U.S. Gov. Printing Office, 1977.

Hunten, Donald M., and Morrison, David., eds. *The Saturn System*. Washington, DC: U.S. Gov. Printing Office, 1978.

Longair, M. S., and Warner, J. W., eds. *Scientific Research with the Space Telescope. International Astronomical Union Colloquium No. 54 held at the Institute of Advanced Study on August 8-11, 1979*. Washington, DC: U.S. Gov. Printing Office, 1979.

Micheux, C. M.; Fish, F. F., Jr.; Murray, F. W.; Santina, R. E.; and Steffey, P. C. *Handbook of the Physical Properties of the Planet Jupiter*. Washington, DC: U.S. Gov. Printing Office, 1967.

Moik, Johannes G. *Digital Processing of Remotely Sensed Images*. Washington, DC: U.S. Gov. Printing Office, 1980.

Morrison, David, and Samz, Jane. *Voyage to Jupiter*. Washington, DC: U.S. Gov. Printing Office, 1980.

National Aeronautics and Space Administration. *NASA Day*. Washington, DC: U.S. Gov. Printing Office, 1962.

_____. *Spacecraft Sterilization Technology*. Washington, DC: U.S. Gov. Printing Office, 1966.

_____. *Mariner-Mars 1964: Final Project Report*. Washington, DC: U.S. Gov. Printing Office, 1967.

_____. *Surveyor Program Results*. Washington, DC: U.S. Gov. Printing Office, 1969.

_____. *Optical Telescope Technology*. Washington DC: U.S. Gov. Printing Office, 1970.

_____. *The Planet Jupiter (1970): NASA Space Vehicle Design Criteria*. Washington, DC: U.S. Gov. Printing Office, 1971.

_____. *Advanced Scanners and Imaging Systems for Earth Observations*. Washington, DC: U.S. Gov. Printing Office, 1973.

_____. *Optics and Lasers-Technology Utilization*. Washington, DC: U.S. Gov. Printing Office, 1976.

_____. *Outlook for Space*. Washington, DC: U.S. Gov. Printing Office, 1976.

_____. *Machine Intelligence and Robotics: Report of the NASA Study Group, Final Report*. Washington, DC: U.S. Gov. Printing Office, 1980.

Pomeroy, John H., and Hubbard, Norman J., eds. *The Soviet-American Conference on Cosmochemistry of the Moon and Planets*. Washington, DC: U.S. Gov. Printing Office, 1977.

Redmond, Charles, and Waller, Peter. *NASA News: Venus Cloud Studies Show Changes in Long-Term Wind Pattern*. No. 81-33. 9 March 1981.

Russell, E. E.; Chandos, R. A.; Kodak, J. C.; Pellicori, S. F.; and Tomasko, M. G. *Study of Spin-Scan Imaging for Outer Planets Missions*. Santa Barbara, CA: Santa Barbara Research Center, 1974.

Waller, Peter. *NASA News: Pioneer Venus 1 Completes Two Years in Orbit, Mission Planned Through 1986*. 1 December 1980.

Wells, William C. *Multiple Discipline Science Assessment*. Schaumburg, IL: Science Applications, Inc., 1978.

Wilson, James H. *Two Over Mars*. Washington, DC: U.S. Gov. Printing Office, 1973.

Jet Propulsion Laboratory Documents

Becker, R. A. *Design and Test Performance of Mariner 4 Television Optical System*. Pasadena, CA: Jet Propulsion Laboratory, 1965.

Brown, Harrison; Stanley, G. J.; Muhleman, D. O.; and Münch, G., eds. *Proceedings of the Caltech-JPL Lunar Planetary Conference held on September 13-18, 1965*. Pasadena, CA: California Institute of Technology, 1966.

Heacock, R. L.; Kuiper, G. P.; Shoemaker, E. M.; Urey, H. C.; and Whitaker, E. A. *Ranger 7. Part 2. Experimenters' Analyses and Interpretations*. Pasadena, CA: Jet Propulsion Laboratory, 1965.

Jet Propulsion Laboratory. *Ranger 7, Part 1. Mission Description and Performance*. Pasadena, CA: Jet Propulsion Laboratory, 1964.

_____. *Development and Testing of the Television Instrument for the Mariner-Mars 1971 Spacecraft*. Pasadena, CA: Jet Propulsion Laboratory, 1971.

_____. *Proceedings of the Saturn's Rings Workshops, July 31-August 1, 1973. The Rings of Saturn*. Washington, DC: U.S. Gov. Printing Office, 1974.

_____. *Proceedings Symposium on Charge-Coupled Device Technology for Science and Imaging Applications held on June 15, 1975*. Pasadena, CA: Jet Propulsion Laboratory, 1975.

_____. *Mariner Venus-Mercury 1973 Project Final Report*. Vol. 1. Pasadena, CA: Jet Propulsion Laboratory, 1975.

_____. *Mariner Venus-Mercury 1973 Project Final Report*. Vol. 2. Pasadena, CA: Jet Propulsion Laboratory, 1976.

_____. *Report of the Terrestial Bodies Science Working Group: Executive Summary.* Vol. 1. Pasadena, CA: Jet Propulsion Laboratory, 1977.

_____. *Report of the Terrestial Bodies Science Working Group: Mercury.* Vol. 2. Pasadena, CA: Jet Propulsion Laboratory, 1977.

_____. *Report of the Terrestial Bodies Science Working Group: Venus.* Vol. 3. Pasadena, CA: Jet Propulsion Laboratory, 1977.

_____. *Mission Summary: Halley Flyby/Tempel-2 Rendezvous.* Pasadena, CA: Jet Propulsion Laboratory, 1979.

_____. *The Deep Space Network: Progress Report.* Pasadena, CA: Jet Propulsion Laboratory, 1980.

Kinct, Donald H., and Staniszewski, Joseph R. *The Design of the Ranger Television System to Obtain High-Resolution Photographs of the Lunar Surface.* Pasadena, CA: Jet Propulsion Laboratory, 1965.

Lorre, Jean J., and Lynn, Donald J. *Application of Digital Image Processing Techniques to Astronomical Imagery 1977.* Pasadena, CA: Jet Propulsion Laboratory, 1978.

Nathan, Robert. *Digital Video-Data Handling.* Pasadena, CA: Jet Propulsion Laboratory, 1966.

United States Government Documents

U.S. Congress. Senate. Committee on Commerce, Science, and Transportation. *National Aeronautics and Space Act of 1958, As Amended, and Related Legislation.* 95th Cong., 2nd sess., 1977.

_____. _____. House. Committee on Science and Astronautics. *Viking Project. Hearings Before a Subcommittee of the House Committee on Space Science and Applications.* 93rd Cong., 2nd sess., 1974.

_____. _____. _____. Committee on Science and Technology. *Briefing on Mars Exploration. Hearing before the Subcommittee on Space Science and Applications.* 94th Cong., 2nd sess., 1976.

_____. _____. _____. _____. *1978 NASA Authorization. Hearings before a Subcommittee on Space Science and Technology.* 95th Cong., 1st sess., 1977.

_____. _____. _____. _____. *1979 NASA Authorization (Program Review). Hearings before a Subcommittee of the House Committee on Space Science and Applications.* 95th Cong., 1st sess., 1979.

United Nations Documents

United Nations, General Assembly, 34th Session, 14 December 1979. *Agreement Governing the Activities of States on the Moon and Other Celestial Bodies.* A/RES/34/68.

_____. Department of Economic and Social Affairs. *The Application of Space Technology to Development.* E.72.II.A.12., 1973.

National Academy of Sciences

Space Science Board. *Lunar Exploration.* Washington, DC: National Academy of Sciences, 1969.

_____. *The Outer Solar System.* Washington, DC: National Academy of Sciences, 1969.

_____. *Strategy for the Exploration of Primitive Solar-System Bodies—Asteroids, Comets, and Meteoroids: 1980-1990.* Washington, DC: National Academy of Sciences, 1980.

Proceedings

Advances in Electronics and Electron Physics. *Proceedings of the Third Symposium held at Imperial College. London. September 20–24. Photo-Electronic Image Devices.* Vol. 22B. London: Academic Press. 1966.

American Astronautical Society. *Proceedings of an AAS/AAAS Symposium held on December 29, 1966. Physics of the Moon.* Tarzana, CA: American Astronautical Society, 1966.

————. *Proceedings of an AAS Symposium held on May 25–27, 1967. Use of Space Systems for Planetary Geology and Geophysics.* Vol. 17. Tarzana, CA: American Astronautical Society, 1967.

————. *Proceedings of the Tenth Annual Meeting of the American Astronautical Society. May 4–7, 1964. Lunar Flight Programs.* Vol. 18. North Hollywood, CA: Western Periodicals Co., 1964.

————. *Proceedings of the American Astronautical Society Symposium on Unmanned Exploration of the Solar System. February 8–10, 1965. Unmanned Exploration of the Solar System.* Vol. 19. North Hollywood, CA: Western Periodicals, Co., 1965.

————. *The 21st Annual Meeting of the AAS held on August 26–28, 1975. The Space Telescope.* Washington, DC: U.S. Gov. Printing Office, 1976.

COSPAR. *Proceedings of a Symposium of 20th Plenary Meeting of COSPAR, June 7–18, 1977. New Instrumentation for Space Astronomy.* New York: Pergamon, 1977.

International Astronomical Union. *Symposium No. 65 held on September 5–8, 1973. Exploration of the Planetary System.* Dordrecht, Holland: D. Reidel, 1974.

Society of Photo-Optical Instrumentation Engineers. *Proceedings of the Society of Photo-Optical Instrumentation Engineers. Effective Systems Integration and Optical Design.* Vol. 54. Palos Verdes Estates, CA: Society of Photo-Optical Instrumentation Engineers, 1975.

————. *Proceedings of the International Optical Computing Conference '77 held on August 25–26, 1977. Applications of Digital Image Processing.* Bellingham, WA: Society of Photo-Optical Instrumentation Engineers, 1979.

————. *Proceedings of the Society of Photo-Optical Instrumentation Engineers held on January 29–February 1, 1979. Instrumentation in Astronomy III.* Bellingham, WA: Society of Photo-Optical Instrumentation Engineers, 1979.

Periodical Articles

Allen, Lewis H., and Salomon, P. M. "Operation of the Surveyor Television System in the Photo-Integration Mode." *Journal of the Society of Motion Picture and Television Engineers,* 79 (July 1970):615–620.

Baker, Ralph L. "Pioneer 11 Saturn Display System." *Journal of the Society of Motion Picture and Television Engineers,* 89 (August 1980):557–560.

————. "Pioneer/Jupiter Real-Time Display System." *Journal of the Society of Motion Picture and Television Engineers,* 84 (June 1975):481–485.

"Bandwidth Economy." *Electronics* (17 August 1970):38–39.

Batson, Raymond M. "Photogrammetry with Surface-Based Images." *Applied Optics,* 8 (July 1969):1315–1322.

Beatty, J. Kelly. "Rendezvous with a Ringed Giant." *Sky and Telescope,* 61 (Jan. 1981): 7–18.

————. "NASA and the Selling of Space Science." *Sky and Telescope,* 63 (March 1982):243–245.

Blanchard, L. E. "The Design of the Postlanding Television System Photometric Charts for the Surveyor Spacecraft." *Journal of the Society of Motion Picture and Television Engineers,* 79 (March 1970):226–229.

Brahic, A.; Breton, J.; Caubel, J.; Cazenave, A.; Cruvellier, P.; Dupuis, Y.; Lago, B.; Minister, I. F.; Perret, A.; and Scribot, A. "Feasibility Study of a Multiple Flyby Mission of Main Belt Asteroids." *Icarus,* 40 (1979):423–433.

Burke, J. J.; Gehrels; and Strickland, R. N. "Cloud Forms on Saturn." *Journal of Geophysical Research,* 85 (November 1980):5883-5890.

Canvel, Henry. "A Slow-Motion Television Film Recorder." *Journal of the Society of Motion Picture and Television Engineers,* 74 (September 1965):770-772.

Carr, Michael H.; Baum, W.A.; Briggs, G.A.; Masursky, H.; Wise, D.W.; and Montgomery, D.R. "Imaging Experiment: The Viking Mars Orbiter." *Icarus,* 16 (1972):17-33.

_____; Masursky, H.; Baum, W. A.; Blasius, K. R.; Briggs, G. A.; Cutts, J. A.; Duxbury, T.; Greeley, R.; Guest, J. E.; Smith, B. A.; Soderblom, L. A.; Veverka, J.; and Wellman, J. B. "Preliminary Results from the Viking Orbiter Imaging Experiment." *Science,* 193 (27 August 1976):766-776.

_____; _____; Strom, R. G.; and Terrile, R. J. "Volcanic Features of Io" *Nature,* 280 (30 August 1979):283-306.

Colin, Lawrence, and Hall, Charles F. "The Pioneer Venus Program" *Space Science Reviews,* 20 (1977):283-306.

_____, and Hunten, D. M., eds. "Pioneer Venus Experiment Descriptions." *Space Science Reviews,* 20 (1977):451-525.

Cook II, A. F.; Duxbury, T. C.; and Hunt, G. E. "First Results on Jovian Lightning" *Nature,* 280 (August 1979):794.

Danielson, Edward G., Jr.; Klaasen, Kenneth P.; and Anderson, James L. "Acquisition and Description of Mariner 10 Television Science Data at Mercury." *Journal of Geophysical Research,* 80 (10 June 1975):2358-2393.

_____, and Montgomery, D. T. "Calibration of the Mariner Mars 1969 Television Cameras." *Journal of Geophysical Research,* 76 (10 January 1971):418-431.

Davies, Merton E., and Arthur, W. G. "Martian Surface Coordinates." *Journal of Geophysical Research,* 78 (10 July 1973):4355-4387.

Dermott, Stanley F. "The Braided 'F' Ring of Saturn." *Nature,* 290 (9 April 1981):454-457.

Dunn, V. Earl; Acton, H.; Conrath, D.; Hissins, C.; and Bain, H. "The Use of Slow Scan Video for CME in a Remote Area." *Journal of Medical Education,* 6 (June 1980):493-495.

Dunne, J. A.; Stromberg, W. D.; Ruiz, R. M.; Collins, S. A.; and Thorpe, T. E. "Maximum Discriminability Versions of the Near-Encounter Pictures." *Journal of Geophysical Research,* 76 (10 January 1971):438-445.

Edelson, Robert E. "Voyager Telecommunications: The Broadcast from Jupiter." *Science,* 204 (1 June 1979):913-921.

Elle, B. L.; Heinmuller, C. S.; Frumme, P. J.; and Neumer, A. E. "The Lunar Orbiter Photographic System." *Journal of the Society of Motion Picture and Television Engineers,* 76 (August 1967):750.

Ellman, Carvyn. "The Surveyor Variable and Fixed Focal-Length Lenses." *Journal of the Society of Motion Picture and Television Engineers,* 77 (April 1968):333-336.

Ennes, Harold E. "Slow-Sweep TV for Closed-Circuit Use." *Electronics* (November 1956):140-143.

Gaffy, Michael J., and McCord, Thomas. "Mining Outer Space." *Technology Review* (June 1977):51-59.

Gault, Donald E.; Guest, J. E.; Murray, J. B.; Dzurisin, D.; and Malin, M. C. "Some Comparisons of Impact Craters on Mercury and the Moon." *Journal of Geophysical Research,* 80 (10 June 1975):2444-2460.

Grammer, Jr., R. A.; Stets, J. F.; Buttner, B. W.; and Filbert, H. C. "Ground Reconstruction of Lunar Orbiter Photography." *Journal of the Society of Motion Picture and Television Engineers,* 76 (August 1967):765-773.

Gunter, Jonathan F. "An Introduction to the Great Debate." *Journal of Communication,* 28 (Autumn 1978):142-156.

Hanner, M. S. and Weinberg, J. L. "Gegenschein Observations from Pioneer 10." *Sky and Telescope,* 45 (April 1973):217-218.

Hapke, Bruce; Danielson, Jr., Edward G.; Klaasen, K.; and Wilson, L. "Photometric Observations of Mercury from Mariner 10." *Journal of Geophysical Research,* 80 (10 June 1975):2431-2443.

Heckel, Donald T. "Unit and System Design of a Lunar Operating Camera." *Journal of the Society of Motion Picture and Television Engineers,* 76 (August 1967):774-779.

_____, and Quandt, Ronald L. "Environmental and Thermal Effects on Surveyor Vidicon Performance." *Journal of the Society of Motion Picture and Television Engineers*, 77 (April 1968):324-332.

Heen, H. K.; Wilson, W. C.; Widmer, J.; Stone, Jr., D. J.; and Boase, E. E. "Lunar Orbiter Camera." *Journal of the Society of Motion Picture and Television Engineers*, 76 (August 1967):740-750.

Herman, D.; Moore, J.; and Tarver, P. "Mission Building Blocks for Outer Solar System Exploration." *Space Science Reviews*, 14 (1973):363-382.

Hoffer, William. "Looking Up to Know Ourselves." *Mosaic* (September/October): 363-382.

Hoffman, R. E. "Vidicon for Space Applications." *Journal of the Society of Motion Picture and Television Engineers*, 76 (August 1967):780-782.

Huck, F. O.; McCall, H. F.; Patterson, W. R.; and Taylor, G. R. "The Viking Mars Lander Camera." *Space Science Instrumentation*, 1 (May 1975):189-241.

Ingersoll, Andrew P. "Jupiter and Saturn." *Scientific American*, 245 (December 1981): 90-108.

IP, W. H. "Physical Studies of the Planetary Rings." *Space Science Reviews*, 26 (1980: 39-96.

Jaffe, Leonard D. "The Surveyor Lunar Landings." *Science*, 164 (16 May 1969):774-787.

James, Warren. "Unveiling Venus with VOIR." *Sky and Telescope*, 63 (February 1982): 141-144.

Jensen, A.; Whitcomb, R. J.; Reinke, R. O.; and Carsom, D. E. "Lunar Orbiter Readout." *Journal of the Society of Motion Picture and Television Engineers*, 76 (August 1967):757-765.

Keldysh, M. V. "Venus Exploration with the Venera 9 and Venera 10 Spacecraft." *Icarus*, 30 (1977):605-625.

King, John S., and Riehle, James R. "A Proposed Origin of the Olympus Mons Escarpment." *Icarus*, 23 (1974):300-317.

Kinzly, R. E.; Mazurowski, M. J.; and Holladay, T. M. "Image Evaluation and Its Application to the Lunar Orbiter." *Applied Optics*, 7 (August 1968):1577-1586.

Klaasen, Kenneth P. "Mercury Rotation Period Determined from Mariner 10 Photography." *Journal of Geophysical Research*, 80 (10 June 1975):2415.

_____; Thorpe, Thomas E.; and Morabito, Linda A. "Inflight Performance of the Viking Visual Imaging Subsystem." *Applied Optics*, 16 (December 1977):3158-3170.

Knollenberg, R. G.; Hansen, J.; Ragent, B.; Martonchik, J.; and Tomasko, M. "The Clouds of Venus." *Space Science Reviews*, 20 (1977):329-354.

Kosofsky, Leon J. and Broome, Calvin G. "Lunar Orbiter: A Photographic Satellite." *Journal of the Society of Motion Picture and Television Engineers*, 74 (September 1965):773-778.

Kreuzer, Barton. "Electronic and Motion-Picture Systems in the Space Age." *Journal of the Society of Motion Picture and Television Engineers,* 70 (December 1961): 961-966.

Krueger, Harold W., and Williams, James W. "Surveyor Television Power Conditioning." *Journal of the Society of Motion Picture and Television Engineers*, 77 (April 1968):337-341.

Leighton, R. B.; Horowitz, N. H.; Murray, B. C.; Sharp, R. P.; Herriman, A. H.; Young, A. T.; Smith, B. A.; Davies, M. E.; and Leovy, C. B. "Mariner 6 and 7 Television Pictures: Preliminary Analysis." *Science*, 166 (3 October 1969):49-67.

Liebes, Sidney, Jr., and Schwartz, Arnold A. "Viking 1975 Mars Lander Interactive Computerized Stereophotogrammetry." *Journal of Geophysical Research*, 82 (10 September 1977):4421-4429.

McCauley, J. F.; Breed, C. S.; El-Baz, F.; Whitney, M. I.; Grolier, M. J.; and Ward, A. W. "Pitted and Fluted Rocks in the Western Desert of Egypt: Viking Comparisons." *Journal of Geophysical Research*, 84 (30 December 1979):8222-8232.

McDougal, Myres S.; Lasswell, H. D.; Vlasic, I. A.; and Smith, J. C. "The Enjoyment and Acquisitions of Resources in Outer Space." *University of Pennsylvania Law Review* (March 1963):521-636.

Malling, Leonard R. "Space Astronomy and the Slow Scan Vidicon." *Journal of the Society of Motion Picture and Television Engineers,* 72 (November 1963):872-875.

"Mariner 9 Mission Summary." *Space World*, Vol. J-2-110 (February 1973):46–48.

Martz, E. P., Jr. "Optical Problems of Television Recording of the Moon and the Planets from Approaching Spacecraft." *Applied Optics*, 2 (January 1963):41–50.

Masursky, Harold. "An Overview of Geological Results from Mariner 9." *Journal of Geophysical Research*, 78 (10 July 1973):4009–4029.

_____; Batson, R. M.; McCauley, F.; Soderblom, L. A.; Wildey, R. L.; Carr, M. H.; Milton, D. J.; Wiehelms, D. E.; Smith, B. A.; Kirby, T. B.; Robinson, J. C.; Leovy, C. B.; Briggs, G. A.; Duxbury, T. C.; Acton, Jr., C. H.; Murray, B. C.; Cutts, J. A.; Sharp, R. P.; Smith, S.; Leighton, R. B.; Sagan, C.; Veverka, J.; Noland, M.; Lederberg, J.; Levinthal, E.; Pollack, J. B.; Moore, Jr.; J. Hartmann, W. K.; Shipley, E. N.; De Vancouleurs, G.; and Davies, M. E. "Mariner 9 Television Reconnaissance of Mars and Its Satellites." *Science*, 175 (21 January 1979): 294–305.

Meredith, Dennis. "Special Effects in the Movies." *Technology Review* (February/March 1982):56–63.

Mesner, Max H. "Television's Toughest Challenge." *Electronics* (17 May 1965):80–89.

Meyers, J. J.; Endter, D.; and Limoges, R. F. "Film Processor-Dryer for Lunar Orbiter Photo System." *Journal of the Society of Motion Picture and Television Engineers*, 76 (August 1967):750–757.

Montgomery, D. T. and Adams, L. A. "Optics and the Mariner Imaging Instrument." *Applied Optics*, 9 (February 1970):277–287.

Murray, Bruce C. "Imaging of the Outer Planets and Satellites." *Space Science Reviews*, 14 (1973):474–496.

_____. "The Mariner 10 Pictures of Mercury: An Overview." *Journal of Geophysical Research*, 80 (10 June 1975):2342–2344.

_____, and Davies, M. E. "Space Photography and the Exploration of Mars." *Applied Optics*, 9 (June 1970):1270–1281.

Mutch, T. A.; Binder, A. B.; Huck, F. O.; Levinthal, E. C.; Morris, E. C. Sagan, C; and Young, A. T. "Imaging Experiment: The Viking Lander." *Icarus*, 16 (1972):92–110.

Nelson, William C. "Contribution of High Technology to U.S. Industry." *Optic News*, 8 (1982):24–26.

O'Handley, Douglas A., and Green, William B. "Recent Developments in Digital Image Processing at the Image Processing Laboratory at the Jet Propulsion Laboratory." *Proceedings of the IEEE*, 60 (July 1972):821–826.

Pellicori, S. F.; Russell, E. E.; and Watts, L. A. "Pioneer Imaging Photopolarimeter Optical System." *Applied Optics*, 12 (June 1973):1246–1258.

"Pioneer Venus." *Telecommunication Journal*, 44 (December 1977):580–586.

"Planetary Bonanza." *Astronomy*, 2 (June 1974):4–27.

Pollack, James B. "Climate Change on the Terrestial Planets." *Icarus*, 37 (1979):479–553.

_____; Colburn, D. S.; Flasar, F. M.; Kahn, R.; Carleston, C. E.; and Pidek, D. "Properties and Effects of Dust Particles Suspended in the Martian Atmosphere." *Journal of Geophysical Research*, 84 (10 June 1979):2929–2945.

Remley, Frederick, M. "Factors Leading to the Choice of a Digital Television System." *Journal of the Society of Motion Picture and Television Engineers*, 90 (November 1981):1054–1060.

Rindfleisch, T. C.; Funne, J. A.; Frieden, H. J.; Stromberg, W. D.; and Ruiz, R. M. "Digital Processing of the Mariner 6 and 7 Pictures." *Journal of Geophysical Research*, 76 (10 January 1971):394–417.

Ruiz, Reuben, M. "JPL Processing of the Viking Orbiter Images of Mars." *Journal of Geophysical Research*, 82 (30 September 1977):4189–4202.

Sagan, Carl. "The Lost Pictures of Mars." *Astronomy*, 2 (May 1974):12–15.

Salomon, P. M. "Applications of Slow-Scan Television Systems to Planetary Exploration." *Journal of the Society of Motion Picture and Television Engineers*, 79 (July 1970):607–614.

Schubert, G.; Counselman, III, C. C.; Hansen, J.; Limaye, S. S.; Pettergill, G.; Seiff, A.; Shapiro, I. I.; Sumoi, V. E.; Taylor, F.; Travis, L.; Woo, R.; and Young, R. E. "Dynamics, Winds, Circulation and Turbulence in the Atmosphere of Venus." *Space Science Reviews*, 20 (1977):357–387.

Science Advisory Group. "A Strategy for Investigation of the Outer Solar System." *Space Science Reviews*, 14 (1973):347–363.

Seaman, L. T., and Klemas, V. "Comparison of Visual Imaging Systems for a Mars Orbiter." *Journal of the Society of Motion Picture and Television Engineers*, 79 (January 1970):7–10.

Selby, Carla. "UPI Newstime Uses Satellites and Slow-Scan TV to Distribute News." *Communication News* (March 1979):60–61.

Sharma, Surya P. "International Law of Outer Space." *The Indian Journal of Law*, 17 (1977):185–208.

Shoemaker, E. M.; Batson, R. M.; Holt, H. E.; Morris, E. C.; Rennilson, J. J.; and Whitaker, E. A. "Television Observations from Surveyor 3." *Journal of Geophysical Research*, 73 (15 June 1968):3989–4043.

Smith, Bradford A.; Beebe, R.; Boyce, J.; Briggs, G.; Bunker, A.; Collins, S. A.; Hansen, C. J.; Johnson, T. V.; Mitchells, J. L; Terrile, R. J.; Carr, M.; Cook, II, A. F.; Cuzzi, J.; Pollack, J. B.; Danielson, G. E.; Ingersoll, A.; Davies, M. E.; Hunt, G. E.; Masursky, H.; Shoemaker, E.; Morrison, D.; Owen, T.; Sagan, C.; Veverka, J.; Strom, R.; and Suomi, V. E. "Encounter with Saturn: Voyager 1 Imaging Science Results." *Science*, 212 (10 April 1981):163–191.

_____; Briggs, G. A.; Danielson, G. E.; Cook, II, A. F.; Davies, M. E.; Hunt, G. E.; Masursky, H.; Soderblom, L. A.; Owen, T. C.; Sagan, C.; and Suomi, V. E. "Voyager Imaging Experiment." *Space Science Reviews*, 21 (1977):103–127.

_____; Soderblom, L. A.; Johnson, T. V.; Ingersoll, A. P.; Collins, S. A.; Shoemaker, E. M.; Hunt, G. E.; Masursky, H.; Carr, M. H.; Davies, M. E.; Cook, II, A. F.; Boyce, J.; Danielson, G. E.; Owen, T. C.; Sagan, C.; Beebe, R. F.; Veverka, J.; Strom, R. G.; McCauley, J. F.; Morrison, D.; Briggs, G. A.; and Suomi, V. E. "The Jupiter System Through the Eyes of Voyager 1." *Science* (1 June 1979):951–971.

Snyder, Conway W. "The Mission of the Viking Orbiters." *Journal of Geophysical Research*, 82 (30 September 1977):3971–3983.

_____. "The Extended Mission of Viking." *Journal of Geophysical Research*, 84 (December 1979):7919–7933.

_____. "The Planet Mars as Seen at the End of the Viking Mission." *Journal of Geophysical Research*, 84 (30 December 1979):8487–8519.

Soffen, Gerald A. "The Viking Project." *Journal of Geophysical Research*, 82 (30 September 1977):3959–3970.

Soha, James M.; Lynn, D. J.; Lorre, J. J.; Mosher, J. A.; Thayer, N. A.; Elliott, D. A.; Benton, W. D.; and Dewar, R. E. "JPL Processing of the Mariner 10 Images of Mercury." *Journal of Geophysical Research*, 80 (10 June 1975):2394–2414.

Solnick, Steven L. "Slicing the Pie in the Sky." *Technology Review* (October 1981):74–75.

Southworth, Glen R. "Instructional Television Over Phone Lines." *Audio Visual Instruction* (April 1970):32.

Stone, Edward C. "How Voyager 2 had been Reprogrammed." *Nature*, 202 (20 August 1981):675–698.

_____, and Lane, L. A. "Voyager 1 Encounter with the Jovian System." *Science*, 204 (1 June 1979):945–948.

Strom, Robert G. "Mercury: A Post Mariner 10 Assessment." *Space Science Reviews*, 24 (1979):3–70.

_____; Terrile, R. J.; Masursky, H.; and Hansen, C. "Volcanic Eruption Plumes on Io." *Nature*, 280 (30 August 1979):733–736.

_____; Trask, Newell J.; and Guest, John E. "Tectonism and Volcanism on Mercury." *Journal of Geophysical Research*, 80 (10 June 1975):2478–2507.

Swindell, William, and Doose, Lyn R. "The Imaging Experiment on Pioneer 10." *Journal of Geophysical Research*, 79 (1 September 1974):3634–3644.

Thomas, P., and Veverka, J. "Grooves on Asteroids: A Prediction." *Icarus*, 40 (1979): 394–404.

Thorpe, T. E. "Verification of Performance of the Mariner 9 Television Cameras." *Applied Optics* (August 1973):1775–1784.

Trask, Newell J., and Rowan, Lawrence C. "Lunar Orbiter Photographs: Some Fundamental Observations." *Science*, 158 (22 December 1967): 1529–1535.

[Untitled.] *Space World*, Vol. I-2-98 (Fall 1972):16–22.

"Venus Observed by Mariner." *Sky and Telescope*, 47 (April 1974): 235–240.

"Voyager." *Telecommunication Journal*, 44 (December 1977):580–586.

Wallace, William B. "Beefing Up Moon Photos." *Electronics* (8 March 1965):130–137.
Yeates, Clayne M., and Clarke, Theodore, C. "Galileo Mission to Jupiter." *Astronomy,* 10 (February 1982):6–22.
Young, A. T., and Collins, S. A. "Photometric Properties of the Mariner Cameras and of Selected Regions on Mars." *Journal of Geophysical Research,* 76 (10 January 1971): 432–437.

Miscellaneous

American Broadcasting Company. "Voyager 2" (television program). *Nightline.* 24 and 25 August 1981.
Colorado Video Incorporated. "Narrow Band Video Systems." (Brochure.)
Embrey, Bernard C., Jr., and Southworth, Glen R. "Application of Narrow-Band Television to Industrial and Commercial Communications." (Unpublished paper.)
"Eyes on the Moon." *New York Times,* 25 March 1965, p. 36.
Frosch, Dr. Robert A. Speech given to the Commonwealth Club, San Francisco on 14 September 1979.
Klaasen, Kenneth P.; Clary, Maurice C.; and Janesick, James R. "The CCD Television Camera for NASA's Galileo Mission to Jupiter." (Unpublished paper.)
Mutch, Thomas A.; Kochendorfer, Fred D.; and Wolfe, John. "Pioneer Saturn Encounter News Briefing" (speech). 21 August 1976.
"Ranger Hits Moon." *New York Times,* 25 March 1965, p. 23.
Rodgers, III, R. L. "Charge-Coupled Imager for 525 Line Television." Paper presented at IEEE Intercon, New York City, on March 1974.
Sony Corporation of America. "Revolutionary Video Still Camera Called Mavica Disclosed by Sony." 24 August 1981. (Brochure.)
Southworth, Glen R. "Slow-Scan TV Teleconferencing." (Brochure.)
_____. "Slow-Scan TV Telemedicine." (Brochure.)
"Surveyor 3 Lands on the Moon and Sends TV Pictures." *New York Times,* 20 April 1967, p. 1.

Books

Beatty, J. Kelly; O'Leary, Brian; and Chaikin, Andrew, eds. *The New Solar System,* New York: Cambridge University Press, 1981.
Carroll, John S. *Photographic Lab Handbook,* Garden City, NY: American Photographic Book Publishing Co., 1977.
Clarke, Arthur C. *The Promise of Space,* New York: Pyramid Books, 1968.
Corliss, William R. *Space Probes and Planetary Exploration,* Princeton, NJ: D. Van Nostrand, 1965.
Davies, Merton E.; Hauge, T. A.; Katayama, F. Y.; and Roth, J. A. *Control Networks for the Galilean Satellites: November 1979,* Santa Monica, CA: Rand Corporation, 1979.
_____, and Murray, Bruce C. *The View from Space: Photographic Exploration of the Planets,* New York: Columbia University Press, 1971.
Dermott, S. F., ed. *The Origin of the Solar System,* New York: John Wiley, 1976.
Gehrels, Tom, ed. *Asteroids,* Tucson: University of Arizona Press, 1979.
Haley, Andrew G. *Space Law and Government,* New York: Appelton-Century-Crofts, 1963.
Jessup, Phillip C., and Taubenfeld, Howard J. *Controls for Outer Space and the Antarctic Analogy,* New York: Columbia University Press, 1959.
Langford, Michael. *Visual Aids and Photography in Education,* New York: Hastings House, 1973.

Millerson, Gerald. *The Technique of Television Production*, New York: Hastings House, 1975.
Murray, Bruce; Malin, Michael C.; and Greeley, Ronald. *Earthlike Planets*, San Francisco: W. H. Freeman, 1981.
Ordway, Frederick I., III., ed. *Advances in Space Science and Technology*, Vol. 10. New York: Academic Press, 1970.
Robinson, Glen O., ed. *Communications for Tomorrow*, New York: Praeger, 1978.
Schultz, Peter H. *Moon Morphology*, Austin: University of Texas Press, 1976.
Scientific American. *New Frontiers in Astronomy*, San Francisco: W. H. Freeman, 1975.
Veith, Richard. *Talk-Back TV: Two Way Cable Television*, Blue Ridge Summit, PA: Tab Books, 1976.
Waters, Aaron C. *Moon Craters and Oregon Volcanoes*, Eugene: Oregon State System of Higher Education, 1967.
Zworykin, V. K.; Ramberg, E. G.; and Flory, L. E. *Television Science and Industry*, New York: John Wiley and Sons, 1958.

Appendix
NASA Space Probes Summary

Spacecraft (no. in series)	Launch date	Visual imaging system	Discoveries and achievements
Moon			
Ranger (9)	1964–65	Six TV cameras	First high resolution lunar pictures
Surveyor (7)	1966–68	Single TV camera with scan mirror	First high resolution lunar pictures transmitted from moon's surface
Lunar Orbiter (5)	1966–67	Film/photo-multiplier	Used film for high resolution photos of entire lunar surface
			ALL three moon probes produced photos that helped select Apollo manned landing sites
Mariner			
Mariner 4	1964	Single TV camera	First photo of Mars surface features at low resolution
Mariners 6, 7	1969	Wide angle/tele-photo TV cameras	High resolution Mars photos
Mariner 9	1971	Wide angle/tele-photo TV cameras	Extended Mars photo coverage; revealed various features (volcanoes, etc.)
Mariner 10	1973	Twin 1,500mm telephoto lenses UV corrected/ Auxilliary wide angle	First low-high resolution photos of Venus clouds, Mercury surface features
Viking Orbiter (2)	1975	Twin telephoto TV cameras	Extended contiguous photographic coverage of Mars; high resolution pictures; photos of Mars' satellites; photos used to locate landing sites for Viking Landers

Viking Lander (2)	1975	Twin facsimile cameras/photo-diode imaging sensors and scanning system	First photos from Mars surface; black & white and color photos; extended missions; stereo-scopic data

Pioneer

Pioneers 10, 11	1972–1973	Photopolarimeters	First spacecraft to image Jupiter/Saturn; black & white and color photos; photos resolving features of Jupiter and Saturn atmospheres
Pioneer Venus	1978	Photopolarimeter with UV sensors	Extended imaging of Venus; recorded Venus atmospheric dynamics/features

Voyager

Voyagers 1, 2	1977	Wide angle/tele-photo TV cameras	High resolution photos of Jupiter, Saturn and moons; record of Jupiter and Saturn atmospheric dynamics; dis-covery of volcanoes on Io; discovery of Saturn's ringlets; potential to image Uranus

Index